A CALL TO ARMS

ANNE LEHOËRFF

A CALL TO ARMS

THE DAY WAR WAS INVENTED

© 2022 Anne Lehoërff

Published by Sidestone Press, Leiden
www.sidestone.com

Lay-out & cover design: Sidestone Press
Cover: Image based on a photo of the Sword mould from Piverones (TO, Italy), 9th century BC, collection Musei Reali Torino (inv. 75004).

Translated by Tim Armstrong

ISBN 978-94-6426-104-2 (softcover)
ISBN 978-94-6426-105-9 (hardcover)
ISBN 978-94-6426-106-6 (PDF e-book)

Contents

	FOREWORD	11
	ENCOUNTERING WAR	13
	How History comes to the Historian	13
	How to explain?	14
	Going to War	15
	History, a Human Science	19
	Archaeology in history	21
	War and European Protohistory Revisited	22
I	**WHAT WARS?**	25
	Story I: Once upon a time, a warrior's weapons…	25
	War Words	28
	Theories of War	28
	The Philosophical Angle	30
	Stateless Societies as seen by Europeans	32
	The 'savage' beneath our Feet	34
	Ever more Archaeological Evidence	35
	Archaeology and History	37
	The 'Primitive' in the City	38
	The War of Origins	40
	The Celt of our Dreams	42
	And there was War…	45
II	**RESEARCH 'EVIDENCE'**	49
	Story II: Keeping Weapons	49
	An Abundance of Evidence…	51
	After the Battle	53
	The Metal Ages in Pictures	55
	Scenes of Combat	57
	The first Battlefields	59

	Sacred Sites and Cult Objects	60
	Skeletons and Splinters	63
	The Lessons of Bones	65
III	**WHEN METAL SPEAKS**	**69**
	Story III: The World of Metal	69
	Fascinating Metal	71
	Choices of metal in Europe	74
	Unpicking Harlequin's Cloak	76
	Hierarchies that dare not speak their name	77
	Deciphering and Understanding	79
	In the Laboratory	82
	Starting the investigation at the end	84
	In the Bronzesmith's Crucible	85
	Under the Metalworker's Hammer	88
IV	**A LIST OF WEAPONS**	**91**
	Story IV: The bronzesmith in his workshop	91
	The Sword extends the Arm…	94
	The sword evolves…	97
	And a Scabbard…	99
	The Spear Thickens	100
	Arrows of Outrageous Fortune…	101
	The Ambiguity of the Hafted Axe…	103
	A Shield to Protect the Body…	104
	The Metal Helmet reinforces the Warrior's Head…	106
	Metal to Embellish the Breast	110
V	**OFF TO WAR**	**115**
	Story V: Taking up arms	115
	Violence in the Palaeolithic	117
	Multiple-Use Technology in the Neolithic	119
	What Kind of Neolithic 'War'?	121
	Declaring War in the Bronze Age	124
	The Revolution in Fighting in 1700 BC	125
	Multifaceted War in the Iron Age	128
	Violence upon violence	130
	Farewell to Arms	131
	Metal Hoards	133

VI	**WAR IN ALL ITS STATES**	**137**
	Story VI: The 1000 BC warrior on the Normandy coast	137
	Women: Goddesses or Sinners?	141
	Masculine Domination	143
	Rich women without weapons	144
	Transgressing Norms	146
	Reasons for War	148
	State, Primitives, the Written Word: Terms of Power	150
	What Sort of Society?	152
	Three Ages of War?	154
	Words and functions for all	156
	The West in the Dynamics of Warfare	157
VII	**THE HUMAN LEVEL**	**159**
	Questions of Scale	159
	War and Peace	162
	A Trip to a Bronze Age Kitchen	163
	ACKNOWLEDGEMENTS	**165**
	NOTES	**167**
	BIBLIOGRAPHY	**189**

Dedication

À la mémoire de Peter Clark, trop tôt et trop brutalement disparu alors nous travaillions sur ce manuscrit au printemps 2021.

Peter était archéologue au Canterbury Archaeological Trust, l'un des pères du 'Dover Boat' mis au jour à Douvres en 1992, et son plus grand promoteur. En 2011, nous avions lancé une aventure européenne autour de ce bateau, de l'Âge du bronze, de la navigation, des relations transmanches qui nous racontaient à quel point nous sommes voisins de part et d'autre de ce bras de mer.

Le projet « BOAT 1550 BC » était une occasion magnifique de travailler en équipe. Peter aimait partager son travail, son temps, sa passion, sa musique avec tous. Avec ses amis, ses collègues, de nouvelles connaissances. Avec les grands et avec les enfants. Il avait une capacité pour aller à la rencontre des autres, simplement, gentiment, avec une ouverture d'esprit et une bienveillance rares. Durant cinq années, nous avons travaillé sans relâche, nous avons eu des fous rires, nous avons bu des bières et disserté sur le « vrai » fish and chips (celui avec la purée de petits pois), nous avons savouré des « cafés gourmands » dont il raffolait. Lorsque des difficultés survenaient, à aucun moment, il ne se départissait de ce flegme qui l'habitait. Calmement, il cherchait la solution, le compromis, le meilleur. Et se réjouissait de ce qui avait été accompli, remerciant et souriant, soucieux de chacun, enthousiaste de tout. Il était un grand professionnel et un homme remarquable.

Je voudrais lui dédier ces pages qui sont infimes face au manque qu'il a laissé, et lui offrir ce petit mot en français, une langue qu'il affectionnait tant.[1]

Le 12 avril 2022

Foreword

The question whether humankind is essentially violent or peaceful has been debated for centuries. Was war invented one day (a suggestion with which this book opens), or has it always existed? How can resilience to violence be achieved? Questions that have become acute and timely since this book was written now that Europe is once again home to unprecedented bloodshed.

Philosophers, political scientists, sociologists, historians and anthropologists have produced what must be libraries worth of books devoted to the topic of war and peace. Archaeology – particularly the study of our deep, unwritten, history -recently joined this group of disciplines investigating it. Many non-archaeologists, in making claims on human nature, go back to that deep history – apparently hoping to find there some perspective on humanity in what is thought to be its most uncomplicated form. So far, this has been a highly problematic endeavour that was often more about using the past to oversimplify and to self-congratulate the present by using prehistory as some kind of antithesis to the present.

Evidence for violence and peace from archaeological sources, however, is more subtle and contextually-defined than one might initially think. In this book, Anne Lehoërff gives many examples of that. In her treatise, she takes us along a personal, loosely written trip along conflicts old and new – with sometimes shocking examples of cruelty from prehistoric societies, but also of superb archaeological warrior outfits displaying outstanding crafting skills. In doing so, she opens the impressively rich archaeology of – especially – Bronze Age France to a non-French readership.

David Fontijn, author of 'Economies of Destruction' and 'Give Peace a Chance'

ENCOUNTERING WAR

I hate weapons and I hate war[2]...

One day, war was invented. Maybe one fine, sunny Monday morning in April. Why not? But what was the date? And how did it happen? And how can historians find out? Any enquiry has to start with an examination of evidence left by the past, written evidence if it exists but also with other forms of archival material left by mankind during the course of history. Studying the invention of war means venturing into the dangerous territory of origins.[3] It also means taking the brave step of analysing the birth of war amidst vanished oral societies known about through physical records – that is, archaeological material.

How History comes to the Historian

In Europe, from the Baltic Sea to the Atlantic and from the plains of the Danube all the way to the Garonne and the Tagus, hundreds of thousands of weapons have been discovered – in graves, hoarded below ground, or thrown into lakes and rivers. Whether ignored or carefully collected over the centuries, these objects have inspired ever-renewing interest since the beginnings of scientific archaeology over the last 200 years or so. Their categorisation according to type has facilitated the periodisation of time and the establishment of chronologies. By seeing weapons in terms of coherent groups and contextualising them alongside other kinds of data, it has been possible to distinguish groups of people (archaeological cultures) who lived together and followed distinctive practices during distinguishable periods. From the start of the 19th century, whole swathes of European history, almost forgotten for lack of written words, have gradually emerged from darkness, thanks to this evidence.

Amidst this enormous mass of data, we see some evidence relating directly to violence, and even war, which a society might see as a legitimate form of violence organised by those who have the power to do so. The advent of the sword between 1700 and 1600 BC in various places in Europe marks a key turning point,[4] more so than any other weapon. This is the first artefact manufactured for entirely unambiguous purposes: wounding and killing people. Its study involves technical questions of how and when it was used, belief systems, the nature of the societies out of which it emerged, and political questions too. This is where this book starts: the study of 'going to war with weapons', not only to understand the means and methods of armed conflict, but also to analyse the societies themselves.

The presence of very large numbers of metal weapons dating from the 2nd millennium BC leaves us in no doubt about the presence of war. Various clues enable us to define how and when they were used. They can be seen as markers in what amounts to an arms race. But is it a birth or a beginning? Can we talk about a 'day' when swords were invented? To get closer to an answer, we have to go back to an even more remote past, to the Neolithic era, and then even further still, to the Palaeolithic. How far back along this path does the material bear witness to 'war'? But rather than retreating into far-off reaches of the past looking for evidence of war then, let us instead take as our starting point the certainties offered by Bronze Age finds, and place them in a broader perspective.

The geographical space involved is vast, covering thousands of square miles over Central and Western Europe. This is the unknown world that the Greeks referred to as 'barbarian', a word that then just meant foreign and only later took on a pejorative meaning. Over the course of time, ever since 'our' arrival on the scene in the form of *Homo sapiens*, this Eurasian isthmus has undergone changes in climate and other profound transformations. This immense space has been a theatre of change, bearing witness to the formation of new land masses, which altered in shape over and over again. People gathered to become settled farmers from the 6th millennium BC, but they never ceased travelling by land and sea. They worked a variety of materials, they prayed, they built houses and architectural structures dedicated to their various beliefs, and they buried their dead in different ways. They also experienced conflict. Evidence for violence between individuals goes back a long way. But the idea that there was 'war' in the full sense of the word raises questions. Questions that apply to humanity as a whole. There is an obligation and a need to look carefully at very ancient human history from before the advent of writing. I am the first to be convinced of this. Nevertheless, this text took shape 'backwards', in a way that puts one in mind of Umberto Eco's crayfish.[5]

How to explain?

This situation is not unrelated to the general question of how a historian chooses their subject matter. Or rather how subject matter comes to choose the historian. Or more briefly – how this encounter takes place. It seems to arise out of a complex system of meeting-points, an infinitely subtle cocktail, an alchemy consisting of something fundamental and immovable and the relationship between these situations that vary from one individual to another. Children are taught at school that they are citizens of their own time, before any of them grow up to become historians. This is obvious, to the extent that things we think about as the same ('funerals', 'party menus', as indeed 'schools', and many other notions), clearly cannot be conceived of as being identical in 1872 or 2022. This is true of chronology and also of place. But such a general truth about spatiotemporal relationships is not enough. Explanations linked to men and women themselves also have to be taken into account, with their own histories and personalities. Our sensitivities, the burdens we carry and our sense of what is required of us, together with our own lived experiences (individual, familial and so on), can all interfere with whatever we are trying to study. Particularly if we are dealing with painful or violent subject matter. Evidently, descendants of holocaust deportees experience a different form of responsibility, consciously or otherwise, when tackling related issues compared with people not directly affected by such events. The same is true for subjects like slavery and racial segregation. Of course, such mechanisms are not simplistic and reactions can vary from one individual to another. Researchers who deal with violence do not necessarily have a greater taste or personal liking for the subject than other people. Simply, they tackle and think about it whilst others do not. Of course, there might be some attachment or sense of connection, or indeed of revulsion; the result being a greater or lesser distancing of certain individuals as they reflect on their historical inheritance – which is inevitably beset by matters that lie beyond that individual's control whilst being part and parcel of their work as historians. People who themselves have been victims of violence might seek out subject matter that help them better understand the mechanisms of what happened to them, or they might be tempted to exclude such issues from their chosen field of study because of the confusion engendered between their personal and research lives might seem uncertain and dangerous, not only to their private lives, but also because the path ahead seems too troubling for them to work effectively as historians. Neither of these choices is any better or worse than the other. Individuals have simply to cope with what they can and cannot do, both as researchers and as human beings. And of course, as time passes, they may well change, and decide to take on material that was once off-limits, or indeed to turn away from what once seemed feasible – all depending on their subsequent experiences, their own development and maturity. One might add that researchers have particular tastes, tastes which have complex origins and these too might make them want to take on one set of themes and historical issues rather than others. Put more academically, and this has often been shown to be the case, historians cannot escape from their own historicity.[6]

There is another question, on a rather different level, but which forms part of this complex mosaic: the question of proof. In the 19th century Prehistory was inconceivable until data began to emerge from the soil. The discovery of objects, hoards and skeletal remains, opened up perspectives hitherto unthinkable in the intellectual, political and religious climate of Western Europe (and related territories). A large-scale and often complex upsetting of certainties ensued, both in the academic communities and in the worlds of ordinary people. This encounter with the very distant past would not have been possible without archaeological discoveries, but archaeology was not in itself enough to make any understanding of the very distant past simple or immediate. The documentary sources available were necessary but not sufficient. Intellectual mechanisms had to be set up and methodologies put into practice.

Going to War

Just as I was writing these lines a book by Stéphane Audouin-Rouzeau was published: *Une initiation. Rwanda (1994-2016)*.[7] He deals with the experiences of a historian, a specialist in contemporary warfare, who studied violence in countries where genocide had recently taken place, and where the aftermath was obvious everywhere, no one knowing what the eventual outcome would be, either in the medium or the long term.[8] Reading texts about subjects relating to one's own – in this case human violence – is quite a normal thing to do, since it helps one to reflect and think more clearly. The subject matter does not have to address exactly the same time and place as one's own subject matter. Indeed, regularly comparing data from areas of study parallel to one's own is an important dimension of specialised research since it helps get a deeper understanding of some questions and a fuller understanding of others. Learning about others' experiences of the world gives us a different perspective, shifting the focus of the way we look at things. The words of Stephane Audouin-Rouzeau make it clear, in the Rwandan context, how anyone studying a war can get caught up in it, even those who have made a long term conscious choice that it should be part of their professional career.

My journey has been different. I have been interested in the distant past and vanished societies since I was a child, like so many others, except that I made this my career. Furthermore, I was fascinated by the oral societies of European Protohistory – the Neolithic era and Metal Ages, from the 6th to the 1st millennia BC (in West European context[9]). Initially, this fascination took on various forms. I wanted to immerse myself in the very distant past which seemed then to be surrounded by a kind of misty halo, because it was so old and so distant from us, so long forgotten. By bringing people from then into the modern world, it seemed one might dare abolish time, directly by means of contact with evidence from the past, and symbolically by giving them some form of life. What is more, as far as oral societies were concerned, the process would not be rooted in the reading of words or texts of any kind. Rather, I would have to be able to read material which appears silent – physical remains left by individual gestures and the social choices concealed behind them – in such a way as to bring them (back) to life. The process seemed all the more attractive because it appeared complicated and quite without indications as to how outcomes might be understood in our present circumstances.

This no doubt somewhat manic enthusiasm was given an extra head of steam by a form of intellectual fervour that gained in strength over the years, because of the widespread failure to understand these epochs and the consequences of their relative marginalisation in the halls of academia. Of course these societies left behind no writing, but they do still belong to our history – their stories are told by historians of *physical* objects whose work is just as valid as that of historians of written texts. The ability to construct a narrative does not depend on the nature of the sources left by past societies, so much as on the work of contemporary historians, and their ability to argue and present a case based on evidence.[10] A researcher's job is to confront and sometimes criticise the current state of play, to find words giving these vanished oral societies a legitimate existence, just like '*others*', in our historical narrative.[11]

Of all the vast number of possible fields of study relating to European Protohistory, I latched on to manufacturing craft, in particular the working of copper alloys during the Metal Ages (that is, the Bronze Age which in Europe lasted from about 2200 BC until 800 BC, and then the Iron Age, which continued in westernmost areas of Europe until 52 BC). I soon became particularly interested in the Bronze Age. This choice of subject came from my interest in what people can do when their minds and skills encounter physical matter that they can transform and fashion. I was particularly drawn by the notion of *Homo faber*, and the various intellectual and manual mechanisms that can give body, volume, function, aesthetics and meaning to the raw materials which nature makes directly or indirectly available to us. By following this path, I found I was also treading in the footsteps of the prehistorian and ethnologist André Leroi-Gourhan. He had never worked on metallurgy (or war), but he had constructed an intellectual tool, the idea of the *'chaîne opératoire'* or 'operational chain'. This enables us to visualise both the non-material activities, which disappear alongside the movements that created them, and hard evidence brought to light by archaeologists.[12] This concept has proved so powerful that it is still used, in the language of Molière, even as far afield as Shakespeare's own country.[13] I never met André Leroi-Gourhan in person, for he died before our paths could have crossed, but I spent much time studying his various works. So, I became a technologist, a specialist in ancient metalwork carried out by people who died several millennia ago. By studying their work, I felt empowered to peer in through the doors of their workshops, draw near to them and try to analyse choices they were making. My first excavation was the site of a bronzesmith's workshop in the oppidum of Bibracte in France where fibulae were made. I went on to study bronzesmiths' moulds in the Po Valley (Italy), then the manufacture of Iron Age fibulae found in various hoards (throughout Europe). Nothing in any of this pointed towards violence and war as a form of organised violence. This was to creep in surreptitiously through a back door.

One object of initial study led to another, and more than 20 years of research on the manufacture of ancient copper alloy artefacts practised by protohistoric societies. During these years, I excavated various sites and structures used in manufacturing. I learned how to look at materials under a microscope. I tried to reconstruct *chaînes opératoires*, and I studied and attempted to reproduce our forefathers' activities, enlisting the aid of contemporary artisans in order to gain a better understanding of the relationship between the physical and the non-physical. I learned all I could about historical methodologies and I tried to combine these approaches in pursuit of my chosen subject – handcraft. My sole aim was to rediscover and understand these people as they were embodied in their skills. I observed ever more artefacts coming fresh from the earth, from museum collections and various other sources. I ended up with a catalogue of various archaeological finds and sites, and manufactured objects of the highest quality, indicating exceptional technical skills.

It soon became impossible to deny the evidence. The metalworkers who fascinated me did not just make high quality objects, like jewellery and vessels requiring great skill and hours of work. They also made instruments for killing – weapons. Of course, I had catalogued these objects, in my inventories or mentally. Yet stupidly, or naively, I never confronted this as a reality, nor did I ever say to myself: 'This sword killed real people, perhaps one, perhaps several'. These bronzesmiths were, literally, engineers of violent deaths.

The truth of this gradually made its presence felt, during the course of my laboratory work and whilst teaching and giving seminars. There were also key moments, two in particular. In 2005 I was making a technical study of the breastplates from Marmesse (Haute-Marne, France), which were discovered as a result of a rather convoluted series of events during the 1980s. The find was dated to the end of the Bronze Age and had been stored in the French National Archaeological Museum in Paris (Saint-Germain-en-Laye).[14] These objects interested me because they were from a metal 'hoard' typical of the Bronze Age and the quality of the metalwork was remarkable. One Tuesday, when the museum was closed, the breastplates were removed from the display cases. To avoid the possibility of damage resulting from excessive handling, they were not taken down to the library as would usually have been the case, but moved up to storage space in the attic. The place looks like an attic from the good old days, like when we were children, full of bric-a-brac, things that are almost, but not quite, treasures. It is freezing cold up there in winter, as it often is in old buildings. Alone, half frozen, I was making a minute study of those breastplates, one after the other, looking at every revealing detail regarding the individual history of each artefact's manufacture. As I put one of them on a small table in order to photograph it, I could suddenly imagine clearly the individual who had worn it, as if projected on to the white wall which was to serve as my backdrop. I had a clear sense that this breastplate had been used in combat, before it became an old archaeological object stuck in a display case in a museum sheltered by a former royal castle. I sat down, and found myself talking inwardly to that anonymous 'person', this 'nobody', hoping to find out what they had experienced and what they had been doing when wearing this warrior's gear.

Another time, another place, but still in an attic. In September 2006, in the museum of the Palazzo di Venezia in Rome, a restorer led me along the corridors of this immense and majestic palace and through a hidden door which opened into a ridiculously small cubbyhole containing a desk on which there was a book for visitors to sign. A metal suit of armour, fully assembled, dating from the 17th century (AD!) seemed to be keeping an eye on the precious register. A very narrow stairway led up, firstly past the restoration laboratory and then up several other flights of stairs, before coming to a sudden halt at the entrance to an incredibly small room, its floor creaking beneath our feet. This was the loft of the tower which looms gloriously over the Palace of Venice and which is also the home of a rather heterogeneous collection of objects. There were about 30 suits of armour, seeming to stand guard over the room, and there were also old wooden display cases. One of these accounted for my presence there, for in it was a collection of helmets, armour, short and long swords, and so on. There were more than 50 pieces which I had come to study at the request of Italian colleagues, again analysing more closely how each had been manufactured.[15] Sitting, as before, at a small table, with a camera, scales, callipers, and various microscopes, the open window overlooking the copula of the Gesù, which stood out against an immaculately blue sky in the magnificent late summer morning light, I had to yield before the evidence: there was nothing neutral about these objects. They were no longer ordinary, but seemed rather imbued by the functions which I could no longer dissociate from their manufacture. Yes, 'my' metalworkers had deployed their skills in the service of artefacts whose purpose was to fight, wound and kill. What is more, Prince Lasdislao Odescalchi, who at the beginning of the 20th century had assembled these items for his collection, now split between the Palace of Venice, the Castello of Saint Angelo and his family properties, consisted exclusively of weaponry. The objects that I was to study had been put together, in a way, to illustrate the origins of war. The message could not have been clearer.

Once I had grasped this truth – finally – questions cascaded through my mind, regarding methods of manufacture of course, but also what it all implied. My thoughts rushed back and forth, hither and thither, trying to link shapes and usages: how might one conceive of these objects in the context of the human societies that had produced them. How and why had they been manufactured? What did they have to say about the people themselves and the choices they had made over the course of time? Why had I missed the subject for so long? Was it just me, or was there some other epistemological dimension? Tackling war then became a necessity, whether I liked it or not. It was therefore 'a Call to

Arms' in the literal as well as literary sense of the word that war imposed itself upon me, with all the questions to which its reality gives rise. So, I did not choose this subject matter, but I did not avoid it either.

History, a Human Science

It is not the historian's job to shilly-shally, particularly when confronted, after years of study, with a form of evidence. At that point one has to use appropriate tools and methodologies to come up with results or hypotheses. Depending on the nature of the subject matter, an enquiry might be more or less delicate both scientifically and from a human point of view. Research distances historians from their subject matter. This is of course far more complicated when this subject matter is still, in every sense, 'living', that is, still present. Rwanda is a very extreme example of this, though there are plenty more situations where there is no functioning distance between past events and present-day reality. A kind of telescoping of time makes it hard to see a way forward, weighing the historian down with emotions and feelings. A researcher has to take a step backwards before, if at all possible, taking over again from the human individual. History is, in the full sense of the word, a human and social science. Encountering difficulties with such experiences is normal, and in some ways reassuring in terms of being human. Insensitivity, real or apparent, would be more disturbing. In the case of Rwanda, this is one of the key questions and anxieties: how can anyone understand behaviour which deviates so far from normal rules and codes, like the murder of neighbours or children denouncing their parents[16]? What cogs of what behavioural machinery spring into action at the time of massacres and mass killings like those witnessed by the 20th century? What kind of hatred can be so powerful as to exclude and deny others who are different from ourselves, to the extent of wanting to annihilate them, make them literally disappear, to dehumanise them in our sight? Anyone whose specialism is the modern world has to confront actions which are difficult to analyse, actions which seem far removed from what we understand as the foundations of humanity in any 'rational' view of the world, that is, a view illuminated by reason.

Rwanda is made even more unbearable by the fact that Western Europe thought it had learnt the lessons of Nazi extermination camps. Here again, the dehumanisation and physical destruction of individuals reached paroxysms of horror which no one thought could ever reoccur.[17] This turned out to be a mistake, both of judgement and of perspective. Instead of an organised genocide geographically separated from the everyday lives of populations, we found ourselves confronted by a massacre in which everyone was involved, into which the whole population was plunged, with no boundary between where life was lived and where killings took place. This was a different pattern, though also rooted in hatred of others because of their difference, in this case ethnic, rather than religious, political or sexual. This makes the role of the researcher particularly difficult – reality overturns all the reference points and certainties of the so-called 'historical method' which we have learned...

Matters are not quite the same for a historian dealing with ancient, or indeed very ancient periods. There is indeed a telescoping of time, but the various levels of sedimentation create a kind of serenity, both symbolic and real. Data takes on an essentially or exclusively archaeological shape. This is direct in the physical sense – bones and the material remnants of past lives. Archaeologists project these traces of the past into present time. They bring these objects to life by trying to give a voice to those who fell silent, recently or very long ago. Archaeologists lend them their words. In the case of more recent periods, thanks to archaeological data, and sometimes various other sources, human beings studied may acquire names, families and a tangible identity, which can be poignant. The dead we study soon become very real, historically speaking, directly because we can see and touch their remains, and indirectly because of the artefacts they made and the houses they built. Yet at the same time, they continue to be literally anonymous. Their identity is made up only by terminologies invented by archaeologists and attributed to them *a posteriori*. Through the centuries, the millennia that have passed, emotions sometimes well up during an excavation, because of a discovery that has been made. But this is nothing compared to what one might feel on finding the remains of someone who died recently, someone identifiable, particularly if their family is still alive and present. The long dead protect the researcher from the pain of their palpable suffering through violence and war, simply by being faceless and nameless. We are cushioned by the sedimentation which transforms and partly dehumanises them over time through the natural process of decomposition. Of course, a skull is still that of an individual – but fleshless, devoid of character and expression, or even if these are present but fixed by death, we see it differently, and the same is true of more extreme cases, for example if the skull in question has been smashed by machete or axe blows. We cannot personify that person, or project ourselves or those close to us onto such dead people. The status of 'documentary evidence' is easily acquired, in the manner of a vase, or the oven of a hearth, even if what happened to such human remains dug up by archaeologists might cause us to question the actions and values of our broader society, which has come to inherit such remains.[18]

One exceptional (and unique) recent discovery quite upset the way we think about such matters, and at the same time sheds light on the complex link between present-day humans and those long dead. It also illustrates difficulties in the way we apprehend death and the various kinds of physical traces it leaves behind, and how this perception shifts and changes depending on the nature of those traces. Ötzi is the name of a man killed 5300 years ago. It was taken from the name of a glacier where he was discovered in September 1991, on the border between Austria and Italy in the Alps.[19] The scientists whose job it was to preserve his body in the museum of Bolzano (Italy) refused to go along with this name. Nevertheless, the public chose to do so because this corresponded to certain expectations. The name gives him some kind of identity. The fact that his body has been remarkably well preserved in the ice for all this time means that he has a face and a human quality which his contemporaries have lost, though many of their bodies have been found in various graves. His skin was preserved, albeit chemically transformed, and still bears the marks of tattoos at strategic acupuncture points. His hair was found. The contents of his stomach revealed what his last meal consisted of. Clinical examinations made it possible to draw up a list of illnesses from which he suffered – Ötzi was about 40 years old and in a poor state of health. Then there are the incredible stories surrounding his discovery, not least the series of deaths of some (but not all) of his discoverers – all the ingredients to make Ötzi into a hero straight from the Late Neolithic, from the end of the 4th millennium BC. He became too the hero of something like a thriller, with multiple hypotheses, seeing him turn by turn, as a murderer, a victim, a man on the run… Whatever the true scenario, one fact remains – that of his death caused by an arrow lodged in his back, probably fired from somewhere below him by one of his pursuers. There is no doubt about the act of violence, even if we cannot know all the details. Yet, despite the tangible reality that makes Ötzi so fascinating, the distance that separates the modern world from his, means we necessarily see his violent death differently from how we see deaths resulting from recent conflicts.

Archaeology in history

Archaeological practice in the context of very ancient periods, particularly with respect to vanished oral societies, certainly does have a distancing effect on historians. Does this change how the researcher works? Up to a point. But what does it change? Probably it means that we do not have to work on an emotional level, at least not one of extreme emotions.[20] But, working on these ancient oral societies deprives us of any connection to the kind of facts that words generate. Without such original words, we have to adapt our methodology and evidence criteria. Again, we have to deal with what exists, what has come down to us from the past.

There is a very old misunderstanding, linked to the role we attribute to writing. When the Western world began to reflect upon and invent history, it used what it knew best: texts. Antique sources provided the cornerstone of what was considered to be erudition. Herodotus was held up as the father of history following a narrow reading of the first sentence of his *Histories*.[21] Since then a lot of water has flowed beneath the bridges of historical practice – archaeology has been invented, vanished oral societies have been identified in the subsoil of Europe, and methods have been developed, making it possible for physical remains to be understood just like any other form of evidence. Some scholars, not least those of the *Annales* school,[22] had strong intuitions about this situation at an early stage, proposing a broader and transformed vision of history. Lucien Fevbre (1878-1956) made this subtle pronouncement:

"History no doubt consists of historical writings. Provided there are any. But history can and must be created with all the ingenuity that historians can reasonably permit themselves... This means words. Signs. Landscapes and tiles. The shapes of fields and weeds. Lunar eclipses and horse harnesses. Knowledge of stones [...] and analyses of swords.[23]

History is in the process. The objective is to understand past human beings in all their component parts, their individual and collective decisions. It does not matter whether the proof consists of a collection of words or objects, old or new, numerous or sparse. The nature and quantity of sources are irrelevant. Documentation is a means, not an end. Documentation is the stuff of research but the objective of research lies beyond documentation, even though documentation has to determine the range of possible conclusions. All past societies have their place in history, and research is never completely finished.[24]

As an individual I have had no direct experience of war, and I admit that I have a tendency to reject it. I keep systematically away from images of violence in any form, cinematographic or photographic. I do not understand why people might have a taste for the morbid... So, it was not as a human being that I approached this topic, but rather as a researcher, compelled by a sense of duty. The sheer age of the artefacts that interested me probably helped – sedimentation had done its work. During the course of my studies of weapons, I had encountered killers and victims, but they remained anonymous, coming to life only indirectly. Besides, it was precisely because of my enquiry into a particular set of archaeological documents – my research specialism – that I came to perceive them more clearly, as something going beyond the metalworkers I initially wanted to understand more closely.

War and European Protohistory Revisited

War is a complex subject which has had an important place in written texts since antiquity, but not necessarily as an object of historical study such as we understand it nowadays. Bibliographies regarding war are abundant, focussing on battles, politics, logistics and strategy. After a time of doubt and the rejection of war following the Second World War, it has now become an omnipresent theme, but the way we approach it has changed. We have moved on from a view of war as something which can be seen and described like a fresco, to a view of war as something experienced from within, that involves suffering. More recent conflicts, both state wars and acts of terrorism have come to the forefront, alongside historical work carried out in the context of various commemorations. For example, the series of events marking the centenary of the First World War which took place between 2014 and 2018. In France, the Algerian War is at last being tackled after years of obscuration. Throughout the world, questions of slavery and colonial wars have been roundly discussed, with vigorous debates taking place in all countries concerned. This plethora can be crushing, creating a sense of guilt, a muddying of paths. Recent conflicts have dominated so much that history and memory can sometimes be confused.[25] Trying to get new perspectives on the enduring phenomenon of war seems sensible if we are to gain a global understanding of wars, and move on from an attachment to the present which sometimes, unless we are careful, means that even the French Revolution can seem very far away in time. Certainly, war is now very much *in*, complete with festivals, reconstructions and publications, commemorating famous battles, like the Battle of Bouvines on 27 July 1214, Agincourt on 25 October 1415, or indeed the Battle of Hastings on 14 October 1066. Such wars conform to the classical 'model' of history. As for the most ancient European societies, our understanding of war has been determined by our own understanding of European history, by our European understanding of 'other' societies, and the way the latter has been conceived by various academic disciplines. Specialists in protohistoric societies are all too aware of how derisory their place is in this landscape.[26] Who even knows what 'Protohistory' means or, at an even more simple level, what Bronze Age societies were like? A brief glance at courses of study in schools (from primary right through to 18+) gives a reliable idea of the importance and space given to various historical periods and human societies. Protohistory's representation is still very small, and still largely excluded from 'History' in the classical sense of the word.[27] But this is not just about which slice of history can be tidied into which box.[28] There are important consequences for the way we think. Two worlds are isolated from one another by one improbable intellectual frontier: writing, which determines the way we look at societies. Any history defined in terms of the existence or absence of texts is mistaken and reductive. Human history is that of all who belong to the genus *Homo*, a genus that has left behind clues that make it possible to see how social, cultural and technical behaviour functioned in the context of the human species. Human history is therefore, at the very least, the history of *Homo sapiens*, our direct forebears. This is who 'we', biologically speaking, are (albeit with variable sprinklings of Neandertal…). The fact that certain societies adopted writing is part of history, but it does not define history. Let us go further and say it is absurd to consider 'Prehistory' as an autonomous field of study, or as anything more than just a convenient and imperfect term defining one period (amongst others), displaying a variety of different aspects and characteristics. Although it was understandable to think like this in the 19th century when archaeological research and academic acceptance of it began, however, more recent developments in methodologies, knowledge and paradigms render such a view obsolete.[29] During the course of this work and the encounters to which it has led, I have become increasingly certain of this, and it has seemed increasingly important to me to criticise and stress just how much this way of looking at history has impeded Europe in the task of writing its own history. For example the history of war.

Originally, this text was purely academic, which meant it had a corresponding protective framework, in the form of its recondite and somewhat obscure technical language, that of 'archaeo-metallurgy'.[30] Several years later, and having completed various other works, it seemed incongruous to leave it to be read in that form. I wanted, as far as possible, to adapt the writing of this book for a readership less familiar with the terminology of what we call 'Prehistory' and 'Protohistory', excluding purportedly specialist jargon.[31] I have tried to guide the reader along more difficult paths where signposts were needed. To reach the goal, certain inevitable assumptions had to be put into perspective, deconstructing some of the readers' certainties, and pointing out various errors often taught as truths, before finally turning to the substance of the book and suggesting new models of explanation. The point was to involve readers too in war, by means of 'a Call to Arms' and metallurgy, but only after acquiring knowledge of the concepts at stake, and understanding what kind of old *a priori* might still be cluttering our thinking. Given the present-day intellectual context, I tried to offer a path between sharp archaeological facts, which for the non-specialist offer little by way of explanation, and a narrative approach that would be too close to fiction and therefore no longer history.

At heart, this book's objective is to be a double history, arising out of my own lived experience (the way war fell upon me out of the blue) and my desire to make a point (that confining history to societies that adopted writing leads to error). In addition, the aim has been to suggest new perspectives as to how history might be written, once freed from dusty old straight-jackets; and, using a new model of study, to explain the advent of war as a technical and social phenomenon that arrived in Europe several thousand years ago.

I

WHAT WARS?

Once upon a time, a warrior's weapons...

War is fought with weapons. Around the year 1000 BC, fighting men in Western Europe had equipment for offence and defence. Their weaponry was varied, with artefacts that left no doubt as to their purpose: helmets, breastplates and swords. Let us take a closer look at a set of weaponry we might imagine as having been in the possession of a warrior in the year 1000 BC. An iconic array of weapons, coherently assembled, even if purists may observe that they are not strictly contemporary, and that they come from regions that are close, but not quite identical (the helmet and the sword come from near the Channel and the breastplate comes from Alpine societies – altogether more continental). To make them seem human and alive, let us spend a moment putting these weapons together and looking at them in situ.[32]

In 1832 in the green lands of Normandy, one Monsieur Maline, who was working in fields belonging to the château of Ailly (Calvados), discovered by chance a series of objects, principal amongst which were nine helmets. He reported his find to Monsieur Vauquelin, the land's owner. The objects were easily identifiable. Local men of learning interested in such 'antiquities' classified the nine helmets as being of the pointed variety, which they termed 'à crêtes' or crested, and as having 'side wings'. Comparisons were made with those found in the necropolis of Villanova (dating from the early Italian Iron Age, between the 8th and 10th centuries BC) in the town of Tarquinia, then called Corneto. They wondered how these artefacts might have been so morphologically similar? They thought that Mediterranean influences must have reached the channel coast by boat and the find was dated to a time not then clearly defined, a form of pre-antiquity, the time of the Celts – the antechamber of history. These nine objects were described as defensive artefacts and associated with combat, the very combat that Celtic populations had dared to unleash in their fight against Julius Caesar – though they had finally to submit to him in Alesia, in 52 BC. 40 years after their discovery, these helmets still seemed to embody such ancient events. So, in 1867, when the French National Archaeological Museum was opened in Saint-Germain-en-Laye, one of the 'Gaulish' helmets was put on display at the Paris Universal Exposition[33]. 30 years later it was still a helmet of this kind which Vercingetorix can be seen throwing at Caesar's feet in the incredible surrender scene painted by Lionel Royer. In this painting, the Gaulish chief is wearing a *sparkling breastplate modelled on a more recent find – the Grenoble hoard from Véria (Jura), also discovered by chance in 1860 – or maybe it was modelled on the one from Naples, decorated with pictures of fighting cocks. In any case, we can exclude the hoard from Fillinges (Haute Savoie), found in 1901 and therefore post-dating our painting.*

Amongst recent iconic discoveries one might mention the hoard of Marmesse (Haute-Marne) which consists of nine breastplates, all of which have been, over a period of time, restored and conserved. This story began in 1974 when sand extraction work was going on – not uncommon in France, then enthusiastically engaged in infrastructure projects (roads, railways buildings, and so on). A digger revealed fragments of decorated metal sheets, not immediately identified, in an area called 'Petit Marais', which were forgotten about for a while. They were taken to the contractor's headquarters, but the owner of the land was not informed. In 1976, other fragments came to light, this time leading to a visit from archaeologists, then a first excavation in 1980. There were more discoveries throughout the 1980s and attempts were made to fit the artefacts together and to restore them. The breastplates rapidly became famous – icons of late Bronze Age defensive armour. At the end of the 20th century, scientific studies made it possible to classify all the metal objects in various ways. It was known by now that these helmets found in Normandy were more or less contemporary to a similar type of breastplate. The Gaulish warrior who had defied Rome had not been forgotten, but his Bronze Age ancestors were still not really seen as warriors, war not being a specific object of study. Everyone was concentrating on typology, dates, and possible stylistic influences. It was as if this the breastplate had not been worn by a warrior, a fighter, a man who tried to kill his enemies and protect himself – the finds were seen rather in terms of 'social elites.'

Our fighter's gear would be incomplete without at least one offensive weapon, which plays an important role here: the sword. Of all the thousands of swords found in Europe, one in particular fits in with the weaponry of our hypothetical late Bronze Age warrior. In 1913, the uncle of a certain Monsieur Wimet came by chance upon a bronze sword at the bottom of the Fort de Croy at Wimereux (Pas-de-Calais, France). Various researchers studied it, not least in the 1970s and 80s when the first general overviews of the Bronze Age were being drawn up. Such close scrutiny and measuring! It was 56.5 centimetres long and it weighed 414 grams. Its shape was pistilliform. It had a complex metal tongue with three distinct parts. The pommel was splayed. The relatively long shaft was perforated at three points so it could be attached to a haft or grip made of organic material (wood or bone), riveted onto the cross-guard. This in turn was elongated and likewise perforated at three points, on either side of the blade. Its remarkable state of preservation was often mentioned, as was its date from the late Bronze Age, around one thousand BC. There was much talk too of how similar it was to a type of sword found typically in the south-west of England and the north west of France referred to as the 'Ewart Park' sword. But no one ever really thought of it in terms of something a warrior might use in action, even though it was referred to as a 'sword'. In 1975 P. Leclerc, writing for a local learned periodical, noted: "The sword is very beautiful." It is true that the object has elegant lines, so such aesthetic criteria were indeed appropriate to describe it – other than in the context of its functional reality of course – killing. Nowadays, when we look at such a weapon, or indeed a helmet or breastplate from the same time period, it is hard to avoid facing up to this fact.

This then is our warrior's paraphernalia, which shifted, in the eyes of researchers, from the status of an object requiring typo-chronological definition, to that of real weaponry carried by an individual who would have to be imagined, at some time or another, fighting on a real battlefield.

It is not yet time to see these weapons being used in battle. Before that, let us take a careful look at the assumptions underlying literary and historical discourse relating to war in the Western World. This incursion into historiographical territory is not whimsical. War was one of the very first subjects narrated by man (certain men, or rather certain participants in war). Yet at the same time, so many aspects of war have been deliberately obscured over the millennia. The paradox is anything but negligible. The impact of writing about the histories of vanished oral European societies has been considerable. In such histories, there was little or no mention of war. This is due to an intricate web of reasons, resulting in silence and errors.

Europe developed a vision of history which saw itself as the centre (superior), compared to the rest of the world (inferior). It chose to see its roots in societies that favoured writing, not least because for a long while there had been no alternative. It also located a model of otherness in distant exotic places which it was in the process of discovering and conquering, without however understanding them. War ran through Europe's history, leaving its mark on people's minds, and imbuing its texts. The construction of this discourse was complex, tortuous even. It determined our intellectual capacity to conceive of 'war' outside models fixed in our imagination. The 19th century saw the establishment of academic frameworks that upset other intellectual norms. But war played no major role in these, so older forms of thought on the subject persisted. The 20th century was torn apart by war. The Western world had to rethink its certainties and moderate its arrogance. The study of societies which until then had no place in the accepted scheme of things finally made inroads. All this was necessary before it became intellectually possible to look seriously at the notion of the invention of war in Europe. Rather late in the day.

Let us now consider, in succession, certain vital reference-points in the course of European historiography, which have marked our thinking, impregnating the process of research, creating a kind of Ariadne's thread in our explanations of the past. Such tools will make it possible for us to understand why European history has failed to deal with the most ancient wars that took place on its soil, and the way this subject has been handled or avoided since 1945. There have been several phases and strata of historical discourse creating essential links between war, politics and society: antique texts, then modern-era reflections linked to European wars but also the discovery of far-off lands, then establishment in the 19th century of academic disciplines, including archaeology; and then in the early 20th century, the way in which history began to reflect upon itself, which offered new ways of thinking before world conflicts undermined and changed Eurocentric triumphalism. But this revolution in thought did not create a fresh space for an understanding of 'indigenous savages' fighting wars on European soil. But first, let us consider the key word 'war' itself.

War Words

Numerous authors have offered definitions of war. Let us start with words or concepts (unpleasant though they might be) that run parallel: 'violence' refers to spontaneous or premeditated acts by individuals, be they healthy or suffering from psychological illness, or traumas which might explain their violent behaviour, isolated or recurrent. The vocabulary and register of discourse describing such acts changes when they are no longer individual, but organised. Then, a different kind of experience is evoked which encompasses yet goes beyond 'violence'. Violence is an integral part of war, but it is not the same thing. 'Raids' refer to intermittent or one-off collective violent actions. A 'massacre' is a violent action involving the killing of large numbers of individuals in a short period of time. If the point of such killing is to exterminate whole populations, this can be called a 'genocide'. Victims may be selected according to categories such as religion, politics, sexuality, or whatever, thus 'justifying' the perpetrators and legitimising their behaviour. 'Conflict' refers to antagonisms or oppositions between the beliefs, opinions or feelings of various persons or groups. Such differences can remain peaceful and find resolution through dialogue and a desire for reconciliation and compromise. Or they can reach an impasse which, if powerful enough, may lead to confrontation. It is within such a framework that 'war' is usually defined. *Le Petit Larousse* offers a definition common enough in the West: *"War is the recourse to armed force in order to resolve a conflict situation between two or several organised collectives, clans, factions or states."*[34]

War therefore implies the deployment of means in the context of a social organisation (including its leadership), and also the actions themselves, through which it is accomplished. In other words, war cannot be conceived as a spontaneous action of individuals outside the frameworks (and norms) of the society to which they belong. This notion is fundamental because it makes possible the concept of the legitimacy of armed conflict and therefore the death of others being brought about by political and social acts.

Beyond the common core of such definitions of war, there can of course be many variations, because societies themselves are not uniform. For this reason, there cannot be just one single, unique, and universally valid definition of the concept of war. Even less so of the forms it might take, the means by which it is carried out, and the many decisions made at various levels. The differing ways in which war – or wars – have been seen, approached, and written about, reflect this diversity. Recently, Umberto Eco suggested a revision of vocabulary and concepts, introducing two new, hitherto unused words to designate contemporary wars, the characteristics of which are different from those of the 20th century – 'palaeo-war' and 'neo-war', two terms which both complicate and shed light upon new realities of war.[35]

Theories of War

As soon as a society comes to express itself through writing, war becomes a regular subject of debate. It is tackled in various ways: possible definitions, legitimacy and justification. In Archaic Greece, Homer, in the 8th century BC, sang of the Trojan War, mingling together gods and humans without it ever really becoming clear, either in the Iliad or the Odyssey, just what role real experience might have played in the fiction that the poet wanted to create. This is the first war narrative in Western literature. It is not a study of war. Besides Homer never defines war. He brings it to life, and has his characters behave in a theatrical manner. This way of writing is not without interest for a present-day historian. It is a documentary source and can be used as such. It is the account of an author telling us *a posteriori* about 'his' Trojan War. The text probably reveals as much about the poet's own world as the war it purports to describe which in fact took place several centuries before.

Numerous authors of antiquity tackled the subject-matter of war, sometimes from vastly different perspectives; their approach is referred to as 'historical', though their criteria and means of proof differ markedly from today's. Let us consider just some. Thucydides, in the 5th century BC, explains his subject and his approach in his *History of the Peloponnesian War*. His procedure is evidently far removed from what any historian would use nowadays. Livy (c. 59 BC-17 AD), in his 150-part book *Roman History*, sets out a history apparently consisting of a series of conflicts, victories, defeats, and great men who shaped and reshaped the contours of power and territories. Tacitus (58-120 AD), in his *Life of Agricola*, never loses sight of themes of conquest and politics, even though his work has a geographical, almost ethnological aspect, with respect to the peoples he describes. In the *Histories* (109 AD), he looks in detail at a young Roman Empire, in which emperors, conquests and victorious domination (Roman) are set out in what one might call a 'classical' manner.

Let us jump forward in time now, though remaining on Mediterranean soil, where the written word was privileged long before it was in other areas. For Machiavelli, war was also a subject of predilection. In 1520 he wrote his *Art of War*[36] in which he announced: "*Princes should therefore make the arts of war their unique and sole preoccupation.*"[37] Much influenced by his reading of Livy, his thinking is that of a humanist and philosopher, convinced of the major role of war in the conduct of power and the government of men.[38] *The Prince* was immensely successful, and it is still up-to-date in many ways, stressing as it does the importance of philosophical reflection on the subject of war, and the need for theorists and thinkers to provide clues as to how it might be understood, if not advice.

The primary participants in war are those who start it, make decisions about it, and lead it. Men of war. As soon as a specific category of individuals was given a special place dedicated to this kind of activity, war became a military phenomenon. Those representing this aspect of society are divided into hierarchies depending on their functions within it, their power to make decisions and their power to command. Some such men have also written about war from a point of view quite unlike that of historians and other scholars. This is a view from the inside, the human view of what goes on and how. The objective here is greater understanding, in order to develop tactics on the ground, to become more efficient. These are the writings of strategists. The best-known book in the Western world remains that of Carl von Clausewitz, a Prussian army general and war theoretician who, in 1832 wrote a text which is still a work of reference today.[39] It was published after his death by his wife and consists of a collection of various descriptions which go far beyond military reportage. He includes a broader vision which explains the book's success since its publication two centuries ago. His ideas have been much commented upon by 20th century philosophers with pacificist leanings.[40]

One of the most ancient writings of this type is not western. Sun Tzu wrote *The Art of War. A Treatise on Military Strategy* in the 6th century AD in China. This was published throughout Europe from the end of the 18th century and left such a mark that it is still studied in military academies today. The text is rooted in Chinese philosophy and defends the notion of victory won by anticipation, preparation, and considering every possible factor – strategy. Nothing must be left to chance. The arguments are astonishingly modern, because they deal with matters beyond the battlefield, encompassing a philosophy of life and of society. Besides, the author believes that the greatest victories are those won before resorting to arms.

More broadly, this text is applicable to a type of conflict which one could call classical, based on the idea of war being declared and conducted by means of direct confrontation, but within a carefully considered framework. Though Chinese societies of the 6th century were not the same as Western societies in the 18th and 19th centuries, it is easy to see why the text had such a strong resonance, and was even consulted for specific guidance.

There are plenty more similar texts, albeit with a variety of assorted styles and rooted in different contexts. Writings about war have appeared regularly, with greater or lesser degrees of success, throughout the history of the West since earliest antiquity. Time is seen in terms of series of episodes of fighting, winning, and losing – and this seems to be what History is all about. It is tempting to go as far as to say that literary writing and the view of war as a series of battles and strategies came into being alongside one another, and that this view of war never quite went away. But the portrayers and theorisers of war never really gave voice to those who fought – with the possible exception of commanders. War is seen to guide the actions of powerful men and we sense it determining whole swathes of the workings of societies.

Such authors describe, formulate, and try to understand war, but never with the eye of a true historian. Neither in terms of procedure, nor in their aims. There have been many wars. The way they happened, and their outcomes have provided food for thought, for writing and for analyses of past events, and their impact on the future. Thucydides was interested in the latter: he wanted to increase understanding to draw lessons for the future and stop future wars from happening. This is an ambition we find over and again throughout time and throughout the world, one that seems doomed to failure. People never fight the same war – they invent other forms of war. This seems proof enough of our immense capacities for adaptation and imagination.[41] There have been ever-increasing numbers of texts about war which aim to avoid future wars; they are interesting in terms of what they are able to explain, but vain in their ambition to bring about a universal and lasting peace.

For centuries, historians have worked with this in mind, following what can be gleaned from available sources: battles, strategy, and politics. The Annales school argued against this view of war at the dawn of the 20th century. But let us not get ahead of ourselves.[42]

The Philosophical Angle

Alongside texts about war, we need to look at thinking about violence from a philosophical perspective, one that looks at human nature in modern Europe. Two contrasting philosophies of war in particular draw upon ancient myths: the myth of progress and the myth of the Golden Age, the first echoed in the work of Thomas Hobbes (1588-1679) and the second in Jean-Jacques Rousseau (1712-1778). Both these philosophies are found repeatedly in the works of authors tackling the origins of war. In the first case, mankind's original state is seen as being one of wretchedness, accompanied by brutality and violence. Progress makes it possible to escape this terrible fate. The myth of the Golden Age, by contrast, depicts mankind's original state as idyllic and pacific. The evolution of society and the arrival of 'civilisations' ends this paradise, which was characterised by simple happiness, and brings violence and war to a corrupt humanity. Studies of 'primitive' societies presupposed that in the early stages of mankind, humans lived in a 'non-civilised' state, according to the criteria of the observer.

Thomas Hobbes put his name to a political treatise in 1651, the *Leviathan*. Here, monarchy – and indeed all kinds of organised state government, are seen as guarantors of peace. For Hobbes, humans are naturally drawn to war, because they are necessarily in competition with one another. The situation for free men, living without a state such as he conceives it, are therefore in a very difficult situation. He writes: *"Man is a wolf to man."* 'Savages' encountered during the process of colonialization are considered to be living in a 'natural' state, one that is 'almost animal'[43]. This is the pre-civilised condition, before the advent of a State, according to the Western definition, which is seen as the sole guarantor of order and peace. They are effectively living proof of his theory: without 'government' and without a 'State', humans are not part of a society. They live in a natural condition where each behaves as a 'wolf' towards others and fighting is a continual reality. The only possible solution to escape from this savagery is the State (such as it was conceived in Europe between the 17th and 20th centuries), the organising principle at the very top of society which makes peaceful life possible. The State therefore guarantees peace, and may also undertake wars, when necessary, but only to preserve a peaceful society. This is how such actions are legitimised. Hobbes' views regarding 'savages' were shared by several of his contemporaries, though Michel de Montaigne (1533-1592) and Étienne de la Boétie (1530-1563)[44] had already made the contrary case. This analysis persisted for a long while and was even found in the early works of sociologists and ethnologists in the 19th century, not least in the positivist vision of human evolution.

The vision of Jean-Jacques Rousseau, which became widespread in France, is the opposite of Hobbes' theory. We find his conception of humankind in his essay *On the origins of languages*. It finds full expression in his *Discourse on the origins and foundations of inequality amongst men* (1755) and *The Social Contract* (1762). People, in a 'state of nature' are good, and inclined to live peacefully with all other living beings. Only hunger, not war, leads people to kill others by hunting them down. To give weight to his theories, Rousseau argues both from comparisons and demonstrations. This was possible thanks to voyages undertaken by Europeans over the previous two centuries, which had generated a vision of 'real' savages. Rousseau based his ideas in particular on the tales of the explorer Louis-Antoine de Bougainville (1729-1769) and his observations of the 'savages' of Tahiti.[45] His view of them, however, had more to do with the way they wanted to be seen by westerners, and the image that it suited westerners to retain. According to Rousseau, violent instincts appear only alongside the corrupting influence of society, that generates envy and social inequality. In his work, political propaganda against the reigning monarchy is scarcely veiled. Artificial laws give rise to a kind of war which natural laws cannot conceive. Here human history is necessarily seen as a form of degeneracy, because of assumptions about an ideal time when humankind was young. Seen in this light, Rousseau was not really offering an alternative to the 'State' such as he experienced it.

Neither Hobbes nor Rousseau lived anywhere near these distant societies, and they lived further still from any era of the 'first' men. War was considered to be first and foremost a political and economic phenomenon bringing together all the various levels of the social structure. This analysis is based on the State and war is treated without question as organised, legitimate and structure-giving conflict. What is more, making war is part and parcel of the way the State was understood as a political tool, necessitating the State's existence. In modern Europe, such reasoning persists in definitions of 'States', past and present. Thus, in 1968, Jean-Pierre Vernant (1914-2007) wrote: *"The classical Greeks considered war to be natural. Because of their organisation into small city states, each jealous of its own independence, and likewise determined to assert its supremacy, they saw in war a normal expression of the rivalry which governed relationships between States."*[46] He then goes on to discuss military issues, strategy, and tactics. The social perspective is not entirely forgotten – particularly regarding antiquity. But this is generally seen in terms of the relationship between individuals and their social status. Hence his view of the *hoplite* in Greece, and the soldier in general, who fosters a sense of citizenship, and with this his own role in the city state.[47]

Stateless Societies as seen by Europeans

The idea of 'primitive man' arose out of a new world-view instigated by colonial European expeditions. However, such 'primitives' remained, in those days, a theoretical notion far distant from everyday life, though an abundance of eyewitness accounts and ideas were available as a result of long-distance voyages. These populations were seen as functioning so differently from European societies that they were described as being based on 'customs'. Since these societies did not pass on their knowledge and their past by means of written texts, Europeans wrote their history for them, as Jack Goody (1919-2015) and Serge Gruzinski demonstrated[48]. The consequences were twofold: for the populations directly involved whose history was 'stolen', and in Europe (and by extension the Anglo-American world from the beginning of the 19th century), we witness the creation of the intellectual model of the 'savage'.[49]

Over the centuries, Europe proved unable to analyse and understand 'war' in the context of these far-off and exotic societies, since there was no correspondence with its own values and specific codes – these being inconceivable in the context of 'primitive' societies. Indeed, since war had to be an organised act reflecting the nature of a society considered as such, it is hard to see how the notion of war could have emerged in texts which assumed that 'non-state', 'primitive' or 'savage' societies could not be 'true' societies. This does not mean that other phenomena were not tackled. Europeans did not analyse 'war' as such, but they did describe it from the perspective of 'violence', rather more in terms of individuals performing actions which were in some way disorganised, seen in an almost biological light. From the moment first contacts were made with peoples encountered during expeditions, and theorised by Hobbes and Rousseau, the fundamental question was formulated: were these 'savages' at the ends of the world, who embodied human beings in their most primitive state, violent by nature? By observing them could we get back to our own origins?

The Western response can be seen as having several stages. The first visitors in the 16th century were struck by the bellicose nature of the populations they encountered. Travellers' tales, merchants' records, and reports from learned people and missionaries all stress the importance of the role of the warrior. Westerners judged this violence very negatively, though they themselves had landed without invitation and with intentions that were not exclusively pacific. Besides, the customs of the 'savages' justified the role of the missionaries, whose job it was to convert them to Christianity, and the presence of Europeans in general, who had come to civilise them.[50]

Hans Staden's travel narrative (1525-1579), forward-looking and ahead of its time, is considered to be one of the founding texts of ethnology, though ethnology did not come into being as an academic discipline until the 19th century. The Spanish ship on which this German adventurer set sail ran aground near the island of Saint-Vincent off Brazil. He remained a prisoner there for nine months, thus becoming an involuntary observer of the customs of the 'Indians' of Tupinamba. So, he became an ethnologist by accident, making detailed descriptions of what he saw, and he was marked particularly by acts of violence he witnessed, and the way conflicts were settled. He described how prisoners were put to death by sword, during the course of ceremonies which seemed very strange to him. Most of all, the practice of cannibalism horrified him and on several occasions he had to extricate himself from difficult situations, aware that he himself might end up on his jailers' menu. Liberated, almost miraculously, he published in 1557 a work which subsequently became popular throughout Europe with titles in various languages including words like *'naked, savage and cannibal...'*. The success was immediate, no doubt due in part to a form of morbid fascination with cannibalism. Though it is not a scientific work in any modern sense of the word that ethnologists would subsequently understand, he narrates his observations in a way that goes beyond mere description. Certainly, his stories are not without judgments regarding the deeds that were committed, but the scenes are analysed in minute detail and a careful choice of vocabulary. Different illustrations are to be found alongside the written text. This opens a new path, based on an interest in the 'other', in hitherto unknown populations, 'savages', so far-off in so many ways. He makes no secret of the violence, even if he does not always understand it, so distant are his captors' customs from 16th century European codes.

There is little consistency in the treatment of the topics of violence and war at the heart of 'primitive' populations during the course of the following centuries, in the context of the establishment of ethnology at the end of the 19th century alongside sociology. Two parallel phenomena come into being at that point, arising out of a previous dynamic, but also moving in a new direction; on one hand the continuing pursuit and expansion of colonialism, overtly political, with new territories (in particular Africa) being opened up; also, the coming into being of various academic disciplines, including ethnology and social anthropology. The 'uncivilised primitive' did not disappear as a concept, and the topic of war was considered, but always within a framework implying that such conflicts were disorganised, having a spontaneous nature as they erupted into everyday reality. *"In the life of savages and barbarians the most important events are wars"*, wrote the Englishman, Herbert Spencer (1820-1903). Neither these societies nor their wars are understood or envisaged with reference to their own values. The models of analysis and classification proposed by early ethnologists illustrate their vision. Thus, in 1877, Lewis Morgan (1818-1881) published a seminal work *Ancient Society*, which looks at Western colonialism from a scientific point of view.[51] He distinguishes three periods, that of 'savagery', that of 'barbarism' with the development of agricultural societies, and that of 'civilisation' accompanied by 'states'. This work is marked in particular by his readings of Jacques Lafitau (1681-1746) and the latter's observations during the course of his mission to Canada in 1711.[52] The debate becomes even more complicated in Europe with the appearance of the concept of 'original indigenous peoples'. No longer with us, of course, but with a real presence, emerging from the depths of pre-history.

The 'savage' beneath our Feet

Modern archaeology came into being during the course of the 19th century. The taste of learned men for antiquities had been evolving since the Renaissance. It was in this context that the first archaeological excavations took place, particularly in Italy. Then, they were essentially looking for fine pieces of beautiful monuments from periods of history and societies also known from antique written sources – very much the fashion. Links were made between the two and connections sought. Knowledge increased and there were some impressive finds. But this does not mean that a totally unknown Mediterranean world was being invented 'from scratch'.

In European countries where classical antiquity had left rather less in its wake, the situation was different. In England, Germany, and Scandinavia, erudition was all the rage, as was the taste for the antique; the 'grand tour' of Italy became an obligatory rite of passage for young Englishmen from good families. Like those who lived around the Mediterranean itself, these people too acquired and collected curiosity cabinets of mysterious or high quality objects which were supposed to combine knowledge, beauty and human genius. The principal difference between archaeological finds in the Mediterranean and non-Mediterranean worlds was that the latter were without explanation in antique texts. Of course, certain types of monuments were present (starting with megaliths), but when they dug down (literally), strange artefacts were found, some of which seemed comprehensible, others less so.

In 17th century Northern Europe, the idea emerged of a world buried beneath our feet reaching far back to a very ancient local history. Scandinavians pioneered both a scientific approach and the establishment of *ad hoc* institutions: groups of people committed to the practice of assembling evidence from under the ground, in order to write a different history. This was to be called 'archaeology'.[53] During the course of the first half of the 19th century, certain key discoveries made in the context of this substrata of intellectual activity undermined traditional ways of thinking. Alongside Mediterranean archaeology, there came into being a form of archaeology known initially as 'antediluvian'. The expression was adopted by Jacques Boucher de Perthes (1788-1868), the director of customs and president of the *Société d'émulation de la Somme*. He was the very image of a provincial man of note and a great lover of geological study and various antiquities, combing his way through fields and valleys looking for ancient remains in the alluvial sediments of the Somme. In 1842 at the site of Mechecourt-lès-Abbeville, he discovered a tool made of flint visibly fashioned by human hands. This discovery was made at an ancient level, alongside remains of extinct animals – including a mammoth's jawbone. The fact that they were present at the same level suggested that they both came from the same time-period. Boucher de Perthes thus had proof of the great antiquity of man, thanks to a method known as 'stratigraphy', which was employed by the first geologists as early as the 1840s.[54] Following the traditions of the time, Boucher offered to present his results at a sitting of the Académie *des Sciences*, convinced that he would receive the academics' congratulations and recognition. What a disappointment! The secretary of the Académie at the time, Élie de Beaumont, (1798-1853) vigorously opposed de Perthes' theories, refusing to admit that humans could have lived alongside mammoths. In 1847 Boucher de Perthes nevertheless published his work under the title *Celtic and antediluvian antiquities*. The key word was unleashed: 'antediluvian'. Humanity was seen as existing before the Great Flood. At the time, Boucher's conclusions were supported by the English geologists Charles Lyell (1797-1875), Joseph Prestwich (1812-1896) and John Evans (1823-1908), the latter also being a numismatist. Boucher de Perthes was not alone in looking underground for very ancient clues to the past.

The violent rejection of this discovery, and the ensuing debates, mark a key point in the birth of archaeology for modern times, or rather very ancient ones. Far more ancient than anything hitherto conceived. No intellectual or religious framework had any space for this 'very, very old world'. Since the spread of Christianity in Europe, Adam had for centuries been considered the first man. He had been created by the hand of God, and this could not have been before 4000 years, ago according to a literal reading of the Bible. This date had not just been dreamed up. Not alone amidst the long series of ecclesiastical 'chronologists' since the Roman Empire, the Anglican Primate of Ireland James Asher had, in his *Annales Veteris Testamenti a prima mundi origine deducti* (London, 1650), and likewise in his *Annalium pars posterior* (London, 1654), fixed the date of creation at the start of the night preceding 23 October 4004 BC. His most important chronological deduction was often considered to be the birthday of Adam himself. Some scholars had talked of an era before Adam as 'Pre-Adamite', in which something of prehistory can, on close inspection, perhaps be detected.[55]

There had been no precedent for what was to follow in the years from 1840-1850 when subterranean evidence revealed giddying new chronological perspectives. Thanks to animal fossils, the history of the world and that of humankind had to be rethought. The birth of a new time-reference had to be accepted, a very ancient time, for which nothing had prepared us, and which no one had really foreseen. It is understandable how brutal the shock must have been for some.

Ever more Archaeological Evidence

These discoveries from the Somme were not isolated. Soon, all of Europe's subsoil was being explored. Varied types of evidence came to light: bones found alongside flint, as in Abbeville, but also different types of objects – graves, remains of dwellings, necropolises containing hundreds of burials, some of which were very ancient indeed. Some sites were extremely important for the exploration of 'prehistoric' times. Regarding the descent of man, bones of Neanderthals (Germany) in 1856 and Cro-Magnon (*Homo sapiens*, France) in

1868 played a key role. In Switzerland, cold and drought led to a drop in lake levels during the winter of 1853-1854. In Lake Zurich, the water-level dropped 30 centimetres below the lowest level previously recorded in 1674. Near the village of Obermeilen, posts appeared, and amongst them, at a very deep, dark level, objects strange to the eyes of the local population, made of flint, polished stone, bone, and antler, as well as ceramics. Ferdinand Keller (1800-1881), the president of the Society of Antiquaries in Zurich, was informed. A few weeks later he went to see what was going on and published two short articles. These discoveries grew ever more important in the world of antiquaries and budding archaeologists. Local men of learning interpreted these remains as having come from very ancient villages. Ferdinand Keller was the first to put forward a general explanation [56] – the existence of settled populations living in dwellings built on stilts. 'Riparian civilisation' had come into being.

Of course, modern archaeology is well aware of mistakes in interpretations made in those days – the means early archaeologists had at their disposal were modest and there were no comparative frameworks available – the science of 'ethno-archaeology' did not then exist. Villages on stilts were not entirely unknown. In Switzerland, fishermen's houses had been built on this principle right up until the 18th century. What is more, and this is a very important point, explorers had reported examples of villages built on water by certain 'primitive' peoples, like those of Kouaoui in the bay of Doreh (New-Guinea) in the works of Jules Dumon d'Urville (1790-1842).[57] He had set off on the *Astrolabe* at the behest of Charles X (1757-1836), explored Polynesia, and published *The Voyage of the Astrolabe*, 1830-1833. Ferdinand Keller drew on this as a source for his Riparian village. He thereby set in motion an important intellectual process: European soil still bore traces of very ancient, long dead 'savages', who could still be observed in worlds considered to be non-civilised. So, the 'primitive' European came into being.

Naturally, the main reason for interest in Riparian villages was the broad span of evidence that became available, and what this might teach us about vanished populations. Fascination with various sites was proportionate to the quantity of discoveries made there. Since finds had been preserved in mud on the banks or beneath the waters of lakes, these remains were extraordinary in many respects: there were lots of them, very well preserved, and they gave glimpses into everyday life. The posts and the planks made it possible to imagine the shapes of the houses, and dugouts discovered hinted at how transport across the lake had taken place; fishing-nets showed means of subsistence, fabric invited guesses about what these people wore; wooden vessels found alongside ceramics gave a very real view of how they ate; shiny bronze artefacts demonstrated the excellence of their crafting skills, the variety of what they could produce and so on. One can well understand the 'lacustromania' that these discoveries unleashed.[58] No one had ever ventured so far back in time, and no one had ever got so close to men and women in this new 'prehistory'. It was possible to enter the daily life of societies no one had ever even mentioned, and about which there were no written texts. And this could be done directly, concretely, through physical remains. The encounter was literally at a human level.

Archaeology and History

This link between observer and observed is one of the strengths of archaeology. It is different from what the ethnologist sees, because (in archaeology) the movement of human action is invisible, immobilised, buried, and takes the form of subterranean data, like the voice of the people which has been lost. But its immediacy, this form of abolition of time between the present and the past which one achieves during an excavation, as one makes one's way down through levels of time, bestows upon the archaeologist an almost demiurgical power. As we reveal buried remains, we bring back to life those who have vanished into silence; we give them a form of discourse through the interpretation we make of surviving evidence, and the stories we narrate about them.

In its early days, archaeology, long regarded by text-based historians as an 'auxiliary science' to history (like the study of epigraphs or numismatics), was largely ignored – or indeed disdained. This 'prehistory' was not seen as worthy. It was about nothing more than studying illiterate savages, dead to boot, who could not even be directly observed. How and by what means could any serious results be extracted from that? At a time when history was setting itself up as a science, archaeology had few devotees in the more traditional and visible parts of the academic world, apart from a few curious and open-minded luminaries. Auguste Geoffroy (1820-1895) was amongst them, though he was under no obligation to do this.[59] He was the second director of the French School of Rome from 1875 to 1882, having received a more or less classical education which shaped his view of history. Nevertheless, he possessed an openness of mind and an insatiable curiosity which led to his interest in the extraordinarily rich and productive[60] work on very ancient times being conducted in Scandinavia, in particular on the Bronze Age.

The archaeology of vanished oral societies followed parallel but quite different paths depending on the country, and the attitudes of various academic disciplines – and the way they related together at the highest level: schools of history, ethnology, sociology, biology and geography. The nature of the dialogue between disciplines and the awareness of prehistory in academic systems had consequences regarding the ways this brand-new science was pursued. Scandinavian Europe and Britain again demonstrated a pioneering spirit. Germany did not lag far behind, accompanied by Austria, where the extraordinary (Early Iron Age) necropolis of Hallstatt was discovered, inspiring great public enthusiasm as soon as it was excavated in 1846. Not only were hundreds of graves very well preserved, and very rich in content, but there was also the nearby salt mine, which explained the importance and power of the site, yielding incredible objects: miners' torches, shoes, leather bonnets, clothes and so on. Salt had preserved these fruits of ancient labour remarkably well, and there was an obvious resonance with the age of the industrial revolution in Europe with its mines.[61]

Mediterranean Europe, being more obviously marked by antiquity, was more divided in its attitudes towards the archaeology of very early times. In northern Italy, riparian settlements were sought in the foothills of the Alps, but the south of the peninsula remained more sensitive to the Greek and Roman worlds. Spain, the westernmost outreach of the Mediterranean area, remained sometimes less keen. The discovery of the painted caves of Altimira in 1868, but recognized only at the very beginning of the 20th century, placed the country in the line of fire as debates raged about the veracity of such phenomena, opening the way to a suspicion that was still present when the Chauvet Cave (France) was discovered in 1994 – the dating of paintings here was so ancient that some began to doubt their authenticity.[62] France was, in a way, at odds with itself. It was the country where Prehistory (in the Palaeolithic sense) had begun and the most important European country in terms of the number of sites discovered. It was also one of the slowest countries to grant institutional space to this new archaeology of the very distant past, so archaeologists had to take refuge alongside biologists and geographers, rather than taking up their rightful place amidst other academics in the humanities and social science sectors. Intellectual and academic barriers were thereby erected, some aspects of which are still with us in the 21st century…[63]

History, for its part, was much reflected upon throughout the 19th century, as it became an independent subject, acquiring greater importance, and establishing itself institutionally and academically, demonstrating the seriousness of its intentions and its scientific values at the dawn of the 20th century.[64] This was history in its triumphant form which persisted until a major sense of disenchantment set in after 1945 – the way it dealt with war followed this general pattern. The subject matter was seen as worthy of attention, because of evident political implications. Those who had played a role in wars continued to offer up their expertise for analysis by historians – who were now also professionals. There was more precision, more exigency regarding details, but war studies remained political and military in spirit; great men of war, from Alexander the Great to Napoleon, continued to command respect – though the professed academic approach meant that this was kept somewhat concealed.

The 'Primitive' in the City

Views of 'primitive man', discovered thanks to long sea voyages, developed following a path broadly similar to that of science towards the end of the 19th century and particularly during the course of the 20th century. This development ran in parallel to that of sociology. France was not that quick off the mark at a time when exchanges between history (classic, based on written sources) and anthropology were taking place as a matter of course in the Anglo-American world. There, humankind was grasped as a totality. Meanwhile, back on the old continent, the links between the two disciplines were much more complicated. There were impressive initiatives, like the museum of ethnography in the Trocadéro in Paris which in 1938 became the Museum of Mankind thanks in particular to its director, the ethnologist Paul Rivet (1876-1958).[65] This Parisian museum, founded in 1878, was one of a series of similar European enterprises between the years 1860 and 1890. In Italy, the creation of the Pigorini Museum was atypical, anticipating a pattern of thought that was just beginning. Founded in 1875 in Rome just after the Italian Unification, this museum was conceived not only to receive ethnographical collections, but also prehistoric collections from the kinds of sites that Luigi Pigorini (1842-1925) had himself excavated in northern Italy (the 'Terramares'), following the model of riparian excavations. In these museums, and in studies they fostered, 'otherness' was studied in the context of ongoing colonization carried out in the countries from which objects and narratives were being brought and which early ethnologists were trying to understand, whilst their political leaders were busy appropriating the territories from which they came. Here too, the triumphalism was evident, reaching a climax at the time of the International Colonial exposition which was held at the *Porte Dorée* in Paris in 1931.The slogan suggested that one might travel all the way around the (French) world in a single day, thus glorifying the power of Paris over these territories and people everywhere in the world. The attitudes of these researchers were not clear-cut, and sometimes verged on schizophrenia.

Some of them were opposed to colonial conquests, though these conquests fostered the advance of ethnological discourse. You could go to the various countries and bring back objects to study. Not all of this took place in a warmongering and restrictive atmosphere. Though the situation in Africa remained complicated for a long time, Latin America and the chilly northern lands were more auspicious for scientific missions on the ground, which soon came to be seen as indispensable. It was no longer possible to do ethnology from a sitting room or office – you had to observe directly, according to increasingly rigorous protocols. From the 1920s, big names in ethnology based their theories on data gathered during their own missions, carried out in a spirit of methodological duty – hence the first sentence of Claude Lévi-Strauss' *Sad Tropics*: "I hate travelling and I hate explorers".[66]

Ethnological methodology went off in a new direction, though still keeping its eye on distant horizons, but it left the topic of war largely untouched. There were a few exceptions, like Broníslaw Malinowski (1884-1942), before the 1940s.[67] The general model was that 'primitive' societies were inclined to be peaceful. They could be affected by forms of violence and fighting. But such acts would be based on instinct and would not find organised expression. In no way could these be compared to the fighting which took place between civilised countries, which was 'proper' war. Amongst the architects of such theories about war in primitive societies one finds Quincy Wright (1890-1970), a professor at Chicago and the author of the study which appeared in 1942 with the title *A Study of War*; also, Harry Holbert Turney-High (1899-1982), a professor of anthropology in North Carolina, who wrote *Primitive War* in 1949. Without denying the warrior-like nature of such populations, the perspective from which they wrote nevertheless made it impossible for combat amidst such populations to be seen as war, as an organised activity – even less then, could it be seen as a legitimate object of study. In the minds of these authors, a kind of inferiority was implied regarding these 'primitive' peoples, continuing the ancient belief that western societies are superior. This form of denial – or refusal – continued for a long time, until the study of war changed profoundly at the end of the 20th century.

In these earlier approaches to the subject there had never been room for a European historical perspective to be directed towards Europe itself. Had this been the case, certain sets of problems relating to the understanding of so-called developed civilisations could have been applied to populations deemed 'primitive'.

In 1977, the French anthropologist Pierre Clastres (1934-1977) strongly criticised the mistakes made in the analysis of 'primitive' societies, and particularly, "*in the field of contemporary ethnology; the almost total absence of a general understanding regarding violence in forms that were at once the most brutal and the most collective, the purest and the most social: war*". From an anthropological point of view, it seemed absurd that "*war should thus be excluded from ethnological discourse*", and that it might be possible to "*think about primitive society without at the same time thinking about war*".[68] He explained how the world of 'savages' was perceived at the start of the 19th century as a wretched one, that could only lead to disorganised and incoherent violence. This is what Clastres called "*economic discourse*" which only "*progress*" could resolve in some way.[69] He discussed one author after another and showed how none of their theories, from Spencer to Leroi-Gourhan (1911-1986), including Lévi-Strauss (1908-2009), was tenable. For his part, he suggested that in fact, war does exist in societies he refers to as 'primitive', that they do adopt rules and that such wars guarantee a kind of balance between groups, precisely because of such regularisation. Recently, the anthropologist Christophe Damangeat[70], reproblematised this notion of 'primitive' war through a study of indigenous Australians, though this still does not contradict the specifically archaeological approach which goes to the very heart of archaeology: on the one hand there is what archaeology sees (and what it makes visible) which has to be interpreted, avoiding the quicksands of fiction; and on the other hand there is what archaeology does not see (that which is invisible because data has disappeared of is absent), and which has to be taken into account, but without necessary lending to it undue importance. Regarding war (and its origins), as for other topics, it is always difficult to strike a balance between the dangers of a fictional approach (overextrapolation or giving voice to something that does not exist) and an approach that is too 'down-to-earth' and over-dependent just on visible data.

The War of Origins

Despite the abundance of archaeological discoveries, which grew continually over the years, war was only ever dealt with peripherally. This was probably to be expected, logically speaking, given the mind-set in which the contrasting perspectives of Hobbes and Rousseau continued to resonate, now in a European context. Were these 'local' primitive societies violent and warrior-like? Could such a question be answered here (by looking at the past)? With the 'invention' of prehistory, and the creation of ancient 'primitive' European man, the binary scheme of European state warfare versus the violence (or non-violence) of exotic allegedly state-less 'savages' was becoming inadequate. Or rather, it should have become inadequate.

This would have been a good time to adopt at least a trilateral approach. This would have meant: firstly, seeing the European in terms of a 'classical' state model; secondly, an openness towards different and geographically distant recent societies; and thirdly an openness to societies that are equally 'exotic', not in the geographical sense of the word (they are beneath 'our' feet), but chronologically. The opportunity to think in these terms regarding European history was somewhat passed by. It was not war as such that was in a state of evolution, so much as academic disciplines themselves and the way they dealt with the subject matter of war – various intellectual steps were not taken, and they still seem hard to take. Prehistoric archaeology – and the intellectual world in general? – was probably not ready to find an answer. Maybe no one really want to find an answer. Perhaps there was no desire to do so. Nevertheless, it has to be admitted that archaeologists did not make war their subject matter, neither at the end of the 19th century nor at any time in the 20th century. They dedicated their efforts to excavating, classifying, and refining methodologies in order to turn archaeological finds into documents that would make it possible to understand the characteristics of ancient people, their affiliations and their evolution. Some archaeologists, sometimes, did ask self-critical questions, usually from new, albeit marginal positions, in areas of study where thinking was more advanced and where evidence was more abundant, but not always easy to interpret. Because there were no words for these things, they did not take the risk of using the narrative mode to represent prehistoric humankind, and indeed everything in the academic world pointed away from doing so. The key word was 'science'. If they wanted to be taken with a modicum of seriousness, this was no time to start telling stories, particularly now that those who had words and sentences in their sources – 'historians' in the classical sense – were trying to escape from the literary mode.[71]

This division had two major consequences. The first was that prehistory as a whole did, by and large, take the 'scientific' road. Archaeologists made rigorous descriptions of their finds, and of their artefacts. Their narrative was technical, morpho-typological, attached to chronologies, and restricted literally to the level of the objects. From 1950 onwards with the development of laboratory science, this tendency grew so strong that some researchers lost any sense of historical perspective. This way of practising archaeological discourse, refusing any literary form, lasted for a long time; indeed it was seen as the only possibility. It still remains dominant today. There are still experts in the Palaeolithic, now at the start of the 21st century, who refuse to be associated with history in any way at all and want as a matter of principle to be seen exclusively as 'scientists', in the illusory hope of being taken seriously. This posturing reflects, almost absurdly, the refusal to integrate oral societies into history (as defined by writing), thus entrenching an obsolete intellectual border from both sides.[72] The second consequence has been that any prehistory of interest outside the academic world had to be narrated by others.

Late 19th century painters appropriated prehistory to construct an iconographic narrative of how they imagined the ancient worlds that fascinated them. Paul Jamin (1853-1903) was amongst the most famous of them: he latched on to the theme of violence. In 1885 he painted a picture which subsequently became famous – a group of men dressed in animal hides and running away from an enormous mammoth which was about to crush them during a hunt which had evidently gone wrong.[73] Then, in 1888, a painting of his caused many grave concern about the fate of a woman at a cave entrance. She was naked and leaning backwards, having been grasped around the waist by a dark-coloured hand that contrasted with her almost milky-white skin. She is defending herself, in a desperate gesture, by reaching out with her left arm towards her attacker, forcing her fingers into his eyes. Her fate seems sealed – unless the man protecting her wins his fight against the wild attacker.[74] Jamin also has us trembling for an unfortunate Bronze Age woman, the diaphanous skin of her right breast on view beneath her torn dress. She is tied up in a dugout canoe, sailing inexorably away from the bank, in Alpine surroundings that could only be lakeside. But violence is far from being the usual preoccupation. In the context of Protohistory, Jamin's *Rapt à l'Âge du bronze* is not part of the mainstream approach.

Although the cave-world of the Palaeolithic does not necessarily exclude violence, the impression which has come down to us of following periods from the Neolithic onward is rather pacific.[75] Lake sides or river banks were the subject of a considerable number of paintings depicting quasi-idyllic Neolithic or Bronze Age lacustrine scenes (Bronze Age referring here to the period between 2000 BC and 500 BC). Men can be seen fishing and women awaiting their return with a child sleeping peacefully in their arms; other men laugh and chat beside the stilts supporting their houses; girls promised to them simper, with flowers in their hair. Light in these pictures is that of a sweet, peaceful, sunset. Nothing in them betrays the slightest desire to fight, or the vaguest predisposition towards aggression. Certainly, the men are powerfully built. But this is no doubt just because they live in a natural manner, healthy and righteous. Rousseau, for whom Switzerland was so important, would have found in these scenes a posthumous embodiment of his theories and a yearning for a lost earthly paradise. In the various scenes, elements of décor are clearly based upon recent archaeological finds. This peaceful vision of an ancient lacustrine world, and more broadly that of early peasants, persisted for an exceptionally long time, practically until the end of the 20th century.

Moreover, archaeologists did not really challenge these fantastic painterly visions, even if they expressed their vision in a different way. For decades, Neolithic societies were envisaged as egalitarian and peaceful. Rousseau's 'noble savage', in a way, had been reincarnated, since ethnologists working on primitive societies had all but excluded questions about war from their investigation.

Though not following an entirely identical path with regard to the specific question of war, contemporary and archaeological 'primitive man' experienced a parallel destiny. Nor did either (of the latter) appear in isolation. However, let us not get ahead of ourselves but rather return to the story of prehistory. Painters and sculptors came and went. As did writers. One 20th century bestseller on the subject of war and violence should not be glossed over: *La Guerre du feu* by Joseph Henri Rosny (1856-1940). Dozens of reprints followed its first full-length publication in 1911, and it is still to be found on booksellers' shelves. Since archaeology had failed to keep a grip on its own subject matter, the general public built up its own picture of a prehistory emerging from the darkness of time. The world of caves was violent and those who lived in it were very simple savages. Scary! Playing scared was fine because the individuals were long since dead! Prehistory was a fluid world capable of harbouring fantasies of every kind, all thrown in with a jolly mixture of archaeological data.

The Celt of our Dreams

The 'Prehistoric' world ended for the greater part of Europe, according to traditional views, with the Celts (Gauls in France). Their world was seen as a kind of antechamber to history. Its final episode was indeed narrated by a war chief, Julius Caesar. And the end was a victory which put a stop to the Gaulish war effort. Or rather, from the point of view of the Gauls themselves, it was a defeat that would decide their future.[76] Before the discovery of pre-history in the 19th century, the origins of France were linked to Alesia – the last stand of the Gauls. France's national hero was a defeated but nevertheless valiant warrior: Vercingetorix. His name was known because it is mentioned in texts, not least Caesar's. From a more global perspective, the Celts had been identified by other authors of antiquity including the Greeks who called them the *Keltoi*.[77] The Celtic period, that of the Middle Iron Age (the *La Tène* period in Europe north of the Alps, which began in about 475 BC), occupied an in-between position. It was mentioned by antique sources, in relation to certain events, but concrete knowledge of this period and its societies, which were oral societies, relied essentially on the new practice of archaeology. So, the two approaches were combined, and attempts were made to deploy excavation methods in the best ways possible. Large-scale excavations took place, and some were very successful.[78] In the Morvan area of France, the oppidum (hillfort) of Bibracte,[79] the capital of the Aedui, was identified and excavated under the leadership of Jacques-Gabriel Buillet (1817-1902) and subsequently Joseph Déchelette (1862-1914). A rampart of a type mentioned by Caesar was discovered, also a *murus gallicus*, and workshops for the manufacture of bronze, enamel, and glass. Houses and places of worship were also revealed. People started looking for other places mentioned by Caesar, in particular battles where mythical victories had been won, Gergovia for example, or lost, such as Alesia. Emperor Napoleon III (1808-1873), fascinated by conquerors, wrote a biography of Caesar and dedicated money and resources to the excavation of the site of the battle. He summoned the very best military specialists and experts in siege warfare. There was a lot at stake. Symbolically, all this was about the place where a new Gaul was founded, a future France! Alesia was identified, whatever the continuing doubts of various conspiracy theorists. Nevertheless, this era, also referred to as the La Tène period (after a site in Switzerland on the edges of Lake Neuchâtel), remained one of in-betweens. Though not part of antiquity, it was still not regarded as part of Prehistory either, the latter being considered a very distant world. In people's minds, as in French school programmes, it was seen as a preamble to national history.[80] It achieved a degree of quasi-nobility, sometimes even elevated to the rank of 'civilisation', as if this were a mark of superiority of some societies over others, thanks to its position at the threshold of history, as if Mediterranean enlightenment shone upon it.[81] This label is still difficult to remove, because of a fascination, indeed an obsession, that goes far beyond archaeology.

While there is no novel quite on the level of Rosny's, late 19th century painters and sculptors enjoyed depicting Gauls.[82] In these scenes everyone is always armed, sometimes quite anachronistically. One of the most famous pictures is probably Lionel Royer's *Vercingetorix casts his arms at the feet of Julius Caesar*, which dates from 1899 and is kept in the Museum of Puy-en-Velay. Everyone in France knows the scene: Vercingetorix's powerful white horse bursts in from the left of the picture. It has only just halted and its hooves still stir dust. Its head is still moving, and its mane is flowing. Its metallic harness, complete with *tintinnabulum* (mobile decoration displayed at neck level), seems to ring out, clicking metallically. The Gaulish chief, looking straight ahead, is wearing a breastplate. His arms reach towards the ground in completion of the movement with which he has just cast his sword and helmet at the feet of the Roman consul, who is sitting on a raised platform, dressed in red. The consul is motionless, in stark contrast to his still moving enemy. His face is marked by a haughty rictus. He looks with disdain at a vanquished foe who refuses to bow his head. Behind him and all around him, his generals also look on severely, whilst in the background, soldiers have raised a forest of standards forming a circle which stands out against the yellow sky. At the foot of the platform, another Gaul is kneeling, torso naked but still wearing a helmet, and looking towards his chief, apparently caught between admiration and resignation. Weapons litter the ground near him. To the left of Vercingetorix's horse, some men are emerging from the half-light; they too are still carrying their helmets, though they are shackled prisoners overseen by troops of Roman cavalry and infantrymen. In the background, Alesia is burning. The sky is tinted pink and grey above the town and over the rest of the scene. It is impossible to tell whether this is the colour of dawn or the colour of defeat. This surrender still figures regularly in publications about the Gauls. It is entirely imaginary and could only have occurred thus in the work of an artist happy to depict weapons over a thousand years older than those which Vercingetorix would have used under such circumstances. Because of its familiarity, this scene was even picked up by Albert Uderzo and René Goscinny to be used humorously in various adventure albums of Asterix the Gaul: Vercingetorix, getting down from his horse, now throws his weapons not at the feet but, as a final act of provocation, onto the feet of Caesar- Caesar cries out in pain.

Every artist appropriated the Gauls in their own way, retaining the characteristics then attributed to them: courage, indiscipline, pride, cruelty and a taste for fine food, drink and so on. Art offered depictions of men and women who had not been encountered through words, people sometimes feared by the authors of antiquity and whose bravery and cruelty were indeed exaggerated by some, like Julius Caesar, because this was to their own advantage – you cannot have a truly glorious victory unless your enemy is scary and powerful, and might themselves have won, had you not been quite so strong and such a clever strategist... Combat that renders 'barbarians' harmless is surely the most legitimate of all. Artists, the public, and historians were divided in the face of these Gauls – no one was really sure if they wanted them for ancestors or not.

Gauls did not use writing (although they were aware of its existence) and they did not live in the kind of state systems normally attributed to societies that we associate with a particular type of government, involving 'war', and with its organised deployment. In a way, the Gauls represent a kind of intellectual frontier in our understanding of the 'primitive' warrior, and this has been so since the start of the 19th century, continuing right up to present times and recent changes in archaeological thinking. The Gaul is a key figure in our knowledge of ancient forms of war, but most of all in the European intellectual construction of values surrounding the concept of war. War takes on its full meaning in societies where (what we conceive of as) 'state' control is present. Such is the heritage that Europe received from antique texts and modern philosophies. Beyond this sphere, the 'primitive', the 'savage', and the 'barbarian' are considered to have indulged in forms of violence sometimes poorly understood and always believed to be beyond the pale of any kind of 'civilised' framework. The Gaulish warrior falls between these two stools, being described as a barbarian but also as a valiant man, who finally lost and subsequently could in turn be 'civilised', peacefully at first thanks to some early contacts, and then definitively, during the course of various stages of Roman conquest.

Different points of view and shifts in perspective over time have meant that one or another of these character traits have been brought to the fore. Thus Polybius sees the Barbarian as a violent individual, ill-disciplined and always ready for a fight, the very opposite of the Hellenistic Greek, who embodies the Roman refinement which he admires. One of the paintings of Paul Jamin, *Brennus et son butin*, (Brennus and his spoils) is probably amongst the most terrifying representations of this vision.[83] The scene takes place during the sack of Rome, at the very moment of Brennus' triumph, when he comes to receive his 'due', which the painter envisages differently here from 'due' in the form of gold as described by texts – it retains only the horror of the supposed 'barbarism' of the Gauls. In a dark room, the door opens, held by a grey-haired Gaul. He is armed. On the threshold, Brennus stands sturdily, and smiles almost greedily. He is wearing a feathered helmet, holds a lance in his left hand and an ivory pommelled sword hangs at his right side. The fastener of his scabbard gleams in the daylight whilst in the background of the scene one glimpses a temple, no doubt on the Capitol Hill. Blood flows over the step beneath his left shoe. The house is Roman, as can be seen from the wall-paintings and the artefacts. The

Gaulish chief is happy because the door has opened to reveal five young women. Four of them are entirely naked, their clothes having slipped to their feet. Two of them are sitting in a contorted position because they have been tied up. The third is reaching towards a pillar on top of which stands the golden statue of a god she seems to be imploring. The fourth, in the centre of the picture, is turning her face towards the door and hiding her eyes from the light and from the man who embodies the violence about to be done to her. The fifth woman is lying down, half in shadow, her hips still covered but her pale breasts bare. At her feet, amidst the gold and silver plunder, lie the heads of two men, skin already grey. The realism is implacable. If one were to suppose it a depiction of a real scene, it would be unbearable. This belief in the cruel and warlike character of the Gauls, and the Celts in general, enjoyed a real success right up to the dawn of the 20th century.

Other characteristics of these populations were revealed by the growing number and diversity of excavations in a national context where the Gauls were now welcomed as ancestors: one could have fun seeing them as enjoying a fight, being a bit rebellious, but basically nice, and certainly not bloodthirsty monsters. Popular depictions of them in the 20th century were very different to those of the 19th century. The Gaul becomes a national hero, a patriot struggling against the enemy, as the French fought against the Germans. The Gaul is awarded a place on packets of cigarettes, beer, Camembert (the French national cheese 'par excellence'), and on chocolate and champagne – all 'made in France'. In 1941, a Gaul grasps the shoulder of a young Frenchman on a propaganda poster *France toujours*, advertising for French volunteer labourers.[84] The Gaulish hero persists, but his image changes. Celtic archaeology gradually took a normal place alongside other periods. There was interest in where the Gauls lived and traded, and in their funerary artefacts. War became a marginal consideration. Weapons were found, but they were catalogued (and detailed typo-chronologies were invented), but there was hesitation as to their true purpose – killing. As with so many domains of the human sciences, the decades following the Second World War saw the opening of new perspectives.

And there was War…

There is something labyrinthine about the intellectual history surrounding war. Firstly, there is 'traditional' history (with written sources) where war was a fundamental theme; then, a view of violence in the context of primitive men and women who were seen as exotic and far away – then, breaking away from these two, a third way of looking at the topic: archaeology. Moreover, archaeology itself must be divided into two approaches: on the one hand the periods for which textual history is present, and on the other, the world of oral societies. In the first case, the archaeology of Classical antiquity was seen as a subsidiary practice alongside a more noble cause, but it nevertheless played a role in research about war. Studies of certain subject areas, like fortifications, were abundant, and added considerably to our knowledge, making new approaches possible.[85] In the second case, the archaeology of oral societies, the situation was different. This again can be subdivided: on the one hand, an unexpected 'Prehistory'. The route to the acceptance of this was complex. But the notion of the 'primitive human' on European soil was accepted, with all it that implied regarding the concept of 'non-societies'). In this case, parallel to global ethnologies relating to societies now referred to as 'indigenous', there was a tendency to reject war, however real its manifestations, even to the extent of denying facts in the evidence which came to light. On the other hand, there was the Celtic world, the antechamber to history and more obviously linked to history. This three-part division (almost four-part if we isolate the Celtic world) in the approach to war, lasted until after the Second World War.

In archaeology and anthropology, it was not until the 1990s that a general change of outlook took place. In 1993, John Keegan instigated a shift in direction in the Anglo-American anthropological tradition, anthropology being affected more deeply than archaeology. This also involved a broad and, one might even say, daring framework of geographical reference.[86] Lawrence Keeley's work marked a major break in historiography. His approach, by implication, was more clearly archaeological.[87] The premise was clear: war is an integral part of the human condition. He wanted to prove this using archaeological evidence, particularly from the Neolithic, considering it vital to break away from the illusion of peaceful societies in the general framework of indigenous societies. Keeley did not hesitate to draw parallels between European prehistory and tribal societies (like those of Latin America), following an approach characteristic of Anglo-American studies, assuming a clear parallel between all forms of 'primitive' societies, past and present, wherever they are found. He was very clear about the constant refusal to admit the existence of war: *"Like most archaeologists trained after the Second World War, I finished the first stages of my studies so firmly convinced of an ontological incompatibility between war-like activities and prehistory, that I was quite prepared to reject any material proof to the contrary."*[88]

The second half of the 20th century and the beginning of the 21st forced researchers and society itself to adopt another view of the way history is written. Society, like researchers, had a divided view of war after 1945. No one spoke about it, but it was present everywhere, and weighed heavily. I belong to a generation which did not experience war on the soil of my own country. Decolonisation had been a reality in France for several years, as was supposedly the case for most other Western countries which, in the 19th and 20th centuries, had engaged in various conquests. School textbooks did not yet carry unbearable photographs of concentration camps. History in French schools at the end of the 1970s up to the end of the 1980s was well-mannered, albeit punctuated by a few grand stories of battles, and a few heroes who were glorious or, by contrast, doomed. Not all households had a television and there was no media over-exposure of everything that happened in the world. Children were informed by what they were given to see. Young intellectuals at the start of the 1970s, whether they were students or had just become parents, militated for peace, denouncing the brutality of the war in Indochina, and demonstrating against wars in Vietnam and Cambodia, which were by then ending in a way that was difficult to stomach. Everyone was against the Cold War. This generation had not taken part in the Algerian War. Large numbers of the children of these baby-boomers or 'pre-baby boomers' (who became my teachers in the 1990s) were born towards the end of such conflicts and had never had any direct contact with war. Unless, of course, their family history was directly affected – not least the children and grandchildren of Holocaust victims.[89] Those reaching the end of their university careers had, however, experienced a different history. They had been adolescents or young adults during the Second World War. Then, they had seen, or taken part in the wars of decolonisation.[90] Their desire for peace was immense. For this generation, the desire to put behind them the traumatising experiences of war was particularly strong or simply unconsciously hidden. The words of Jean-Pierre Vernant in 2004 are very poignant: *"François Hartog asked me recently if, when I wrote about a 'good' death, I did not have, at the back of my mind, my experience in the Resistance. I had to stop and think. Then I realised that he was right. I had simply not realised this."*[91] And this was in Europe. Keeley makes a similar point when he writes: *"like most archaeologists educated after the Second World War',* for a long time he had been wearing *"blinkers".*[92] On 9 November 1989, the fall of the Berlin Wall made it possible to imagine for a moment that it might be possible to believe that our long history of conflicts had finally come to an end. The hope was short-lived. War returned to European soil, in Bosnia, three years later. My real first contact with war as a contemporary reality came about as I was preparing for my *agrégation*[93] in history: decolonisation was on the syllabus. This was in 1994, the year of Rwanda. This was a very important date, for thought in general, and for studies about war.

A whole adult generation wanted peace. They had inherited an intellectual history on the subject rooted in antiquity, from which no one could entirely escape. The first chinks in the armour, if one might put it that way, appeared not so much because of the political aspect of war, but because of the violence and suffering at the heart of conflicts, massacres and torture.[94] The anthropological perspective played a role too, both with respect to the subjects it focussed on and in the methods it used, since laboratory techniques made it possible to look at physical evidence and skeletal remains in a new way. A current at the heart of Anglo-American *War Studies* set new thinking in motion as early as the 1960s – but under circumstances which meant it was kept under wraps: this was in the context of an academic world in which research on war had never really ceased. It was human motivation that evolved. These studies were part of the self-questioning and the sense of malaise following the Second World War and subsequent decolonisation. European and Eurocentric history had for a long time been triumphalist and pedagogical. But the period after the Second World War was painful. There was a need to look carefully and to understand; there was a desire not to forget. Intellectuals were to play their role.[95] The change was not immediate. Those who had been traumatised had to be reintegrated into society and learn to live again; time was needed for a new generation to get involved. The experiences of countries still at war in the 1970s provided further motivation, but also acted as a brake. At the start of the 1980s, a sense of duty developed, to make sure that the victims of atrocities in the Second World War would be remembered. In France, the historian Pierre Nora took the initiative of publishing (1984 to 1992) *Les Lieux de la Mémoire* (La République/La Nation/Les Français) in three volumes, subdivided into numerous short, thematised articles.[96] This work was a reflection, and an introspection too, which included a form of repentance in the face of particular events.[97]

The 1980s and particularly the 1990s marked a turning point. War again became an object of study. In history, ethnology, and archaeology – but in a new way. This came out of a desire to look at certain topics on a human level, from the intimate perspective of those involved, rather than from the point of view of politics and strategies. Another decade passed before university publications and teaching programmes were truly affected. Meanwhile, the world plunged into new forms of war and violence. In 2001 the attacks in New York shattered any certainties to which one might still wish to cling. War was no longer neglected or approached obliquely. War research came to the forefront of the Western intellectual scene, and nowadays it is omnipresent, invasive, and stifling. The war that has just broken out in Ukraine (under attack from its Russian neighbour) is yet another painful demonstration that war is not, alas, just a matter for historians, but a human phenomenon that can always return to haunt us.

Contemporary wars receive vast amounts of attention, though they are only – if one may dare say this – part of a pattern of behaviour that has come down to us from very ancient times. For this reason, it is perhaps not a bad idea to take a step backwards, to go back in time in order to place them in a far-reaching perspective, bearing in mind that in the scale of human history the 21st century represents an almost insignificant fraction of a second. Before we became the 'we' that we see ourselves as being now, how did our ancestors behave, and how did they come to invent this reality of violence which is at the same time organised and structure-giving?

II

RESEARCH 'EVIDENCE'

Keeping Weapons

Our 1000 BC warrior's weaponry is just the kind of archaeological find that also provides evidence for the study of the origins of war. The helmet is typical of buried metal hoards most often found by chance in the past, usually during the course of agricultural work. The group of objects found in 1832 in Calvados, Normandy, were so astonishing that the farmhand who came across them, unsure what to do with them, reported them straight away, even though he was clearly able make out what they were amongst other less easily recognised fragments. The curious manner of the objects' arrangement also attracted immediate attention: the nine helmets, their crests pointing skyward, were in groups of three, the groups also forming a triangle. The intentional nature of this layout was unambiguous. The objects were well preserved and in their original state. They immediately became famous by the standards of the day. Of course, this was no archaeological excavation in the modern sense of the word, but rather a collection of objects. They were unusual enough for us to suppose that the man who found them and then the landowner took time to check there was nothing else buried there. The find was then split up, rather than kept as a whole as would happen nowadays. Each object found its way to a different place. The landowner, Monsieur Vauquelin, gave one of the helmets to each of his sons-in-law. The first was given to Monsieur D'Acy who wanted to bequeath it to the French National Archaeological Museum of Saint-Germain-en-Laye; but it ended up being sold in 1907 to Monsieur Costa de Beauregard and is now to be found in Philadelphia in the United States. The second was given to Monsieur de Glanville. It was exhibited at first, then sold for 1700 francs in June 1902 to Count Ladislao Odelscalchi. There is some historical irony in the fact that precisely this helmet was used to symbolise the national Gaulish hero during the course of the Universal Exhibition in 1867. Now it has come sleepily to rest in the attic of the Palace of Venice in Rome – a somewhat belated piece of booty taken from the very Gauls whose heads it was supposed to have protected in 390 BC.

The helmet embodies one of the most widespread categories of data for the study of war: weaponry and armour. But one should not oversimplify. Firstly, we need to add in the two other components, found in wetland hoards or under water, which make up our chosen set of weaponry: the breastplate and the sword. The breastplates of Marmesse were buried in land that was boggy at the time, but partially dried out as a result of quarrying work – a familiar scenario for archaeological discoveries before legislation was drawn up to deal with clashes of interest between the modern economic world and research into the past by means of buried data. The Wimereux sword is categorised as an 'isolated' object, of the kind that often surfaces during dredging, or work of a similar nature. The circumstances of its discovery make it difficult to be precise about its origins. It was kept, typically for the time of its discovery, because of what it meant to the people then, and so it ended up as part of a scientific collection – in this case that of the museum of Boulogne-sur-Mer. Nowadays there are thousands of examples of swords throughout Europe, though the way they come to light is growing less and less fortuitous, for they tend now to be found in the context of archaeological excavations – of course chance does sometimes still cross swords with archaeologists. Helmets, on the other hand, are far fewer in number, and breastplates are fewer still.

The finds chosen to symbolise our warrior were discovered in part or wholly by individuals who had nothing to do with archaeology, so it was only by chance that these objects found their way into the history of archaeological collections. This is how things happened for a long while and how they still happen now from time to time, even though legislation has made it illegal in France (since 1941) to attempt archaeological excavations without authorisation. Most recent legislation (dating from 2016) attributes the status of 'public good' to any archaeological discovery. This has probably made data from under the ground something of a long-term special case: such goods might be discovered by anyone, not least on their 'own' land. The collections of metal objects we have today came to light as a result of old-school chance discoveries. The constant renewal of archaeological practices (the professionalisation of archaeology) and the kinds of study carried out has brought about a progressive evolution in the nature of sources, particularly in the context of violence and war. The sets of weaponry we have chosen here yield evidence only about themselves as objects and, more particularly, as weapons identifiable as such. However, this group fails to represent the category of objects that were deliberately broken before being buried. For example, the fragments of the Ewart Park-type sword found in two important Bronze Age hoards from around the end of the 1st millennium BC in Crundale and Hollingbourne (Kent, England) alongside objects including axes and also fragments of metal ingots. These objects were for the most part deliberately broken, not least the swords and spears. In Crundale the total of 182 objects and fragments weighed in at about 14 kilograms. Nor do such objects constitute the totality of 'evidence'. What is more, the objects we are taking as examples are disconnected from any battlefield, unless we imagine a battle was fought round the place where the hoard was buried, for which there is no evidence. Lastly, our objects are literally disembodied, to the extent that the warrior who used them is present neither in the place where the hoard was found nor in any grave. There are no human remains, and there is no direct information about any wounds which an individual might have received.

The main dividing line between fiction and historical narrative is *evidence*. Reasoning and demonstration depend on evidence, which is a form of documentary source, even if its form is literary.[98] Such data is required for a researcher to undertake any inquiry and, as it unfurls, develop hypotheses, and draw closer to certain phenomena, maybe even the truth about them. But what data does war leave behind that might constitute historical proof? Or more precisely, what material objects can excavations reveal that might further our understanding of vanished oral societies?

History is not defined by the written word alone. However, the absence of words, names and narratives creates methodological difficulties, and a real a real sense of frustration. Historians working on very ancient periods in fact have access to nothing that might yield biographical information or give details relating to certain domains (social customs, feelings and so on). A description of an unknown individual, for example a Bronze Age Louis-François Pinagot, would be very much more complicated than it was for a historian like Alain Corbin.[99] I do not know whether the metalworker who made the Grenoble breastplate was handsome, tall, brown-haired or blond, whether he was good- or ill-natured, or if he could be entertaining. I cannot tell if he fell wildly in love with a woman from the neighbouring village with whom he had five children, two of which died at a young age, nor do I know if his son took over his profession. I know nothing about any of this and the only point in mentioning it is to highlight my own powerlessness and ignorance. I might indeed choose to embroider my text with anecdotes, but such details would be fiction, not history. What I can write is constrained; I am in a world of wordless sources. Here the gap between archaeological writing and contemporary history is obvious, palpable even. My colleagues who study contemporary history, even when they are working on shadows of people no longer alive, nevertheless have the advantage of the kind of data (names, dates, places, lists, photographs, memories, notebooks, newspapers, and so on) that I shall never have. The title of this book could not make matters clearer: the most important form of 'evidence' I have at my disposal is weaponry. While weaponry has much to teach us, it cannot be seen in isolation from other data which might come to light, and which could, studied alongside it, have something to teach us, in various ways, about war.

An Abundance of Evidence...

One sword does not make a war. Or rather not the totality of war. It sheds light on a physical aspect of the subject. It bears witness and provides evidence. But evidence of what? The historian's fate is to be plagued by questions. This is at the very heart of what we do. It is the domain of the *"fertile enigma, intuition, and tiny ideas that won't go away"*.[100] As such, in addition to questions about the kind of data that might be permissible as 'evidence' with regard to war, we need to ask what sort of evidence might make it possible for us to identify new sets of circumstances, new beginnings, a 'birth', or 'invention'. Here we are faced with a considerable set of unknowns at the heart of the initial questions, the very idea of what constitutes a 'beginning'. To avoid going round in circles, another question has to be asked: does it make sense to take various types of physical *things* as a basis upon which to investigate such ancient times. This in turn presupposes answers to two further questions: how far do we need to 'go back' in time, and what kind of sources will we need?

We have to make the most of data available on (or in) the ground and what has been preserved over the last 200 years and then, from all the material available, decide what it seems most sensible to study from which perspective. All vestiges of the past are fragmentary, which is to some extent fortunate because otherwise there would be no space left for the present. We would be literally overwhelmed, overrun, stifled. It would be impossible for us to live and to move forward into the future. Quantities of data available vary greatly according to type and period. A minimum data-threshold of some kind is vital. If researchers look carefully at what they have inherited from the past, it might turn out that the only option is pure fiction. Not in the sense of the 'constructive fiction' (or narrative) inherent in all writing but 'imaginative fiction' in the sense of crossing the line to a point beyond the pale of history, that is, crossing the red line between reasonable hypothesis and wild imaginings.

For centuries, megaliths have maintained their presence in our landscapes, but without any 'instructions for use', so that they have been contemplated at various stages without being understood, because of the lack of a coherent archaeology to help interpret them. Such monuments have been associated with gods, monsters, and various legends in vogue at the time which generated others in turn. They were seen as the work of giants, trolls, in England as the creatures of Merlin. Even the first scholars who tried to analyse them ended up with theories marked by an esotericism which can only be justified in terms of the data then available, for example William Stukeley (1687-1765) who carried out pioneering work in the area of Stonehenge (England), but who then came up with conclusions quite removed from any scientific or rational justification.[101] It was only because of scientific excavations carried out from the end of the 19th century, dating methods deployed from the 1950s, experimental archaeology which began only in the 1970s, and the development of funerary anthropology which only got underway in the 1980s, that various threads converged so that reasonable hypotheses could be developed regarding such Neolithic constructions.

Regarding very ancient periods of history, and certain aspects of them, it was long considered a difficult and dangerous thing to go beyond technical descriptions (avoiding narrative in order to protect oneself from the charge of purely imaginative fiction). In archaeology, an isolated skull, an anatomically complete skeleton, or a sword, may be useful taken on their own, but more is needed for them to be understood in connection with one another. As more discoveries have been made and more studies carried out, the process of source accumulation has made it possible to go beyond some intellectual sticking-points and to legitimise new objects of study. It is clear moreover that researchers today are in a better position than a century ago to put forward certain types of interpretations. This is not just to do with the quantity of material available. It is also a question of information, repetition, and analogies regarding what has been established based on physical data. Medicine offers a good analogy. Symptoms are identified in one case, which may also occur in a second, and may then again be repeated with other individuals, apparently corresponding to patterns on the basis of which a pathology might subsequently be identified. Archaeological data is silent, but its various markers are similar to those of medical symptoms. In addition to the question of minimum data-thresholds, new methodologies are now making it possible for archaeological data to yield more information. With this in mind one can see how it has become possible nowadays to deal with sets of problems which could not have been envisaged half a century ago.

It goes without saying that war is dangerous, since danger is the primary goal of war: mutilation and killing. This is a truism. You do not go into the middle of a battlefield without risking your life… So, how can data be gathered about such a perilous activity? Let us differentiate between two types of sources, direct and indirect, which relate to two timescales, war as it is happening, and sources generated either directly afterwards or later still when the fighting is over, and peace has returned.

After the Battle

Direct sources of various kinds originate from people and places. They can be captured immediately, particularly nowadays with sound and visual recordings (photographs, videos), though this involves risk to life and limb for whomever is gathering the data. Such people may be directly implicated (combatants) or eyewitnesses (civilian populations, reporters and so on). The danger inherent in theatres of war goes some way to explain the absence of ethnologists who are more likely to be present in places where peace reigns, so it makes sense that they have paid less attention to the kinds of situations which are relatively difficult to observe. But for our studies, there exists no supporting evidence of this nature. No participant in Bronze Age warfare, and no eyewitness, has escaped to share photos taken at the height of action…

The category of data produced *a posteriori* by such individuals is, however, worthy of attention. Such types of data have one thing in common: as soon as action ceases, memory kicks in, creating a more or less powerful and conscious distance between what was experienced and how it is remembered. Work that comes into being in this way modelled not only by real experience, but also by emotion and pain, even if the purpose was to seek out truth or pay attention to detail. Though motives for reporting might well exclude introspection or any suggestion of intimacy, the aim might still be to recall the sequence of military events (dates, names, pictures, choice of strategy, tactics and so on), from the point of view of the narrator. The mode might be descriptive, yet the tone endorsing – or indeed judgemental – implying a 'good' course of events, a 'bad' strategy, and so on. The texts of some antique authors come close to this in their propensity to move away from evidence-based descriptions. For our study, though written texts obviously cannot be excluded, their role can only be marginal. Because of their very nature (the fact that their authors lived in antiquity, that they wrote about the vanquished from the point of view of the victor, the distance from evidence and so on), and the fact that such sources date from very late in the period (the last centuries of the 1st millennium BC), they can only represent an infinitesimally small part of what we have to study.

The narrative of participants or witnesses can also be in pictorial form, directly bearing witness to action or composed afterwards. What a shame that we can benefit from no equivalent of Mathurin Méheut's (1882-1958) watercolours, sent from trenches at the Front during the First World War, which give a vividly poetic account of his actual experiences. For example, his *Guetteur au bois de la Gruerie* (Argonne) from autumn 1915 where the scene of action is partially obscured by a very beautiful green grasshopper in the foreground: the artist, being unable to hold back his talents as a naturalist, invested in this fragile insect all his love of life. Yet there is no shortage in Europe of figurative representations in very varied media, the oldest dated to 36,000 years ago, demonstrating a need for expression going back a long way, well before the advent of writing. Not all these representations involve war and violence. However, a certain number of them do deal with conflict, scenes of violent death, and individuals bearing arms. They occur over a considerable arc of time, from the Late Palaeolithic right up to the 1st century AD. They are to be found in caves, on stelae, on rocky outcrops, stone objects, pottery, wood, and metal.

In each case, *a posteriori* narratives (texts and pictures) intentionally or otherwise contain transformed versions of the lived experience which gave rise to them. They are reconstitutions involving greater or lesser distancing from the time and place of action, either because of an individual's situation (the need to 'wipe' traumatising scenes from memory, for example), or because of exterior expectations and norms relating to the society within which the writing or images were produced (what may or may not be said or depicted, in one way or another). Paintings and engravings are not literal translations but codified scenes, which show aspects of war. The man depicted in Pech-Merle (France) is one of the most ancient iconographic representations, dating from about 20,000 years ago.[102] Wounded in three places, he stretches his arms forward and seems to be about to collapse onto the ground. One of the best-known Upper Palaeolithic paintings with a human subject is the 'shaft' scene in Lascaux, dating from about 15,000 BC.[103] A man with a rigid posture and arms spread stumbles backwards. In front of him is a bison, its head lowered, though one cannot tell whether this is because it is attacking or wounded. It too seems on the verge of death. In both images the precise nature of the confrontation – real or symbolic – between the animal (imaginary or not) and the man, are ambiguous and we do not know what kind of violent scenario it represents. Other isolated and less famous examples show that this is recurrent. The symbolic aspect comes more strongly to the fore on the cave wall in Addaura (Sicily), painted in about 10,000 BC.[104] At the bottom of the scene a bull, standing practically upright, seems to be reaching forward with its feet. Above it an individual is about to use a spear or long stick against the animal. Overlooking these two there is a stylised depiction of ten individuals. Their heads have birds' beaks, and they are in a strange dancing position. Six of them at least are visibly men and at least two of them clearly have erect phalluses. The strangeness of the scene has led to many hypotheses, from ritual dance to sexual activity, or even sacrifice, the men being the ones about to be sacrificed, bound by ropes and wearing masks that may shortly suffocate them. We shall never know. But it is worth noting that the depiction of men as opposed to women grows more important at this stage and seems to be associated with times when acts of violence, ritualised or not, are frequent, not only in Europe but also in the near East: a scene in Çatal Höyük (Turkey) from the Early Neolithic shows some kind of procession of men surrounding and bringing under control an immense bull.[105]

The Mesolithic period gives us the first depictions in Europe of men without animals. Many caves, particularly in eastern Spain, have walls decorated with astonishing silhouettes of male archers, shooting, falling, running, and dancing with incredible dynamism, almost ballet-like.[106] Once again, these should certainly not be understood photographically, but as a narrative of events and practices given special meaning by being represented. Moreover, some silhouettes, like those in Minateda (Albacete, Spain), are riddled with arrows, yet still standing and walking towards a group of adversaries whose right knees are bent and whose left legs are stretched behind them as they continue to fire arrows. This is a clear depiction of conflict, whatever the symbolic significance. Violence is at hand.

The European Neolithic was less prolific in imagery relating to our topic. Cave walls were not used to depict this sort of scene. Now, we find considerable numbers of women, men less frequently, depicted usually in the form of figurines or on ceramics.[107] This style tended to highlight body-shape, sometimes in a very stylised way, which no doubt contributed to the notion of the Neolithic as one of peaceful if not idyllic agricultural activity.

The Metal Ages in Pictures

By way of contrast, the Bronze Age offers some extraordinary groups of images. There are decorated rock faces, particularly in Scandinavia and in the Alps. There are hundreds of them, and those in Scandinavia have still not all been accounted for. Amongst them are armed men in groups or in isolation, often with erect phalluses, sometimes alongside boats. They play a key role in our understanding of Early Bronze Age societies. Such compositions mingle figurative elements: some are clearly modelled on reality, whilst others have more to do with the world of religious beliefs. Men confront one another, swords or axes in hand, conveying a real sense of fighting. The choice of explicit depictions of erections in a large number of them has to do with the symbolism of potency by biological means, not any real state of affairs on the battlefield. The frequent presence of boats carrying men, weapons, animals, and types of dancers bent double, as well as signs and figures which seem to delineate spaces, demonstrate the complexity of such iconography – and the importance of such combats in the Bronze Age. Decorated cave walls in the Alps (Mount Bégo, Val Camonica) are more varied, with representations dating from the end of the Neolithic to the beginning of the Iron Age. Though there are scenes of violence, one can also make out complex tableaux of such agricultural societies' everyday life, where fields, stars and communication routes all have their role to play. Combat is represented by means of weapons, sometimes carried, sometimes simply lined up in greater or larger numbers, but not in the form of an explicit confrontation. Animals are everywhere, represented either just by heads with antlers or horns, or in a more complete manner, including scenes in which they have been put to work. As in Northern Europe, these cave walls are full of signs which are more or less easy to interpret, since as a whole these are linked to human society, in which combat and war form an integral part, though these are not the sole subjects. The Bronze Age is also characterised by the existence of engraved stelae on which men are depicted bearing weapons: there is little doubt as to their role. But there are no combat scenes. These are no more than silhouettes, phantom-like, disappearing behind their equipment which consists of a sword, a helmet, a shield, and sometimes a spear or even a chariot. This choice is far from anodyne. There are many such stelae in the Alps, but they are particularly abundant in the Iberian Peninsula.[108] Here, sets of weaponry are recorded as if in the inventory of a solicitor who has been drawing up lists of a warrior's property on the occasion of his death: sword, shield and helmet compose a trilogy to which other items, spears and two-wheeled chariots, may or may not be added. The iconography linked to combat varies according to geography and the mode of representation of the participants, their equipment, the ways in which they are depicted and the symbols which locate them in their roles at the heart of their society. In some regions no such pictures, but this does not mean that they were entirely peace-loving. Weaponry is to be found everywhere. It is the iconographic narrative which varies from one place to another, from one cultural tradition to another.

In the Iron Age there was a great increase in what was depicted, how and where. Though rock art grows less important (the latest scenes found in the Alps date from this period), objects were often decorated, and indeed scenes of action were portrayed on them. Many materials were used, some perishable like wood, which have rarely been preserved. Metal objects appear to have enjoyed a privileged status in iconographic representation, including those of war. Some well-known examples date from the 1st millennium BC and the Celtic world. The backrest of a bench on which an inhumed body was laid to rest in the luxuriant tomb of Hochdorf (Stuttgart, Germany, dating to the end of the Early Iron Age) is decorated with stippled ornamentation made with a punch.[109] Close to the far edges two four-wheeled wagons confront one another, each bearing a man pointing a sword in his right hand and holding a shield in his left. The central scene consists of three male couples facing one another, each man with a short sword in one hand and a sort of stick in the other. These adversaries confront each other dynamically, almost dancing as if in a boxing match. The way the movement is presented makes the combat seem realistic. It takes on an almost metaphorical character. In another burial there is another scene which mingles the real and the symbolic, the Cult Wagon from the Strettweg grave (Styria, Austria) dating from the 7th to 6th century BC. The ensemble consists of two elements, a metal vessel with a round bottom and a four-wheeled wagon astonishingly well-equipped: two symmetrical groups stand back-to-back, one in front of the wagon and one behind it. At the centre, a stag is framed by two women each holding one of its antlers. Behind this first plane a second consists of four persons, two women framed by two helmeted men riding horses, with a shield in one hand and a spear in the other. At the centre there is a woman who stands twice as tall as the figures surrounding her, naked but for earrings, and a belt round her waist. Her sexual features are clearly visible. Her arms are raised, palms held flat towards the sky; on her head, which is protected by a small cushion, she carries a sort of headpiece on which a metal vessel has been placed. This procession is realistic as far as the detail of the persons is concerned, but the relative sizes of the groups of figures, compared to one another and to the stags, betray a sense of hierarchy which goes beyond the figurative. It also shows clearly that although conflict is at the heart of the scene, this can only be understood in the context of a spiritual and social dimension. Everyone has their role to play, a place in the social order, including women who are only rarely depicted at this time.

South of the Alps, two regions are marked by an extraordinarily rich iconographic production using metal as a medium: in the Po valley, metal vessels are decorated with bands of various kinds often involving banquets and processions. But the warrior is not forgotten. In Sardinia at the end of the Bronze Age and at the beginning of the Iron Age, small statuettes (*bronzetti*) depict warriors bearing arms as well as boats and animals (often with horns or antlers), showing that, despite regional differences, generic types of representation and common associations existed over vast areas.

During the second half of the Iron Age the iconographic repertoire grows fuller and more complex still.[110] Alongside human figures, geometric and vegetation motifs now find their way into scenes alongside a fantastic bestiary including many chimeras. The scenes are depicted on many different types of objects, including small ones like fibulae, metal vessels, statues and so on. One of the most astonishing artefacts from the end of the period, certainly not to be passed over, is the Gundestrup Cauldron, discovered in 1891 in the peatbogs of Jutland (Denmark). It has been dated to the 2nd or 3rd century BC. Its diameter is 69 centimetres, and it is made from 13 silver plates clasped together to form the interior and the exterior; it is decorated, each piece forming an individual picture (twelve rectangles, the 13th being circular and forming the bottom[111]). The style is extremely rich, typifying the relationship between reality and symbol which characterised the Celtic world. Many interpretations have been offered. Gods and goddesses, imaginary scenes, chimeras, decorative motifs, all in a style which is at once realistic and very graphic, such as the animals' fur and manes, or again the clothes, beards, and hair on the heads of gods and humans. The ensemble is so extraordinary that a whole book could be devoted to it. Getting back to our topic, on one of the plates three men are brandishing swords. Another is even more astonishing. On the central plate there is a two-level scene. On the higher level there are four mounted men moving towards the right and on the lower level we see six foot soldiers moving towards the left. This procession is framed by two further representations. The one on the right depicts three men busily playing carnyxes (war trumpets). On the left hand a giant (a divinity?) has hold of what seems to be a foot soldier by the waist and the leg and is throwing him into a large cauldron. In terms of the composition, this individual interrupts what is otherwise a static harmony by being the counterpart of the person who is at the front of the musicians' march (or the end of the foot soldiers). It is worth noting the importance attached to the equipment, all archaeologically verifiable, to the hierarchisation of the participants, and to religious beliefs associated with combat and warriors.

These examples represent only a modest percentage of the scenes once depicted, those which have been preserved and discovered. No doubt we shall never see a large repertoire of motifs and scenes depicted on wood, a material very much in use during these periods, but which easily perishes.

Scenes of Combat

There are various kinds of 'theatres of war'. Some involve killing. In this category, one can isolate places dedicated to fighting, 'official' battlefields, for want of a better word. This kind of direct source has recently become a part of archaeology, but the process has been difficult and often controversial. The greater the distance in time, the less accessible data there is – either on land or at sea, where just as much fighting must have taken place. The First and Second World Wars now constitute a legitimate part of archaeological research, and this has helped to develop new ways of looking at such events, thanks to the study of places where battles took place, which began to be excavated towards the end of the 1980s during the course of large infrastructure works (roads, railways, industrial or commercial areas, and so on). The archaeologists involved were confronted with trenches and remains of active explosive devices which created safety problems. What was to be done if such things were to help contribute to knowledge? How to approach such spaces and the historical vestiges uncovered in them? The matter was often complicated by the fact that archaeology was seen as a science only of very ancient things, whilst such wars were an up-to-date, controversial subject. Contemporary archaeology had every bit as much trouble gaining legitimacy as archaeology of more ancient periods, though for contradictory reasons: archaeology was not useful since we had texts; it yielded data too slight, fragmentary, and silent for it to contribute to history. Despite such timorous reservations this is now one of the most dynamic sectors of archaeology in the sphere of combat,[112] including conflicts that took place at the end of the 19th century, and Napoleonic wars on European soil. Such studies are now reaching beyond Europe.[113]

Wars of the 20th century were mass wars from every point of view. Their impact on the environment is still visible in some places, even without archaeological excavation. Landscapes have sometimes literally and permanently been reshaped by bombing, trenches, and fortifications. Battlefields in previous centuries were for the most part localised, at least as far as the most significant battles were concerned. The same is true in the United States, where the approach to archaeology has always been linked to anthropology. Regarding the Middle Ages, the British were pioneers. Nowadays there are some mythical sites that one can see clearly, Bouvines or Hastings for example.[114] As for antiquity there has been a longstanding tradition of trying to identify battlefields and associated physical remnants on site. No doubt the battle-narratives of poets and historians are linked to the importance attributed to them. Archaeology was called upon to help investigations into antique battles earlier than for other periods. Possible sites were excavated, and battlements, fortifications and other military constructions were identified.

Progressive sedimentation over the course of the centuries and millennia, even if there was no large-scale development on the site of the battlefield itself, makes it increasingly difficult to localise areas specific to war, particularly if the name of the site has been lost and there is no reason to keep the memory alive. Georges Duby (1919-1996) was right to highlight this: *"If the memory of Bouvines has not been entirely lost, this is because it was cultivated, and carefully so."*[115]

Once again, the end of the Iron Age constituted a threshold in many respects: the locations of mythical battles are mentioned in written sources, and the 19th century went looking for them, for ideological as well as scientific purposes: Gergovia, Alesia, and Teutoburg. Napoleon III himself encouraged excavations on the sites of victories and defeats which marked the end of Gaulish independence. Colonel Stoffel, the emperor's aide-de-camp, played a major role in both. He led investigations on the plateau of Merdogne and areas nearby in order to demonstrate that this was indeed the site of Gergovia, the capital of Arvernia and the place where Vercingetorix was victorious in his conflict with Caesar in 52 BC. Real traces of the battle can be seen on the site: two Roman defensive ditches, two projectiles fired by catapults, and missiles from bolt-throwers have been found *in situ* in the Roman ditches; a projectile fired from a catapult is still lodged in the ground of the oppidum just to the rear of the rampart, a military construction. Alesia received even more attention from Napoleon III's 'national archaeology'. The emperor entrusted the excavations to Stoffel in 1862. More than a battle site, Alesia symbolises defeat and the end of Gaulish independence, regarded in the 19th century as the first national epic, with Vercingetorix[116] as its first hero. Research did not aim just to understand the logistics of occupation, the functioning of the oppidum or even how the battle was fought. The starting point was textual study, complemented and verified by excavations, in a Europe characterised by exacerbated nationalism. In 9 AD, Armenius and the Germans ambushed the Roman army. The defeat of the Romans at the battle of Teutoburg marked the point where Roman expansion stopped. The location of the place where more than 20,000 men confronted one another is still the object of several hypotheses. Tacitus mentions Detmold. War booty found in 1868 led some to opt for Hildesheim. The German historian, Theodor Mommsen (1817-1903) thought it was in Kalkriese in Lower Saxony and recently the town of Paderborn has been suggested. Only the site of Kalkriese has so far been excavated. So, no unanimous agreement has been reached as to where this battle might have been fought.

Alesia and Teutoburg are both symbolic sites – a defeat and a victory – which have been used for ideological and political purposes. Even from an archaeological perspective such places derive some of their status from being 'sites of memory' with all the symbolism this implies.[117] The present definition of 'sites of memory' (in France) is primarily concerned with 20th century conflicts and the location of traumatic events which took place in them, but the term can be extended to include places of combat and death which have long been important in a society's history. Thus, in ancient Greece, the *trophy* marked the heart of where the fighting took place, the very centre of a battlefield; it took the form of an offering made of weapons taken from the enemy, it marked the centre of the battle symbolically and physically. Battlefields were not just places of fighting and death. They were also places for rituals linked to warfare, celebrated on the site of combat, in addition to consecrated spaces elsewhere.

The first Battlefields

What evidence is there for battlefields in Central Europe before the 5th century BC, the beginning of the Middle Iron Age, when migrating Celts crossed paths with 'literate' Mediterranean cultures? An interesting question, but the answer is not immediately obvious. A good 2500 years have passed since the end of the Early Iron Age, and 3500 years since the middle of the Bronze Age, 7500 years since the beginnings of Neolithic Europe. And what of our earlier presence in Western Europe 40,000 years ago, when *Homo sapiens* first encountered and then replaced Neanderthals?[118] Is there any evidence for battlefields then? Nowadays archaeology can locate very small clues which are nevertheless rich in meaning: and some such clues have indeed been found. However, we need to be particularly vigilant, and maintain a questioning attitude as we excavate, hoping that succeeding populations over all the years did not destroy everything, not purposefully but simply by living their own lives.

Amongst the most ancient features are ramparts, defensive walls, ditches, and fortifications in general. Examples which can be dated to the Early Neolithic have been identified and excavated during the course of the 20th century. When such Neolithic societies were deliberately viewed as egalitarian and peaceful, this type of find was considered to mark out boundaries to dwelling places, particularly in Northern Europe in the 6th millennium BC, the so-called 'Linear Band Ceramic Culture'[119] period. Nowadays such constructions are considered more likely to have come from a desire to protect living space, at a time when encounters between individuals were perhaps not entirely peaceful! Similarly, the large enclosure-like structures of the Middle Neolithic (the 5th till the 4th millennia BC) found throughout most of Europe have been reconsidered in the light of evidence of conflict, leading to similar conclusions. Such large-scale constructions are relatively easy to spot archaeologically. As for the Bronze Age, they are found in the context of monumental burial mounds (tumuli), but they are much rarer for human dwelling places; these were apparently unprotected against possible enemies by such constructions as ramparts and ditches. The fortified site of Velim in Bohemia is exceptional for Europe in this period, since it has a true system of well preserved fortifications.[120]

Protohistorians most often find themselves paying attention to negative indicators: hollow structures and changes in texture and colour which indicate human activity. Difficulties arise not only because of the antiquity of such remains, but also the nature of the materials themselves. For thousands of years in non-Mediterranean Europe structures consisted mostly of earth and wood, other than in certain specific cases (for example the megaliths). Such perishable building materials are often poorly preserved, other than in exceptional cases when underground conditions favour the survival of organic materials, for example in lacustrine sites or more recently discovered lakeside sites like the dwellings of Must Farm in England.[121] So archaeologists need all their knowledge and skill to transform these brown traces in soft soil into clues for the presence of, for example, a palisaded rampart… seeing in them defensive structures against enemies, evidence for acts of violent destruction, perhaps even human remains, weaponry and so on, clues that a battle might have been fought here.

Amongst other recent excavations a site in the Valley of Tollense (in western Mecklenburg-Pomerania, Germany) was identified in 2006 as a possible Bronze Age battlefield.[122] Well preserved in muddy sedimentation, various weapons were found mingled with skeletal remains of about 200 individuals, indicators *in situ* of a conflict which apparently took place in about 1200 BC. Work is still being carried out on this site and at present it remains a one-off. However, it gives grounds for hope that future discoveries might yield more consistent and precise data regarding how war was fought, thereby radically improving our knowledge base.

Sacred Sites and Cult Objects

All around places where battles were fought (restricted areas, battlefields, living places where fighting happened – dwelling places in particular), spaces and constructions linked to warfare can be detected, which were, one might say 'on the front-line'. Religious activities and places fall into this particular category. The most complete expression of this is the sanctuary: a consecrated place reserved for ritualised practices, connected with beliefs and divinities. Any form of violence that a society might identify as such can figure in such places: the exclusion of violence (for example the interdiction of killing in Christian churches), or by contrast the association of violence with the sanctuary by means of rites, sacrifices and so on. To transgress such norms is to go beyond the practices of war which are more or less recognised, even if only tacitly. In Rwanda people took refuge in churches because they thought that killing would be most strongly prohibited in these places. The fact that they were massacred was shocking not only because of the violence unleashed, but also because it happened in places where it was not supposed to. In Oradour-sur-Glane in June 1944, the height of horror was enacted when the village church was burned with women and children assembled inside – killed deliberately in the most monstrous way imaginable because, from the point of view of their killers, they represented the enemy, and this went beyond any other consideration. Theoretically there are places where violence cannot take place, but only provided that the rules are known and respected. Such interdictions structure and channel societies and human behaviour. Norms are often difficult to accept for those outside the society in question. This is particularly true of cannibalism or certain funerary rituals which can seem very strange to observers. The line between what is and is not possible arises out of social norms, rules, and laws with which every society endows itself. War does not escape this mechanism. The soldiers who went to the front in 1915 knew the dangers and the rules. This does not mean that they regarded the war in which they were risking death as justified, but their situation and their actions meant that certain things just had to be done.

A society may well choose to associate wartime violence with specific sacred spaces. Sacrifices to the gods can be understood as part of an act of war connecting the divine world to the human. The latter can seek the gods' goodwill by making offerings in order to gain victory over their enemies. Research about such activities in the antique world is plentiful, particularly in Greece where large sanctuaries from classical times have been studied from a number of different perspectives: architectural, ritual, and sacrificial.[123] Sacrifices linked to war preponderantly consist of weaponry.

There are five kinds of place where such objects have a role to play, and thus five 'archaeological contexts' with respect to archaeological finds: the workshops where they were made; the dwelling places of those who used them (habitats); places where they were used in combat; ritualised spaces where they were symbolically reused, either with a strong connection to their first use (the battlefield) or in their role as objects sacred to the gods (specially constructed sanctuaries or sacred places), and finally places where their functional life ceased and they were abandoned alongside the persons who used them whilst certain specific procedures were enacted, that is funerary rites.

For even more ancient periods, it would be a mistake to suggest that there were no such beliefs or religious places. As soon as humans become conscious of themselves and of others, they project themselves into their environment and become aware of the notion of time, and of life-cycles – including their own, lasting until their deaths and those of others – we see ourselves as part of a dimension which goes beyond mere biological identity. This type of process is a combination of biological potential which comes into being during the course of long-term evolution – for example the human ability to form words which only became possible when the organs of speech came into being – and cognitive development which could be translated into specific actions. In order to identify the relationship between the self and others, researchers have observed signs which are almost the reverse of those associated with violence and war. We see actions which demonstrate an acceptance of responsibility for individuals other than the self: these find expression most markedly in the advent of funerary rites and care for others, identifiable at least since the time of the Neanderthals who were careful to offer graves to their dead.[124] Such acts find concrete expression in the development of graves and in human bone repairs (scarring, post-fracture bone-mending and so on), impossible unless the injured person had been cared for and fed during their recovery (or attempted recovery if the individual died). As soon as humans became involved in this kind of activity, they were doing something which went far beyond their own identity, or their place in a group or an environment, which one might refer to as spiritual or religious. Hypotheses in this area are perilous and can easily yield chancy explanations because evidence is so slight. A researcher must work rather by a process of deduction. By looking at available data (graves, evidence of medical care, the manufacture of objects, food consumption practices and so on), it is reasonable to think that humans developed beliefs which made it possible for them to explain their world and find a place in it.

The production of objects and representations which are 'uselessly' aesthetic and figurative is a significant factor in human history. In Europe, evidence has now been found for this dating back as early as 40,000 years ago.[125] The Chauvet Cave, which chronologically represents the first example of this, is sometimes interpreted as a sacred place or at least a place where 'ceremonies' took place, since there is no evidence of anyone ever having lived there, nor even of a burial site – unlike other more recent caves, for example the one at Cussac (in the Dordogne, France). The representations on this cave wall have no link with war or violence between men, unless one chooses to interpret confrontations with animals (female lions in particular) metaphorically. The state of preservation of sacred sites, like all deliberately constructed spaces, is largely dependent on the materials employed and the local conditions. Palaeolithic caves, as it happened, were sometimes deliberately blocked up at a particular moment in their history, so for millennia it was impossible to get into them. Stone-built architecture has better chances of preservation than wooden structures. Megaliths definitely had some religious role and are sometimes explicitly associated with funerary rites (e.g., dolmens). Some monuments from the Middle Neolithic, which are not made of stone but evident because of their enormous size, also have this function.[126] Many ceremonial places have no doubt escaped our notice, being smaller in scale and built of earth, wood, and so on. Knowledge of such ancient European societies is limited by the absence of certain data, which does not mean they did not exist. They have disappeared, leaving archaeologists to do what they can with whatever remains, trying to fill in as best they can the many gaps and occasionally to put forward hypotheses, risky at times. Written history is not the only source available to us without due consideration.

From the Metal Ages onward (the end of the 3rd millennium BC) there is ever-increasing evidence, including some related to war, both in terms of place and societal behaviour. Sanctuaries in Picardie (France) from the Late Iron Age (Ribemont-sur-Ancre, Gournay-sur-Aronde, France) leave little room for doubt. These are dedicated spaces, surrounded by ditches and palisades; they enclose deliberately laid out human remains and broken weaponry, combining purpose-built places of worship and trophies. Discovered in the 1970s, such sanctuaries gave fresh impetus to archaeological studies of war.[127] They brought about a re-examination of ancient sites where weaponry and individuals bearing marks of violence had been found, starting with the eponymous La Tène site in Switzerland.[128] Human remains and objects discovered there more than a century ago are nowadays interpreted as a kind of trophy built on the site of a collapsed bridge.[129] Such discoveries also led archaeologists to be increasingly vigilant and to pay more careful attention to all indicators of weapon-use, human remains or atypical burial places, which could be associated with rituals linked to war or warriors. In the last few years groups of objects from the Late Iron Age have come to light and very much enriched the data we possess, like the grave of Gondole in the parish of Cendre (Puy-de-Dôme, France) where the bodies of eight warriors were found resting near eight horses which no doubt belonged to them; also the hoard of Tintignac where a collection of carnyxes (war trumpets) and weaponry bears witness to the continuation of the very ancient practice, going back to the Bronze Age and as far as the Neolithic,[130] of burying metal objects and objects of a symbolic nature in hoards. Such finds are almost in a category of their own, since they relate to the question of war as well as broader issues, not least metalcraft and religious observances in places not initially intended or constructed for them. Here, we are dealing with objects whole or broken, buried, or submerged, which we have to see as evidence for religious acts in consecrated spaces, though all that remains is the ensemble of objects themselves. Amongst such groups of items characteristic of European Protohistory there are many weapons which highlight the role played by religious acts in the practice of war.

Skeletons and Splinters

One more indicator of violence with a possible link to warfare remains to be tackled: human remains of combatants – those killed in battle, massacred non-combatants, and indeed survivors who died well after the end of conflict – found in places of conflict, or religious or funerary spaces. Such physical remnants are what each human eventually becomes: a corpse, a skeleton, bone fragments and so on.

Though they are biologically – literally – the remains closest to us and the most intimate, they have nevertheless long been neglected. The way we look at human remains has followed the general history of archaeological research, its ways of framing questions and its paradigms. Even at the time of antiquarian collections, crocodiles were preserved in curiosity cabinets, but the place for most human remains was the cemetery (except relics in the West and the occasional mummy). In the 19th century, human remains were kept for a specific purpose: to establish human connections to 'antediluvian' times; going back ever further to construct increasingly detailed chronologies. Skeletal remains that looked like people of the time, particularly those found in tombs, met with variable interest. There was a tendency to conserve human remains preserved in humid conditions (in Scandinavia for example, or in the peatbogs of Jutland) or dry conditions (particularly in Egypt). Otherwise, what happened was haphazard, depending largely on decisions made at the time of excavation. Often, objects found in graves entered collections, but not the human remains found with them, even though they were recorded, drawn or even prettily painted in watercolours, as happened in the necropolis in Hallstatt (Austria). In other cases, they were conserved alongside the finds. This was generally what happened with finds from the Palaeolithic, Mesolithic and even the Neolithic. The conservation of skeletal remains was less systematic the more recent they were. Also, researchers' views of such remains were conditioned by their own relationship with death: by the start of the 21st century the attitude of Western European societies to death was no longer what it had been at the beginning of the 20th century, when there was greater familiarity with such things and no doubt less anguish (or greater fatalism). In any case, ordinary human remains did not really come to constitute the main corpus of archaeological data for a good century – until 1950, this situation scarcely changed.

The major development came about not on an archaeological site but in a laboratory. The American Willard Libby (1908-1980) developed a system of radiocarbon dating by calculating the decay of carbon-14 present in living organisms, the quantity of which stays stable in living organisms and subsequently diminishes following a predictable rate after death. This makes it possible to calculate how long ago an individual died as long as one possesses a sample of their tissue.[131] Before then, in the absence of written sources, there had been no means of accurately dating ancient archaeological materials, so this method opened up revolutionary possibilities. Skeletal remains acquired a new status and unhoped for potential. Gradually, they ceased to be disposed of. Better still, from the 1970s and 1980s, they became part of new developments and archaeological approaches. Funerary rites were studied taking such data into account. Death gradually became a central preoccupation, at a time when human and social sciences were becoming more sensitive to anthropological perspectives, both in the worlds of 'history' and 'archaeology'.

When war became an object of study in its own right during the 1990s, attention was logically directed towards human remains found in some places. What is more, such remains made it possible to open (or rather re-open) the question of violence at the heart of very ancient populations, because some bones bore marks which left little doubt as to the none-too-pacific nature of their deaths! Palaeoanthropologists began to play a major role in all archaeological fields, ancient and modern. Their skills and their understanding of taphonomy and the sedimentation of bodies was – and still is – used in the study of burial sites resulting from 20th century conflicts. They even play a role in criminal investigations where their expertise leads to a better understanding of what happened to corpses post-mortem and how they were buried. Moreover, recent developments in the study of ancient DNA have contributed further still to the interest shown in human remains, opening further perspectives, in particular regarding kinship. Skeletal remains are used in other investigations too, not just archaeology. There is now an all too real fascination, bordering on the morbid. Investigations into violent deaths – including modern-day criminal cases – now both involve the fullest possible analysis of (skeletal) human remains. Methods used at crime scenes, moreover, are troublingly similar to those of archaeologists: the study of place, snapshots of clues at the scene, the relative positions of objects to one another and human remains, lines of causality, detailed chronologies of events, and so on. The data is similar and treated in similar ways. Only the timescales are different. The presence of violent death accentuates the parallels,[132] not least in theatres of war. A study, which appeared in 2016 under the direction of Jean Guilaine and Jacques Sémelin, set out these methodological changes that have had major consequences in France for the way problems are framed regarding war and its study.[133] It sheds light on the recent interest in newly excavated human remains and the place now occupied by palaeopathology and physical anthropology in studies of violence as a component part of war. The study's authors discuss the different types of find: places of combat with bodies found *in situ* and bodies buried in pits where usual funerary rituals have not been carried out; and also tombs in the more classic sense of the word: the more normal option in the treatment of human bodies, less exclusively linked to war. The study's discussion of violence in the Palaeolithic is relatively brief, looking exclusively at human remains which bear traces of violent blows as causes of death, somewhat following the 19th century construct of the savage. Amongst recent archaeological discoveries several finds show that executions and massacres did take place, not on the scale of more recent periods, but which, provided they continue to be studied carefully, will no doubt shed light upon such human activities, what motivated them and how they were carried out.[134]

The Lessons of Bones

Skeletal remains dating from the Early Palaeolithic are – currently – too few, too fragmentary and sometimes too damaged, for example by animals, for there to be any certainty about the role played by violence during this period.[135] Usable information dates from relatively recent times in terms of human evolution; there is nothing before the end of the Early Palaeolithic, and this is patchy. Amongst the oldest examples there are six individuals, *Homo antecessor* (a branch of human fossil remains), discovered in Gran Dolina (Atapuerca, Spain), all aged under 18 and all decapitated.

For the Middle Palaeolithic (from about 350,000 BC), in central Western Europe, the age of the Neandertals, there are scarcely any more sites. In around 100,000 BC on the site of Baume Moula-Guercy (Ardèche, France), six Neandertals met a violent end. At about the same time, in a cave in Krapina (Croatia), at least 14 individuals were killed. The skeletal remains are very fragmented, and deliberately broken. Evidence of violence seems essentially to concern isolated individuals, and some were wounded in such a way that we cannot always tell how much this was deliberate or the result of various accidents. A certain number of very ancient violent group deaths (Gran Dolina, Spain and Krapina, Croatia) yield evidence of cannibalistic practices at the heart of societies, without it being possible to tell whether these took the form of aggressive acts or simply social and religious activities, which might well shock Europeans nowadays, but which do not necessarily have any link with war. From the Upper Palaeolithic, evidence is a bit less scanty and therefore a little more varied in Europe and beyond: violence played a real role: towards the end of the 1960s on the right bank of the Nile, between Wadi Sahada and Djebel Sahaba, site '117' revealed the remains of at least 59 skeletons of men women and children dateable to between 12,000 and 10,000 BC. Over half had been killed violently, with blows to head and thorax, in ways that could scarcely have been accidental. The majority of these individuals were struck by projectiles which wounded or killed them: arrowheads were still present in some bodies. Researchers did not hesitate to refer to this place as the site of humanity's 'oldest massacre'. If these graves were indeed contemporary with one another, this may well indicate group violence, or a mass atrocity given the population levels at the time. In 2012 the Nataruk site (Kenya) was discovered, where 27 individuals had been killed around 8000 BC; their bones were left *in situ*, leaving no doubt at all about the cause of death. Skulls had been struck showing various points of impact, bones had been broken, arrowheads and spearheads were stuck in bodies, hands tied when they were put to death, and so on. The episode was no doubt linked to a violent confrontation which affected individuals other than the combatants themselves. Amongst the victims were eight women, one of whom was pregnant, and six children, who certainly could not have been defined as warriors.

Cannibalism – and the killing which preceded it – did not disappear. Between approximately 13,000 and 12,000 BC, five individuals were killed before being eaten in Gough Cave (Somerset, England). In the cave of Perrats in Agris (Charente, France), at least five adults and three children met this same fate during the Mesolithic (between 9000 and

7000 BC).[136] In the Early Neolithic (the so-called 'Linear Band Ceramic Culture'), human remains associated with wild animals (the cave of Hanseles Hohl in Baden-Würtemburg, Germany and Zauschwitz in Saxony, Germany and so on) seem to highlight a continuity in cannibalism, at least at the beginnings of the Neolithic. Debates about cannibalistic activities remain open: food needs, ritual, maybe associated with funerary practices, perhaps related to conflicts between opposing groups, reprisals against the vanquished. Possible scenarios are many and varied but, apart from the last, not necessarily to do with war.

During the transition from the Mesolithic to the Neolithic, skulls are noticeably over-represented in some places, for example in Ofnet in Bavaria (Germany) where two excavations yielded respectively 27 and six skulls, some of which bear evidence of blows to the back of the head, implying violent deaths. In the Neolithic, often wishfully thought of as peaceful, there is also evidence of violent deaths, which has been growing stronger as more excavations have been carried out. In the 1980s the site of Talheim (Heilbronn, Baden-Württemberg, Germany) put an end to illusory ideologies insisting that the most ancient agricultural societies in Europe consisted of harmless and peaceful populations. A pit was found containing the remains of 34 individuals, all of whom had died violently. Various fragments of pottery confirmed that these belong to the very early European Neolithic, referred to as the 'Linear Band Ceramic Culture', the end of the 6th millennium BC. The mingled skeletons all had multiple blows and injuries which suggested some form of frenzied attack upon the victims who were subsequently and without further ado thrown into the pit. The greatest number of blows were to the head, but long bones were also affected. The killing in Talheim is not an isolated example. In Asparn-Schletz (in Lower Austria), the upper level of a ditch which surrounded a settlement contained 67 bodies of people who perished as a result of violent blows to the head and whose bones also demonstrated the marks of multiple impacts. In Herxheim (Rhineland-Palatinate, Germany), about 300 individuals have been identified, the majority of them in ditches outside or within dwelling areas, showing signs of blows and also post-mortem mutilation, particularly centred on the head. In the Middle Neolithic, (around the end of the 5th millennium BC for the west of the Continent), other examples highlight the fact that in the Linear Band Ceramic Culture zone, violence and post-mortem mutilation continued, albeit taking place in a different manner. In 2012 in Bergheim (in the upper Rhineland, Germany), pit number 157 contained human remains demonstrating a strange set of circumstances: amongst the skeletons of eight individuals (men, women, and children) there was a man who bore the marks of many blows, and one of his arms had been cut off, either while he was still alive or when he was newly dead. At the bottom of the pit, beneath the eight skeletons, eight additional left arms had been buried, also similarly cut off. In 2016, in excavations at Achenheim (Lower Rhineland, Germany), one of the hundreds of agricultural storage pits (number 124) contained the complete skeletons of six adult males which showed signs of having suffered many blows and were accompanied by four extra left arms. Of course, a list of sites and inventories of broken skeletons is not enough for us to speak of 'war', so we shall come back to this. However, it is certain that interest recently devoted to human remains has made it possible to envisage some kinds of violence taking place over a long period of time, as well as the fact that corpses were deliberately mutilated, and that this continued after the Neolithic.

From the beginning of the Metal Ages (end of the 3rd millennium BC), we see increasing numbers of sites and a growth in the amount of data as the two millennia progress, but this is not uniform and there are some paradoxes. The skeletal remains of individuals who died violently in the Neolithic have received increased attention, but those from the following period not so much. Or rather, not so much importance has been attached to this type of source when it comes from before the Late Iron Age, particularly regarding ossuaries in religious sites. As for the Bronze Age, human remains scarcely play any role in relation to the study of violence and war. Indeed, there are few significant sites of massacre or signs of violent deaths. The site of Tollense (Mecklenburg-Pomerania, Germany), where skeletal remains of several hundred people clearly involved in conflict were discovered, is exceptional. It is the only European site from those times currently identified as a potential place of battle. The excavations were completed only very recently, and the study is as yet unfinished. This does not mean to say that skeletal remains have been excluded *a priori* from research, but rather that they have been used as data essentially only in the context of funeral rites: rich burials from the Early Bronze Age, or the numerous and complex cremations of the Late Bronze Age. Such data was not studied in relation to conflict and war, though the opposite was true for previous periods.[137] Such remains were seen in a different light. No doubt the practices of the time (in terms of ritual and burials) makes the study of such skeletal remains more difficult, which were moreover often incomplete. So, given that the majority of excavations studied to date were not carried out until the 1990s, perhaps we should look to the future when there may well be changes in the light of new data. So far, we have Tollense, still only partially investigated, and also early Bronze Age burial sites like Wassenaar in the Netherlands, as well as the very Late Bronze Age site of Illerup Adal near Alken in Denmark, reckoned to be a series of collective graves for warriors killed in combat.[138]

Skeletal remains have an important place in the study of violence and war during the Iron Age, in particular the Late Iron Age, when they come to light in sanctuaries, *en masse* or carefully placed, not least the crania in niches or doors as in Roquepertuse[139] (Bouches-du-Rhône, France), individual graves (for example in Gondole, France), or even in places where a battle took place. For this period, it is possible to establish parallels and analogies thanks to data from the antique world. Moreover, the burial of individuals in agricultural storage pits remains a frequent practice in the Late Iron Age. The heterogeneous nature of such finds of human remains, alongside other archaeological data of the period, is evident: one simply has to work within such constraints.

Physical proof of confrontations between people follows a course not unlike that of archaeology itself: it might be scarce or abundant, heterogeneous, varied, fleeting, imposing, fragmented, precise, silent, dispersed over time and space, and constantly subject to review in the light of new discoveries and the development of new methods. Although complex, each piece of evidence is nevertheless precious. In this context, the Bronze Age is particularly rich in such evidence. Objects, depictions of the warrior as a key participant in action, such specific pieces of data about a period underline the importance of metalcraft in the conduct of war and the power of this new beginning in the history of European societies.

III

WHEN METAL SPEAKS

The World of Metal

None of the three items that make up our 1st millennium BC Bronze Age warrior's weaponry disappeared or were re-cast in the forge of a 19th century AD bronzesmith. Theoretically this could have happened. Some Bronze Age objects discovered by chance must have found a new life in such a way, never to make it into an archaeological collection. Perhaps they were fragments, axes, tools in general which had no use for those who discovered them and so they melted them down. Other items made from various materials have no doubt been passed over or thrown away. Some discoveries did escape this fate, including various tools, usually when they fell into the hands of scholars. Not least metal weaponry and objects considered to be 'precious'.

The three sets of objects we have gathered together were considered as ancient paraphernalia rather than recyclable raw material. The value attached to them in the ancient world was added to the value attributed them in the modern world. Such relics found protection in this way, as is often the way with metal objects. It was indeed a 'beautiful sword' that came to light in Wimereux, France. Defensive arms received the benefit of similar epithets. Not least so-called 'works of art' in collections with all that this aesthetising vocabulary implies. Archaeological collections are rich in bronze swords, not just because they were manufactured in large numbers during the Metal Ages, or the way they were deliberately buried by their users, but because two or three millennia later people who were not necessarily archaeologists thought that it made sense to keep them. This happened all the more with gold items, but rather less with iron objects (including swords): the latter were in a poorer state of preservation, and there is a hierarchy of materials from which our 1000 BC warrior's equipment could not escape.

Different visions imply different perspectives. Archaeologists studying weapons nowadays examine them, as did their predecessors, by looking for certain types of details, particularly those of a morpho-typological or chronological nature. As with all historical sources, the sword, the helmet, and the breastplate need identification and dating. We need also to consider as carefully as possible the context of the find. The object on its own is not enough, as it was in the time of antiquarian collections. Nowadays archaeologists seek to glean just as much information from the objects' arrangement in relationship to one another, and the ground in which they are buried, as from the objects themselves, because of what this might teach us. This is taken alongside information from other types of data sources. Here, all our attention will be directed towards our helmets found in Normandy, France. We should therefore be careful to consider the way the items in this hoard were laid out, just as for a grave created deliberately before being abandoned. Of course, the helmets should be taken together, as an inseparable group: there can never be any question of giving a couple of them away to someone else, family members or not. Different times, different customs.

The history of such armour and weaponry illustrates the ambiguity of the status of archaeological objects; until very recently they were somewhere between object and archive, between private property and public good. Now, the business of long-term loans between institutions is what counts for these emblematic items. This is why one of the Marmesse breastplates is currently in the Abu Dhabi Louvre, quite a long way from the bogs of the upper Marne Valley in France…

When a specialist in such materials, an archaeo-metallurgist, comes to study such a set of equipment, it is because other types of information are being sought, technical in this case, not least information that can be found in the heart of matter. The helmet from Normandy that ended up in Rome has been studied in this way.

Similar studies have been carried out on the Marmesse breastplates. Ideally these should have started on site, on the day the finds were discovered, incomplete and fragmentary, avoiding the risk of deterioration after excavation. Researchers have to make the most of what they have got… It can be shown that the making of each object represents more than 150 hours work by the standards of the day.

The manufacture of the Wimereux sword is quite a different story, and the ways in which it can be studied are different too. It is a massive piece of equipment, in one single section, very well preserved. The current state of surface corrosion makes it difficult to study certain details. Nevertheless, halfway up and in the expanded part of the sword blade towards the point (it is known as 'pistilliform'), there are small signs of impact on the edge of the blade which could be marks of use and therefore its actual deployment as a weapon. It was made by casting, but it is difficult to determine the type of mould used on the basis of a single object. Its morphology means that all solutions would have been possible. Thanks to our awareness of practices in around 1000 BC, we know that there were two options: casting in a two-piece mould of fired clay, or lost wax casting using a non-permanent mould. The decision would have been made by the bronzesmith and the workshop…

There are many swords in museums but there are few analyses of the materials they are made from, and even then, only when micro-sampling is possible, obviating the risk that a sample might contain too much corrosion (and therefore increased tin levels), which is what happens when just the surface is analysed, or small samples are scraped from the surface. Such samples of micro-fragments of metal from within also yield useful information about the micro-structure. Paradoxically it is almost easier to take samples from helmets or breastplates, though these items are rarer. For such defensive armour, the sheet metal often has gaps which make sampling easier (the gap is made a tiny bit larger, about 2 millimetres approximately) and the operation remains invisible, other than to whomever carries it out. On a sword, making a notch on the blade or hilt leaves a mark which can easily be filled in by restoration, though this always gives rise to *reservations regarding an object's role as a museum piece. Sampling a small piece never to be replaced in the original is an infringement of the object's integrity. This is fine so long as metal remains are seen as normal data sources with knowledge to offer that will contribute to history. However, as soon as some people define such objects (subjectively) as 'works of art', then the situation grows more complicated, though not entirely hopeless. The Wimereux sword has not been analysed in this way. Other examples of this kind of Ewart Park sword contain about 10% tin.*

Such technical preoccupations were probably not something that concerned 'our' warrior, but they did, in their way, concern the metalworker who made this equipment. For weapons have to be weapons and they have to be able to kill.

Every manufactured object embodies a number of facts. It is made of one or several types of raw material and it is the fruit of labour, resulting in a form which is at once general and particular. It also represents uses, one or many. Ever since the 19th century such truths have been important for the pioneers of this discipline.

In 1819, the new director of the National Museum of Denmark in Copenhagen, Christian Jürgensen Thomsen (1788-1865), began the classification of objects for which he had to write an inventory and present in showcases.[140] How was he to proceed? What logic was he to deploy? His starting point was precisely this certainty: objects are characterised by the materials they consist of, and the way these materials are worked necessarily corresponds to a logic whereby they become more complex over the course of time and human history. Therefore, an object considered technically simpler is dated earlier than an object which is more complex. Facts and truths are seen as contained within the source. By establishing a classification of materials using such criteria it became possible to suggest chronologies. Thomsen formalised these in the 1830s dividing periods not yet called 'prehistoric' into three: the Stone Age, Bronze Age and Iron Age. The idea was not entirely new since Hesiod, the Greek poet, had already come up with something similar in *Works And Days* in the 8th century BC. He talks of five successive races in the history of humanity, four of which were metal (gold, silver, bronze, and iron) and also a race of heroes placed between the bronze and iron ages. Thomsen belonged to a different time and was pursuing a different goal.

The intrinsic link between physical archaeological data and periodisation finds its first formal expression here. The terminology has been questioned, and this has sometimes involved heated debates (Heinrich Schliemann being amongst those who cast doubt upon the three period model), so there have been attempts at refinement[141]. Over the course of the past two centuries, archaeological paradigms have changed but the importance of material data and the weight of certain concepts remains essential: it is through the study of physical things, the archaeological data, that one can reach back to real people.

Fascinating Metal

The starting point for our enquiry into war must then be physical, the working of 'copper alloys', a precise term which encompasses different combinations of copper and other metals, known for example as bronze or brass. Such alloys are multifaceted and can be used in different ways depending on the precise nature of the mix, the type of working, and the final state in which the metallic material is left, which can itself be associated with other materials (glass, enamel, ivory, and so on). The term covers simple forms and extraordinary ones, made in one piece or assembled from many. They come into being through a series of varied stages which require time and skill, but also decision-making that sometimes has to be very rapid. The raw material used has to be worked; it has to be extracted from stone before it becomes metal, and is liquified in the crucible; after casting it then it solidifies rapidly, and is worked when cold, or reheated to avoid fissuring, so it becomes malleable, and can take on a new shape. The alloys can occur in a number of colours from almost whitish yellow to orange, and many variations of green or brown depending on the patination. They can be matt or shiny, creating a mirror-like surface if carefully polished. Light reflects off them in a unique way, intensely, capable of dazzling if the sun shines directly into them. The metal can be cold, lukewarm, hot, slippery, malleable, or coarse; it can be flat, straight, or curved and voluminous. It can have the delicacy of a sheet of paper or the solidity of a rock wall. There can be a combination of metallic nuances or an ensemble of contrasting colours in the same object, to which non-metallic materials can be attached, wood, stone, amber, glass, enamel and so on.

The same object can consist of white and yellow metal, and contain within it pieces of coral, like the helmet from Amfreville-sous-les Monts (Eure, France), which dates from the 4th or 3rd century BC. Such polychromy is not strictly useful and seems to have had other purposes. In any case, classifications of this nature are not straightforward. The definition of aesthetic criteria is complex. The same outcome might not be 'beautiful' to all eyes. The same goes for the term 'functional', for one has also to include functions that are not utilitarian as far as an observer might be concerned, but which have a role in its use, including, for the societies in whose context they belong, symbolism or display the owner's identity.

The possibilities seem almost infinite. They depend only on the metalworker who manufactured them. This is the key. All copper alloy manufacture is an individual outcome from an extraordinary range of possible variations and requirements that have been well understood. The result is a combination of decisions, actions, and the assembly of pieces of metals one to another. But for the fear of being labelled a belated positivist, one might claim that the object, the metallic material, tells the truth – which is accurate, but not sufficiently so. The object bears within itself a great multitude of data, but just as many half-truths. Hours can be spent staring at an object without understanding anything, and various people working together might each see something quite different in the same item. Deciding to study metal alloys means being crazy enough to try to make an apparently mute object talk, which then can turn out not to be short of things to say after all. The key is to know which questions to ask.

Nowadays, by means of much improved techniques of analysis it is possible to enter into the heart of matter itself. Materials are obviously not seen as they were in the 19th century, though the notion that they contain an 'intrinsic truth' has not entirely vanished, which is just as well. Going beyond the matter itself, we need to consider the actions necessary to transform raw material found in nature in a crude form into a human product following a series of operations, both non-physical (actions) and physical (leftovers, splinters, rejects, tools, workplaces, and so on). This is the notion of the *chaîne opératoire* coined by André Leroi-Gourhan in the context of Palaeolithic stone working.[142]

In addition to the craftsman's activity and what he leaves behind, there is the craftsman himself. This individual is doubly interesting: both on a personal level because of what he tells us of his skills when at work in his workshop, and as a member of his community – a society which has expectations, behaves in a certain way, and makes decisions, all of which have a bearing on the work he undertakes with his crucible and with his hammer. So, the study of ancient copper alloys means being interested in a type of raw material with its special features and requirements, the individuals who carry out the work and also the society where such individuals belong, which is itself part of a long historical continuum. Three, or indeed four levels of analysis, all starting with old bits of mute metal – an ambitious project...

The working of copper alloys figures alongside two other key metals in the global context of metal crafting. The first of these is gold, worked from the Early Neolithic, having less potential in technical terms and yielding therefore a smaller range of products (jewellery, ornamental decoration, and so on). The second is iron, used in a great variety of ways, from architecture to tools, and including a vast range of other products. The spread of iron was relatively late, beginning only at the start of the 1st millennium BC in Europe, meaning that its long-term history is more circumscribed (particularly with regard to the Neolithic). Also, the state of preservation in which iron objects are found, generally means they need cleaning by restorers before they can be studied, adding to logistical constraints and increasing costs. But then, the skill of the La Tène ironsmiths (the Middle Iron Age, from the 5th century BC) is undeniable. That of bronzesmiths, whose creativity runs parallel to theirs, is fascinating. Copper alloys can therefore be seen as part of a family of materials which unite complexity, diversity, and beauty, thus providing information that can give an overview of the history of copper alloys in Europe over three millennia, not least in the context of warfare.

The movement from object to society is not an easy one. It means moving from static and silent physical things towards something garrulous and constantly moving. Alain Testart (1945-2013) claimed in 2012 that the only way for an archaeologist wanting to *"go beyond the reconstruction of actions and see them in terms of social practices"* was ethnographic comparative studies.[143] This suggestion can make sense, provided due precautions are taken to avoid meaningless comparisons between societies living neither in the same place nor the same time. Lessons drawn from primary comparative studies in the 19th century have shown the dangers of such an exercise. It can be helpful in broadening one's horizons, deepening one's thought and getting archaeological data into perspective, but only if the researcher keeps coming back to real data, getting to know it well, and not trying to compare everything in one go, but just individual points chosen carefully after mature reflection.

As for copper alloy artefacts, the question is tricky: scarcely any contemporary society exists nowadays that an ethnologist might observe which could shed light on the Late Neolithic and the Metal Ages, least of all the Bronze Age. There might be interesting information regarding some artisanal procedures (casting techniques in India for example), but not in the context of societies comparable to those in Europe in the first and 2nd millennia BC. Sub-Saharan Africa is particularly interesting since ironworking started early there, in some areas before the introduction of copper alloys, and there are areas too where the development of alloy-working took a different course, for example in Nigeria. Here, casting processes at the end of the 1st millennium AD were exceptionally good, but these did not evolve alongside hammering techniques, which hinders comparisons helpful to the understanding of Eurasian developments.[144] To sum up, no other Bronze Age society equivalent to that of continental Europe seems ever to have existed, particularly in terms of relationships between technology, social and political models, and then finally to war. So, looking elsewhere will not really help us find answers even though openness to other societies is always useful in the process of logical deduction. Here we need to do something different: firstly, to weigh up the facts about Europe in terms of what they can tell us and then to pursue our investigation based on archaeological finds and the data they yield, in particular metal weaponry.

Choices of metal in Europe

Europe made a deliberate choice in committing itself to metal. There was nothing predetermined about this process. It was a chosen invention in human history with motivations and consequences serious enough to 'make the world go round'.[145] Many societies throughout the world have lived without metalcraft until very recently.[146] What is more, the order in which metals appear is not a universal given, necessarily coinciding with their order of appearance in Europe. Such a new development could not have happened just any old way. Many and varied forces were at work: populations adopted such materials for different reasons. A phenomenon of this nature would be inconceivable unless the societies in question had the requisite cognitive and physical capacities, not to mention the will to set up the means and exchange networks.

The earliest metalcraft appears in Europe in the Neolithic, but chronologically out of step with the process of neolithization, that is to say the advent of the agricultural world.[147] In areas which became agricultural, the organisation of life created ever more specialised spaces: those dedicated to crops were not the same as those dedicated to livestock, or the places where people lived, or necropolises, nor even places of religion. Everything had its 'own' special place. This process happened in stages, in fits and starts, between the 7th and 5th millennia BC, then at increasing speed in a sort of second 'revolution', which is also called 'the Late Neolithic'.

People were not static, immobile. They moved over land and by water. Neolithization itself spread by these two means. Reasons could be very varied. Looking for raw materials and exchange were part of the process. None of this was an entirely new phenomenon – the use of exogenous materials is found from the Palaeolithic onwards. Nevertheless, over the centuries, raw materials grew more diverse and were exchanged over increasingly large distances and in ever larger quantities. People were happy to cross the lands and seas of Europe in order to get greenstones from the Alps or amber from the Baltic. The interest in various rocks that can be transformed by fire (by techniques already known from ceramics) went hand in hand with the increasing complexity and intensity of traffic on European exchange routes.

Copper metalworking was more likely to start up in areas rich in copper ore. A good mastery of extraction and reduction techniques is clearly vital, but in a way, this was the only requirement. The working of copper alloys by contrast, (since the raw materials to be mixed are not all present in the same place) required a reliable and well-structured system of long-distance exchanges. These began to be set up in Western Europe at the start of the 2nd millennium BC, the very time when new forms of objects linked to combat became widespread. It is worth pondering the need to organise networks of this nature and to imagine the power of those who controlled them. This was the backdrop for the simultaneous appearance of a new family of technological processes and a new type of warfare.

Travel then was fundamental and archaeology bears witness to this, showing that societies attached great importance to it, both physically and symbolically. Pathways from the beginning of the Neolithic have been located. Dugout canoes (made from a single piece of a tree trunk) bear witness to movement across lakes and rivers. During the Bronze Age, thanks to a dynamic process of specialisation in many domains, technically elaborate boats came into being. Examples are few in number, but very rich in lessons for us, like those made from planks stitched together by yew withies unearthed in England, the oldest dating from the start of the Middle Bronze Age, between 1600 and 1500 BC for the oldest. One of the best preserved examples was discovered in Dover (Kent, England) in 1992.[148] In Scandinavia combatants represented in rock art characteristic of the 2nd millennium BC, are often seen as fighting on boats which are not dissimilar, in their general form, to those discovered in Britain.[149]

In Northern Europe, however, no Bronze Age boat has yet been discovered. The only known example comes from later. It has much to tell us. This is an Iron Age boat (5th century BC) discovered in Hjortspring (Denmark), in a boggy area: it too demonstrates a certain number of morphological and technical analogies with the more ancient Bronze Age boats. It contained a hoard of metal weapons and armour, both offensive and defensive (swords, shields, and spears).[150] It bears witness to an ensemble of practices, the meanings of which are hard to untangle: a boat relating both to real and symbolic travel, exceptional copper alloy working, copper specific weapon production and a ritual, deliberate and final burial in a hoard that combines these various elements.

Chariots and wagons were the terrestrial equivalent of these boats. Their function was twofold: real and part of a belief system over and beyond their functional use. In Denmark the six-wheeled, horse-drawn Trundholm sun chariot (14th century BC), bears a bronze disc covered in gold which is at the same time a shield and a possible representation of the sun. Made of bronze covered with decorated gold leaf, it was manufactured by the lost wax technique. In the tomb of Kivik (Sweden), also dating from the 14th century BC, one of the ornate panels also depicts a horse-drawn, two-wheeled chariot, with a man holding the reins. Animals have their place in this bestiary of travel: deer, horses, waterbirds, and marine animals. They turn up alongside others (the boar and chimera in the La Tène period), and in ensembles which are much later than the Iron Age where they continue to play a role alongside the warrior. Finally, such travel would not be possible without some representation of space and the stars, indispensable for those venturing overseas and along roads. The Nebra disc (Mittelberg, Saxony-Anhalt, Germany), dating from about 1600 BC, is about 30 centimetres across, made of bronze, and bears circles and arcs of gold. It is considered to be one of the most ancient representations of the heavenly firmament.[151]

In the hoard, it was found alongside two swords, amongst other things. War, metalcraft, and travel: the overlap between the three is a powerful one.

One thing is certain: people and goods are on the move so much that travel becomes part of such societies' religious structure. Here we are going beyond metallurgy, but metalcraft could not have existed as it did if such systems of exchange had not been established.[152] But there is something of a contradiction here: a minimal degree of stability is necessary for such exchange-networks to function. Yet these arise at the very moment when war becomes formally organised, though war is *a priori* a source of instability, indeed a form of insecurity at odds with travel and the provision of raw materials. Metalcraft cannot be conceived without technological considerations in the purest sense. Nor could it have grown to such an extent unless the societies involved had evolved appropriate economic systems. This indeed goes beyond war in the strict sense, yet to the heart of the system of which it was part.

Unpicking Harlequin's Cloak

Let us return to specific questions regarding the working of copper alloys and try following the precepts of André Leroi-Gourhan to 'unpick Harlequin's cloak'…[153] Data, in the case of copper alloy metalcraft, consist essentially of finished objects which were used, or not, at the end of the manufacturing process and which were deposited or abandoned in various places ('contexts' in the archaeological sense): graves, religious spaces (burials being one of these), living spaces (houses, workshops), spaces given over to a particular activity (like battlefields). In short, all spaces which humans occupy at some time or another, though differences in numbers vary considerably. For every sword found in the context of a dwelling-place, there are at least a thousand swords (whole or broken) in hoards, and no more than about a hundred in graves, with very considerable fluctuations according to regions and periods.

As well as the numerical heterogeneity relative to places where they are found buried (many religious sites, practically no workshops) there is a variation in the number of objects in each of these situations. Sometimes there is just one object, sometimes an ensemble consisting of several hundred items. The state in which these are found is also variable, some whole objects, some fragmented, including those found broken when originally buried, not just because of damage resulting from burial.

The sum total of data which amounts to millions of items in Europe as a whole reflects a collection process which stretches over 200 years, indeed more if we include the (beautiful) objects in curiosity cabinets dating from the days of antiquarianism.

Such objects began to be kept well before other types of archaeological finds and for three main reasons: they were beautiful, they were understandable (because they could be identified) and they were made from a material that could, if necessary, be recycled. So, they were favoured over and above other archaeological objects, though others too were considered fascinating in their way from early on. So-called 'thunderstones' for example, which were very much objects of scholarly debate from the beginning of the modern period. What was going on? Were they natural rocks which had fallen with thunder and lightning or were they created by human hands? In 1723, Antoine de Jussieu presented a lecture called *The Origins of Thunderstones* in which he identified the knapped flint and polished axe blades as the works of men rather than nature.[154]

There was continued generic interest in 'bronze' objects, but there was also greater concern about finds accompanying such objects that would help to explain them. For decades in Europe no workshop was ever excavated, but then some were found in England not long after the Second World War, then in France, in the 1980s. They were firstly identified in exceptionally well preserved strata as for example in Fort-Harrouard in Normandy, unmistakably a place where metal was worked, given the kinds of structure, remains of moulds, and various waste products.[155] Nowadays workshops, or at least remains from them (moulds, casting crucibles, waste and so on), are regularly discovered, gradually filling gaps in the data relating to this craft.[156]

Amongst the metal objects found since the 19th century some resulted from a strange practice prevalent in the whole of Europe from the beginnings of the 2nd millennium BC until the Iron Age (at least) : the metal hoard or deposition[157]. This ambiguous and no doubt all too imprecise word designates specifically the assembly of objects (whole or broken), and sometimes metal ingots, in greater or larger numbers, which were deliberately buried in a single operation. There were thousands of these during the Bronze Age, amounting to tons of metal. These are typical for the 2nd millennium BC, and they have never ceased to intrigue and to be interpreted in different ways. Many contained items of weaponry, no doubt constituting key pieces of the puzzle regarding the conduct of war and its accompanying rituals.

Hierarchies that dare not speak their name

There are large numbers of items made from copper alloys. Various kinds of values are attached to such materials, consciously or unconsciously. Professional archaeology has to struggle against judgments of this nature, and rightly so: all finds are equally valuable and have something to tell us about human history. So much for the theory. In reality, these implicit hierarchies are harder to get away from. A gold torc attracts more attention than a polished stone axe, a rich grave generates more interest than a modest settlement. The problem would be a minor one if it had no consequences for the methods used to study such objects. Not to mention the lamentable theft and sale of archaeological finds which has done real damage, creating a substantial economy parasitic on research.[158] Metal hoards in particular are the choice targets of detectorists (hunters of treasure and archaeological goods). They are often intercepted, and their booty recovered. Nevertheless, such behaviour deprives us of information about how the objects came to be buried. The damage is real – and definite – because each hoard is a collection of items whose every component part represents a set of actions, a deliberate procedure, which gives meaning to the collection as a whole.

Metal occupies a special place in these hidden hierarchies. During the course of archaeological excavations, the discovery of metal can give rise to behaviour that is not always what it should be: envy is kindled. Sometimes even media frenzies are unleashed. An archaeologist gains prestige from the discovery of a grave rich in vessels, weaponry, jewellery and other metal objects – far more so than a colleague who has excavated a settlement characterised by post-holes, storage pits and ceramics, even if the settlement is of a totally unusual type and advances knowledge far more than yet another grave belonging to a category often seen before.

A final inequality in the treatment of various families of metals results from their relative scarcity and state of preservation after centuries of lying buried. Copper alloys have less prestige than gold but more than iron. Gold is at the very top of the list because it is still yellow and metal-like (not altered by corrosion) at the very moment when it is discovered. It is rarely found in large quantities and its use is limited to jewellery and ornamentation; in any case it would be hard to use it for anything else. Silver would take second place if there were enough of it in ancient pre-Roman European societies (some such objects do exist, from the early Bronze Age, in particular in tombs in Armorica, France). Copper alloys then are *de facto* in second place, sometimes still shiny if found in peatbogs or rivers, sometimes green in colour, wrongly called 'green bronze' since this material is naturally yellow: it turns green as it ages and corrodes.[159] The use of bronze alloys is very varied with respect to the range of archaeological objects: jewellery, vessels, weapons, ornaments and so on. Finally, though iron is used in a number of different ways, it still boasts only a limited aura. It is more abundant in the European subsoil than metals which form copper alloys, but it does not age well. When excavated, it is covered in accretions of earth and stone which means that it is not always possible to tell what the object is. Sometimes, radiography and laboratory cleaning are needed to do so. This is often a difficult and costly procedure which almost excludes iron from the top three metals. Long ignored, such objects began to arouse interest in Europe when it was realised that, beneath the accretions, surprising things were often to be found, like decorated sword scabbards from the La Tène period.[160]

This is the key: what is, or not, considered to be a 'work of art'. By French law, an ordinary fragment of pottery is considered to be a 'movable chattel'. And generally, it is considered to be an archaeological find. A beautiful Bronze Age helmet by contrast is often seen as a 'work of art', so in people's minds (but not in French law) it can almost shed its status as a normal archaeological find. Exhibitions of archaeological objects more than demonstrate the different ways in which various materials are looked at. Showcases with gold 'treasures' receive far more attention than a weaver's loom-weight (a weight needed to stretch threads), made of stone, though such items are very important to understand weaving, clothing and so on. Visitors have their expectations, so the nature of museum displays, and security measures, have to adapt to them.[161]

The consequences of this unequal consideration of data from under the ground are substantial. Archaeologists have to learn to cope with this unspoken state of affairs. For a metallurgy specialist the implications are far-reaching. We are probably lucky in some ways because metal objects have been collected more systematically and fewer have gone missing from collections; also, people are more willing to offer financial support for the acquisition of such 'works of art' and research into them. But it is also a truly limiting factor because, being too much admired, these objects are also coveted and stolen. Studying them sometimes involves rules which are difficult to put into practice (accessibility, handling, laboratory examination protocols, and so on). All research is dependent on such contingencies which are not strictly scientific, but have a direct bearing on what we can study and how we can study it. Metal weaponry used in war is directly affected by such requirements.

Deciphering and Understanding

Metal is studied according to protocols which have much in common with those used in the analyses of all archaeological objects.[162] The first question is identification. What kind of thing is it? When does this object date from? Questions which seem simple at first, but for which replies are not always obvious – the absence of words, of any 'instruction manual', can make the task arduous, particularly if the object is unfinished, broken, and so on. Deciphering, understanding, accounting for developments in language and vocabulary over the centuries, is not a risk-free exercise. Nevertheless, words are a starting point, a guide which gives historians the opportunity to make a start without having the impression – or the illusion perhaps – of jumping entirely into the unknown.[163] Faced just with some old 'thing' buried in the ground, then raised into the light of day, you have to start by giving it a name. If the object which appears in the ground suggests something already known, the person finding it will be able to use current terms of vocabulary, comprehensible to his contemporaries, in order to talk about ancient realities. This is usually what happens with swords, for example, which everyone can identify in general terms of function.

Archaeologists then add sub-groups drawing on the overall family of swords, linked to places and periods. This is typo-chronology. The concepts of 'type' and 'sub-type' correspond to place of discovery and date. First adopted in the 19th century in order to place discoveries in time, such chronologies were refined over the decades. Metal, more than any other material, was used in the 19th century to draw up such lists of names which were specifically created for archaeology. One of the pioneers of this exercise, the Swede Oscar Montelius (1843-1921), subdivided the Scandinavian Bronze Age into six periods, on the basis of numerous metal objects which had been discovered, particularly in graves.[164] New words, archaeological terminologies, were thereby invented not only for objects, but also for periods – this also happened in the case of Thomsen's tripartite system, and Boucher de Perthes' concept of 'antediluvian' and so on. As for archaeological 'cultures' (that is to say societies known from their material culture), names have been based on stylistic details. For example, the form of pottery (Bell Beaker, Linear Band Ceramic Culture) or indeed the name of a first or iconic find place (Hallstatt, La Tène) and so on. There seems to be no limit to archaeologists' imagination in their quest for words, which are indispensable for work to be carried out and for the communication of results. Metal objects were classified and baptised in such ways as soon as this became possible. A researcher nowadays usually has many typo-chronological reference-points to work from. Nearly all archaeological evidence with a possible relationship to war has been labelled on the basis of such categories.

This exercise is more complicated when finds cannot be assigned to known functional categories, either because such objects are not used in the present day and therefore bear no resemblance to anything in the world of the archaeologist (as with 'thunderstones'), or because the items are unfinished, or waste products, or fragmentary, making identification difficult. So, a fragile, fragmented piece of ceramic lost wax casting mould is not likely to count as evidence, unless the archaeologist is particularly sensitive to this kind of find. Archaeological knowledge never ceases to develop and extend as new discoveries are made and methods invented. All archaeologists have a common ground of knowledge which they share with their colleagues and a background which is their own, linked to training and specialism, added to over time in very varied ways.

Once identified, named, and classified, finds can be studied from various perspectives. Some archaeologists concentrate on stylistic questions, others try to refine chronologies or think in terms of exchanges. Opting for a technological approach means understanding manufacturing processes, the 'catalogue of possibilities'. And in the case of copper alloys there is much to learn: the mixture (alloy) can be binary (made up of two metals), ternary (made up of three metals), or more, with very varied proportions of constituents. This initial decision determines the parameters within which the material will then be worked (casting, hammering, finishing) and the characteristics of the finished product: colour, sonority, resistance, capacity to withstand impact and so on. Moreover, a metalworker is faced with a range of options, certainly considerably reduced depending on the initial choice of alloy, but critical, particularly regarding how the work can be carried out in order to give it its shape, and the final state in which the material is left (to sum up: rough-casting, annealing, reshaping). This second stage (annealing) determines the characteristics of the material and therefore the uses to which it can be put and whether it will function appropriately or not. Making a sword from a binary alloy with 20% tin content would be nonsensical in terms of a weapon's functionality. Not only would it be impossible to hammer its blade, but it would not withstand impact well; at worst it would break as soon as fighting started! A finished object is therefore an individualised result from a combination of possibilities. There is an important additional point: the quality of the execution of the work. Are there any faults, porosity, fissures? What do the joins and finishings look like? To sum up, the question is whether the technical decisions (alloys, manufacture, final state) seem to fit in with the object's intended uses.

Is it important to find answers to such questions or are such details really only of interest to a technologist? The answer is clear. It is absolutely fundamental in order to understand what we have in front of us, what we are speaking about and more important still, what can be said about it. It is only by mastering such technical parameters – this particular type of language – that we can ask historically relevant questions. To risk an analogy, it is hard to do without ancient Greek if we wish to study the time of Pericles, or without medieval Latin to show an intelligent interest in the history of the Western Church in the 10th century. This is worth highlighting because it is not immediately obvious. It is because of the nature of the data and the *a prioris* of metal. Anyone who has not mastered Mandarin confronted with a text in that language will immediately realise that it is going to be difficult to begin research into contemporary China. With objects, the situation is more paradoxical. If I am looking at a sword, I can see that it is a sword. Even if I am not an archaeologist, I can measure its dimensions and I can be pretty sure about its function. A large part of the information is accessible to (almost) anyone regarding a whole range of objects. If I am an archaeologist, I can easily add a typology and a date. If I want to attempt explanations regarding the materials themselves (which is necessary to get to grips with societies characterised by the use of such materials), understanding such requirements becomes indispensable. Copper alloys are a very demanding group of materials, despite the ease of reference in the early stages: their typo-chronology, and the fact that they seem familiar because they are still used today. However, their technical characteristics, the basis of all reflection about their manufacture and their function, are often little known, or at least insufficiently so for us to avoid contradictions or mistakes if we wish to advance hypotheses allowing us to move from the metal to the human dimension.[165]

Metalcraft presupposes a choice of materials and manufacture according to four principal parameters: technical, functional, aesthetic, and economic. Who decides what? According to what kind of process, in which order? What are the rules? When, why, for what kinds of societies? Such questions are important in the study of metalcraft, not least in the context of research into the origins of war. The choice of metal, manufacturing, and production processes is a complex combination involving raw materials and humans in their societies. In order to arrive at hypotheses about the latter, we have to start with the former. By what strange and mysterious ways am I going to move (if this is in fact possible?) from metal objects to the conduct of war? There are many possible analogies between metallurgy and cooking – also fundamental to what defines a society. In both cases, it is difficult to talk about the end product without some knowledge of the list of ingredients, methods and times. No doubt one can happily enjoy an apple tart without necessarily knowing the secrets that went into making it. On the other hand, if the aim is not 'just' to eat, but to understand (or indeed re-enact the production procedure), it is vital to identify stages of manufacture in order to build a bridge between finds that at first seem silent and human activities upon which we can base an understanding of the societies which made them.

Like all researchers working on a topic, I choose a set of material to study, and I set myself problems to solve. So, I have travelled round Europe, its museums, its collections, and I have seen, observed, and handled thousands of objects, fragments, and various finds. There is no point here in drawing up a detailed inventory. The hours I have spent, sometimes in unexpected circumstances, are beyond count: for example, in the entrance porch of a church on the plane of the river Po, a theatre in Hungary, in the library of the Royal Society of Antiquaries in England, sitting in front of the safe of a prestigious bank, or amongst finds in a windy archaeological site, and so on. Technologists have to touch things to be able to understand them. Ideally, this process should happen the moment the find leaves the earth.[166] The time researchers spend with archaeological finds are times of reading in the literal sense of the word, exactly as if they were a texts. Whatever the object. It could be a fibula (a brooch for fastening clothes), a sword, a vessel, a bracelet... The process is always the same: I handle such things carefully, for these are like delicate old people; I take measurements; I weigh them; I photograph them or if need be, I sketch them. Then I continue with the investigation. I look at the number of component parts, assembly, decorative details. I spend time looking at faults, pieces that were not meant to be seen when the object was finished (the inside, covered parts, and so on), signs of impact, repairs perhaps. I take notes. I look through written or pictorial data relevant to the find and I consider the sequence of events during excavation, if there is such a thing – not always the case for less recent excavations – particularly when I was not involved on site. Sometimes I have to make do with inventories with dates of acquisition or deposition, and scraps of information about the people involved, sometimes even prices when dealing with purchases. In a word, I do what all historians do, though my sources are not textual. My job is that of interpreter between the language of the object (or what remains of it) and the language of words.

It is impossible to tell how long this stage will last. Sometimes one has to come back and take another look, check things out, make comparisons. This is the point at which the analysis of the object's manufacture begins. What can be seen with the naked eye? Quality? Use? Any marks of impact? Clues spotted with the naked eye are like so many words which have to be joined up to give meaning, to write a sentence. Sometimes, for this to succeed properly, there is a need to go beyond just looking, however experienced one might be. There is a need to get close to the matter, even inside it.

In the Laboratory

This is the point when laboratory study comes into play, though not necessarily for all objects.[167] The point is not to carry out as many technical investigations as possible but to choose those that will tell us most (be most representative). Even so, several procedures might be needed in order to compare data. Laboratory studies have a real cost. High-technology machines are needed, which can be very burdensome, and they are nearly always in science laboratories (chemistry, technological, sometimes medical) – by no means typical of humanities (Classics and beyond). Specific laboratories for heritage materials are rare (this is becoming less true in the context of archaeology courses where many specialities now include laboratory study components). Researchers trained to carry out such processes are also few and far between.

Interdisciplinarity (or pluri-disciplinarity) is nowadays officially a good thing. Researchers are encouraged to cross normal academic boundaries. In human and social sciences such encounters between different disciplines take place in the form of dialogues in which vocabulary can have different shades of meaning, whilst still remaining comprehensible. This is all about words. Dialogue thrives on nice distinctions regarding definitions and debates about the scope of terminologies. Collaboration between human science and experimental science in laboratories, however, can be much more difficult because language used and problem sets are quite different. Laboratory apparatuses are high-performing and those operating them are very skilled. But what are they looking at, what are they analysing and what problems are they tackling? The difficulty is to combine laboratory techniques with questions relevant to the historians. This is a considerable challenge. In many situations cooperation is difficult for many reasons. Material research scientists are not necessarily fully aware of archaeological ways of thinking, let alone the nature of the specific finds that they are asked to analyse. They are late arrivals in the study of the data, which is brought to the laboratory – they will not have been present at the excavation, even those that are ongoing. They do not always know the chronological or cultural framework relevant to the objects they are analysing. On the other hand, archaeologists are unfamiliar with laboratory machines and their potential, other than methods they use repeatedly (like radiocarbon dating). As such they probably do not get as much out of laboratory investigations as they could.

When applied to the metallurgy of copper alloys, exact science (or laboratory science) usually concentrates on the compositional analysis of certain items. This generally is motivated by one single question: where did the materials used in the alloy come from? There is nothing new in this. Napoleon III already wished, in the 1860s, to create a professorship of applied science at the École des Beaux-Arts in order to analyse Roman and Celtic weapons and find out which alloys were used. This could be seen as legitimate because such ought to yield better understanding of European transportation networks. But it would also be to disregard certain fundamental facts: metal can be recycled. Archaeological finds do not allow us to state with certainty whether an object was produced as a result of one or several processes of recycling. As such, there is no way to be sure we are not analysing four raw materials of the same kind coming from different places brought together over time to form a single object. It is difficult to state with any degree of certainty that such and such a piece of material came from such and such a single place of origin, even if we attempt to rely on lead isotopes, which are supposed to be effective in this respect. In theory the procedure should work. Given the nature of archaeological data (usually in the form of complete objects), we have to look critically. Concentrating on this attractive (but probably utopian) question of the origins of materials may lead us to forget the most important thing: this information source results from a series of actions and choices (which can include recycling) right up to the final abandoning of the object. Rather than seeking answers in terms of numbers, perhaps we should look rather at human involvement.

In archaeology hierarchies of materials play a major role regarding laboratory studies of finds. There are two groups of objects. First of all, there are artefacts to which no particular value has been attributed, yet which one hopes might yield good information. Such artefacts may be subjected to all available forms of analysis, including the removal of a samples, which will subsequently not be replaced back into the original object (so-called destructive analysis). This happens for example with the great majority of ceramics, be they potsherds, architectural fragments, or a bronzesmith's mould. The second group comprises finds considered in the first instance to be 'works of art': over and above their role as data they are considered to have a powerful aesthetic value. In such cases it becomes much more difficult – and sometimes impossible – to proceed to any analysis requiring the extraction of samples.

The vast majority of copper alloy objects belong to this second group. What is the difference? In the first case, there is no reason not to analyse them – one might sometimes even cut straight through a potsherd because of the scientific and historic data this will yield. In the second case it is hard enough even to get up close to the object and trying to take samples becomes a combat sport in which no one can be sure of victory. Archaeologists are responsible researchers, and they care for the preservation of our heritage. No one would ever want to carry out laboratory studies without a good (scientific) reason set out in advance. Nor is there any point in allowing oneself to be persuaded to analyse an item that is more damaged than others: metal corrosion falsifies analysis, giving excessively high tin readings, for example. This can change everything, or almost – it has been mentioned that a binary bronze piece with 5% tin is not the same as bronze with 15% tin. Compositional analyses are meaningless unless there are some guarantees regarding the results, otherwise why spend the time and the money? It is essential to be clear about the sample to be analysed and to sample it from the heart of the artefact, which will yield the best information about the 'microstructure', the kind of snapshot facilitating the deduction of an object's thermo-mechanic history and therefore details regarding the *chaîne opératoire* of the manufacturing process. The parallel here between cooking and casting is that in addition to the obvious list of an apple tart's ingredients, we are also looking for a baker's secret. Did they or did they not put in cinnamon, or vanilla…?

The manufacture of an object is an encounter between materials and the metalworker working with them, as a cook works with ingredients. The study of an archaeological object is similarly an encounter between a manufacturing process and a researcher. In both cases the requirements are facts that can be ignored, and one can just carry on in order to get results. For each cake or study, decisions are made consciously, as in baking. One might well choose to ignore the fact that leaving a cake in an oven at 200°C for three hours will render it inedible for consumption – or that surface analysis involves risks of error. But not without consequences. The deeds will be done but deprived of their purpose: no eating; no proper results.

Starting the investigation at the end

Human actions, like residual materials, are parts of more or less complex *chaînes opératoires*. Technologists studying data, on site or in the laboratory, try to reconstitute and visualise stages of work, decisions made by metalworkers and the societal considerations which brought them about. Metal experiences a long history from its initial form in nature to the final destination which people in a society choose for it. In the classifications of materials, it is defined as a 'complex synthetic material', which means not only that it is obtained by means of a high temperature operation including chemical transformation, but also that the result obtained is reversible. It is thus distinguished from other 'natural' materials which are worked without chemical transformation (stone for example) and 'simple' materials which are also obtained by subjection to high temperatures and chemical transformations, but where the process is irreversible (ceramics for example). The possibility of recycling (the reversibility of these processes), though it does not tell us everything about a (raw) material, is nevertheless a fundamental piece of data for our understanding of that material's use in ancient and modern-day societies.

Metal rarely exists in a pure form in nature (native metal), but essentially in the form of composites which are part of raw materials containing one or several metals imprisoned in a rocky coating – the ore – and which can be isolated by a series of operations referred to as 'ore reduction'. There are considerable variations in the presence of ore resources from one region to another, their specific nature, and the metals they comprise. Also, they can be relatively accessible, lying on the surface or on the contrary available only at a certain depth. It is difficult to get an overview of these aspects of ancient metallurgy because the data is complex and mineral extraction has never ceased to be a part of human activity in Europe for thousands of years. More recent extraction sites have sometimes erased all traces of ancient ones.

Studies of metals were, logically enough, initially directed towards European regions mentioned by antique texts, the mines of Laurion, Cyprus, Spain, the English Cassiterides, Tyrrhenian Italy, both on the continent and neighbouring islands (Elba, Sardinia) and so on.[168] Mines and indeed metallurgy form part of a far larger philosophical and literary discourse. The subject has been discussed in writing for centuries, highlighting not only places but also technical procedures which were of interest at a given time.[169] In archaeology the years from 1960 to 1980 were very lively with respect to metallurgy, thanks to the development of laboratory study methods, focussing essentially on the question of mineral origins.[170] Major changes in recent years regarding the way we look at mines came about largely because of archaeological discoveries on site. A new map was drawn up of places of extraction at different points in Europe, together with a new chronology. Work carried out since the 1990s has shown that mining is a very ancient phenomenon going back to the Neolithic. Metalcraft for which there is evidence in Bulgaria from at least the 5th millennium BC is no longer considered to be a very localised special case, but rather a very early manifestation of metallurgy, involving an active search for ores which continued to develop in Neolithic Europe from the 4th millennium BC.[171] Special materials were actively sought, and technical and human resources were set up to achieve this. Regarding extraction itself, parallels can be drawn between processes to extract metal and processes involving other rocks, particularly flint.[172] Though what happens in the ensuing stages of the *chaîne opératoire* differs profoundly.

Once the ore has been extracted, one essential operation is complete, but this is only the beginning of a long process. The 'piece of rock' is still useless in its present state: we still need to extract the metal content and then create a product corresponding to everyone's expectations, the metalworker's and the end-user's. The work referred to as 'reduction' is an operation or chemical transformation aiming to eliminate the oxygen from the metal oxides so that only the metal will remain. In this way, for example, the copper atoms of the ore are transformed into metallic copper. The temperature and the conditions needed for this operation vary according to the ores and the metals they contain.

All metals from ancient periods contain traces of the original ore, sometimes in infinitesimally small quantities. They are not completely refined as our metals are nowadays. This does not necessarily mean though that an analysis will lead to the source of the ore, for we do not have enough detail about the location of ancient mines. Moreover, one material might have been mingled with others, with new ingots or metal from 'old' recycled objects. In ancient metals, traces of these processes, which were less thorough than they are nowadays (the presence of so-called sulphurs for example), give us very useful clues because they tell us about the type of work carried out by the bronzesmith.

In the Bronzesmith's Crucible

Once the metal has been obtained from the ore (in metallurgical terms: 'elaboration'), we have to move from the metal to the object ('transformation'). Globally, metalwork in ancient societies can be divided into two main kinds: non-ferrous on one side and ferrous on the other – the casting process is at the root of this division into two groups.[173] In general terms, though all metals can be heated so that they become liquid and can be worked in this state, the melting point is very varied, so solutions have to be found and methods adapted.

The melting point of iron is 1535°C, a temperature that could not be attained with the technological means available to ancient populations, neither from the Mediterranean region nor from Northern Europe. In consequence, for ancient societies in Europe, two different schemes of work were for a long time necessary throughout the *chaîne opératoire*. Iron was obtained by a process of roasting, during the course of which the ore was heated in order to extract contents like sulphur. This operation facilitated subsequent beating and folding, when the ore was crushed to obtain fragments that could subsequently be loaded into the furnace. The purpose of this bloomery was to reduce the metal by the 'direct method' which produces a block of iron or steel (pure iron combined with a small quantity of carbon, which makes it much harder), an incomplete product ('blank') that was subsequently reworked. Archaeological traces might take the form of 'molten slag' or 'light slag'[174] and, though this is rarer, the furnace itself. The development of the modern blast furnace at the end of the 15th century AD in the region of Liège (France) was made possible thanks to hydraulic bellows which facilitated temperature increases higher than iron's melting point. This made possible the first cast iron bullets, and then cannons which revolutionised artillery. War again...

Non-ferrous metalcraft includes gold, copper, silver, tin, zinc, and lead, used alone or as the greater or lesser element in alloys, not just present in small traces. Gold stands out for several reasons. It is particularly rare, sometimes taking the form of metal flakes or spangles, and occurring naturally in conjunction with small quantities of silver and copper. Its melting point is 1064°C, between that of copper (1084°C) and silver (964°C). Ancient societies that had mastered the art of firing ceramics had equipment that would allow temperatures in the region of 1200°C to be achieved. This was sufficient for the melting of all non-ferrous metals. The structure of the furnaces in which such temperatures were possible could be quite rudimentary, for example pits or hollows dug in the soil.

The distinction between the two metallurgical groups continued throughout the *chaîne opératoire* of an object's manufacture; this continuity is because of the metals' different melting-points and the methods ancient societies had at their disposal to obtain them. Iron could not be worked in its liquid form at such times. Only technical advances in the modern era and the industrial revolution made it possible to achieve hitherto unattained temperatures, which meant iron could be worked in its liquid, molten form, the result of smelting, then allowed to cool and harden. During ancient periods, an object was made in the forge by annealing when hot, starting with a blank or semi-finished version. Thanks to the smith's work, the object gradually took shape, during successive operations and repeated hammering (hammering whilst hot), heating (annealing), quenching, and further hammer work (to reshape the object). During the hammering process, hammer scale, which is small pieces of iron oxide, became detached, which could remain in a workshop site long after it had been abandoned enabling it to be identified as such in the course of an archaeological excavation.

Non-ferrous metals were worked differently once the metal had been obtained, for they were always given their essential shape by casting, even in very ancient periods. Knowledge of how to extract metal from ore meant that the melting point of non-ferrous metals, all below 1200°C, could also be achieved. This required only relatively simple structures not necessarily characteristic of one artisan rather than another. Such a furnace, then, is very different from a reduction furnace – it is important not to confuse the two.

Casting made it possible to produce an almost complete object or blank which could then be reworked and shaped so as to correspond to the designs of the metalworker who would have planned future work, right up to the completion of the item. There were two kinds of casting in ancient societies: using a permanent mould (also called chill-casting) or a non-permanent mould. In the first case, after the cooling of the metal, the cast item was taken out by opening the mould, which was therefore preserved, whilst in the second case, the 'shake-out' operation (opening the mould at the end of the casting process) was done by breaking the mould, which could not be used again. Lost-wax casting belonged to the second category. Permanent moulds could be made of stone, earth, clay or even metal. Non-permanent moulds were usually made of a specifically prepared fired clay, fine enough for the object to be well defined, porous enough to allow air and gas to escape at the moment of casting and resistant enough to support the shock of the metal at melting point. The advantages and disadvantages of these two technical solutions were not the same. Permanent mould casting – when the mould was filled thanks to the weight of the melting metal – meant that the mould could be reused for several further castings, but it only worked for relatively simple shapes that presented no problems with 'undercuts' (complex structures making straightforward opening impossible), which would have meant that the object could not be removed without destroying the mould – unless the mould itself were to be made from a larger number of parts, which would have created other technical problems. Non-permanent mould casting got round this difficulty and meant that complex items could be produced, but it involved a long phase of mould preparation which had to be repeated every time an item was manufactured.

Ancient European societies used both these procedures. Permanent mould casting was the earliest, but the development of lost wax casting, in the 2nd millennium BC, did not supplant two-part mould casting which continued to be used for smaller items of metal weighing less than 1-1,5 kilograms, either as finished products, or as units to be assembled later. Both techniques could be used together for different parts of the same object, including simple shapes like swords (the blade being made by one technique, the hilt by another). Gold could be worked by an additional casting process since it is workable in droplets (granulation), unobtainable from other metals.

Copper can be alloyed with other metals like tin (making bronze), zinc (brass), and lead. The alloy can be binary (two metals) but also ternary (three metals) or more. The mix cannot be arrived at arbitrarily without consequences, particularly with respect to solubility above certain percentages. Thus, tin reaches a critical point at 15.8% in normal conditions. Bronze with 20% tin is technically feasible – the melting point of the alloy is even lower – but the mix cannot be homogenised. On the other hand, the alloy obtained is harder, more brittle, and brighter than bronze made with 10% tin. It is therefore important to take into consideration the purpose of the object, its function. In a good quality workshop, the bronzesmith will adapt his mix to the eventual function of the object, or the weapon for our purposes; if on the other hand the aim is to manufacture musical instruments to make a noise on the battlefield the choice has to be more judicious still, because a metal rich in tin is harder and more sonorous.

The casting operation was a strategic moment in the *chaîne opératoire* because (unless the casting process was started again from the beginning) it definitively determined the initial internal parameters of a piece of metalwork (its composition, homogeneity) and the outcome in terms of use and subsequent post-casting processes. The quality of casting was also essential, particularly if this was only the first stage of the manufacturing process.

The choice of metal or alloys and the way they were worked was therefore the result of complex and overlapping judgments between various technical and manufacturing considerations, requirements for eventual use, and whatever desires might have been expressed by an end-user, regarding for example shape and colouring. There is no reason to imagine that all societies opted for alloys that were standard at a particular time or place, whichever items were being made: axes, swords, breastplates, helmets, or spearheads, to mention only objects related to war. In addition, one would have to add a warrior's jewellery and ornamentation (fibulae, bracelets and so on). It is hard to imagine uniformity here, that there might be some single normal and identical alloy both for a furnace-made weapon designed for attack, and for another, produced principally by hammering, made to withstand blows, or indeed a piece of jewellery conceived principally according to aesthetic criteria. There is a logical correspondence between techniques of manufacture and particular alloys. A failure to take this into account would be to deny the metalworkers' knowledge and to ignore the specific nature of metals which the archaeological data requires us to understand.[175]

Under the Metalworker's Hammer

After casting, an item might require much more work or very little. Sometimes the Bronze Age metalworker has only to grind and polish it, like some kinds of axe for example. Sometimes by contrast the piece is only an intermediary product, a 'blank', the starting point for work that will take longer than that which preceded it. The metal is to be reworked. The metalworker may thereby create long thin products (wires) or flat ones (sheet metal). It may then be necessary also to rework the material to obtain levels of hardness or indeed malleability which various metals allow depending on their nature. Gold, for example, which is treated by heating, cooling, and working, remains malleable rather than elastic. Copper is half-way between and can for this reason be combined with other metals – tin, zinc – in various quantities for various purposes. Depending on the nature of the alloy, bronzesmiths will have at their disposal a material which might be harder or softer, offering different kinds of opportunities for reworking. Bronzesmiths, unlike the ironsmiths, normally hammer metal when it is cold. They use to their advantage the more yielding plasticity of the metal which is at its best when cool. However, this work can only go on up to a certain point. Beyond this there is a danger that the material will break. This can be avoided by reheating (annealing) so as to give the metal back its malleability, since the crystalline structure in the material itself will be reshaped.

The experienced bronzesmith knows from practice what kind of metal-hammering to deploy. By looking, listening, and touching. Working with metal is just like being a cook with saucepans and preparatory work, the sole difference being that tasting is not possible. Both experiment with the ingredients which they mix, work and re-work... Bronzesmiths and ironsmiths use a range of metal and non-metallic tools. A bronzesmith might choose to leave constituent materials in a harder state (rough-cast or annealed) or one that is more elastic (through hammering) depending on their purpose. A shield, a helmet or a breastplate must be able to withstand blows whilst the pin of a fibula, made to keep an article of clothing in place, needs to be opened and closed easily without losing its shape. Decoration can be added to a piece of metal at various points in the *chaîne opératoire*. At the casting stage or afterwards, by a process of removing material which can be more or less invasive (punching holes, engraving) or through work that involves crushing, so far as this is possible in terms of the material's plasticity (chasing).

In the final stages of manufacture, the object (if it is in more than one piece) is assembled from its constituent parts, likewise by a variety of means: soldering, brazing, crimping, fixtures for metallic components, and fixings for other materials like horn, wood, amber, coral, and enamel. Finally, as we account for all the stages of work in the *chaîne opératoire*, we should not forget the finishing which has to be carried out at the end of each phase, nor indeed such repairs as might have been needed during manufacture (which are not the same as those made when the object is in use), these being viable if the damage is not too serious and if an advanced stage of manufacture has been reached, so that the metalworker is justified in not going back to the very beginning of the operation: casting.

This long manufacturing *chaîne opératoire* implies an accumulation of means, time, and skill, with decisions being made at each stage, and for every type of manufacture. All this shows just how much we need to study manufactured objects individually, as one-off productions planned and thought through by the bronzesmith. The researcher usually has to start an inquiry at the end, with the object, going backwards as far as possible, exhaustively, step by step in the *chaîne opératoire* for each manufactured object, observing with the naked eye, with a binocular microscope to study details. Thanks to the microscope it is possible to gain entry into the material; then each clue can be followed to yield a general vision on the basis of which an overarching view can be achieved, and conclusions drawn.

IV

A LIST OF WEAPONS

The bronzesmith in his workshop

Let us change perspective again and try to track down our 1000 BC warrior's weaponry and armour to the kind of workshop where we might perhaps glimpse a bronzesmith at work. No workshop with completed objects awaiting distribution has so far been discovered. So, we have to do what we can with traces and gaps, making deductions based upon what such metalcraft required. This is rather different for the various phases of mineral reduction (from ore to metal), which are better documented because constructions have been found in situ. The bronzesmiths with their various metals were quite different from their colleagues who extract metal from ore on a site closer to deposits. The maker of our weapons needed a space organised into at least two distinct zones: one for fire and one where there was light. The first was used for the various stages of casting (mould preparation, liquid metal) and for annealing, and the second was used for making moulds, hammering the cooled metal, for adding decoration by working the metal in various ways, and for finishing work. We also need to add a space for storing tools and raw materials, and drying moulds, so one that is sufficiently well-ventilated, and then perhaps also a storeroom for finished or almost finished products. Fitting all this into just a few square metres would be difficult, particularly if we take it that the bronzesmith does not always work alone but wants to pass on knowledge. So, let us imagine two men working. Men, rather than women because, even though we have no indication regarding the sex of metalworker, no present-day or past parallels have ever suggested the presence of a female person in a bronzesmith's workshop. An experienced craftsman and his apprentice would, in view of material requirements for small scale manufacture, also have required a covered area of about 20 square metres, provided that they had a sheltered space in front of the workshop for some tasks.

We might imagine such a workshop in the kind of Late Bronze Age village which grouped together about 30 houses within an enclosure and palisades, funerary, religious, and even political spaces in some cases. The main difficulty in understanding such settlements comes from some materials' poor state of preservation, truncation in some areas, or in others continued occupation since the Bronze Age. More recent constructions may be found on top of older ones, because the latter needed replacing, or were out of date; then again, the newer structures might not be directly above, so there will be criss-

crossing levels of remains creating complex stratigraphic problems. Houses were made of wood and earth, (mud for the walls), with organic roofing: none of these materials lasts well. Such structures are found only in waterlogged conditions, which are favourable to the preservation of organic materials, and which can therefore give us a snapshot of such villages. For example, we find settlements at the edges of Alpine lakes for example, where wood, bark or even textiles have been preserved. Amongst recent discoveries of villages in such favourable contexts we have the Late Bronze Age settlement of Must Farm in England which is roughly contemporary with the bronzesmith who made the weaponry that interests us. Indeed, an exemplary sword was found here, remarkably well preserved. If a workshop was well run, remaining structures will not be too obvious: what there was to be recycled would have been recycled, leaving behind few traces of activity (pieces of casting that went wrong, metal fragments, moulds and so on.). The Must Farm furnace (used for casting and annealing) is an ordinary one and has nothing to do with ore reduction. When a village and its various buildings were abandoned in a deliberate, planned, and organised manner, such sites become particularly hard to locate.

Our bronzesmith has just hung up his hammer after striking a final blow to a piece of sheet metal which will be part of a helmet. He feels it, to check. The sound tells him that the sheet metal needs to go back into the furnace at about 600°C before he starts hammering again. His apprentice watches and listens, trying to help decide the right moment to stop so that better progress can be made later. They exchange few words. The atmosphere in the workshop is warm. Both are attentive, keenly aware of movement, sounds, and colours. The apprentice has just made wax models which will be used to create casting moulds for the fins on the helmet, which will be cast later, then fixed by riveting. It is important work but less risky than hammering which leaves almost no room for error. He knows this only too well because they are also making breastplates. These are complicated.

First, they had made a blank version from the rough casting, deliberately relatively thick in the case of the main parts, since they were to be reworked by alternate hammering and annealing (reheating): the eventual thickness will be in the order of 0.3-0.8 millimetres, with some variation from one area to another. There was a trial run during the casting process: they plunged the mould containing the hot metal into the trough of cold water. The plan was to make hammering easier, but the result was not as good as they had hoped. So, they had to anneal (reheat) several times over and hammer gently because the metal seemed more fragile than usual. This was the third breastplate. Six to go. Taking into account additional tool work and details of ornamentation and decoration, the work will go on for months. When they finish hammering the blank, the next job will be to turn the two flat sheets into three dimensional shapes, cut them down, and add small bosses to highlight the anatomy of the warrior who will wear the breastplate, then roll the edges so that he will not cut himself, and then rivet the breastplate on the left so it can be opened on the right side and at the shoulders, so that it can be put on. The model is not new in principle, but the decorative work will be fuller and more abundant than usual, which will make this item slightly different from similar ones made in the previous century. These will look rather like some breastplates made in the Alps.

The craftsman and his apprentice also have a sword to make. It will certainly require all their attention, but in a different way. The bronzesmith has decided to use the lost-wax casting technique. He has been a master of this procedure ever since his years as an apprentice. He will shape the wax and build up the mould around it, leaving a hole for pouring in the molten metal near the point. The fired earth mould will be allowed to dry slowly. The mould is made of sand, earth, and fine pieces of organic matter. When it is dry, he will melt the wax, creating a void which the metal will then fill; next he will fire the mould making sure it does not crack. In the crucible he will then prepare an alloy with a tin-copper ratio of one to nine. First, he will place a ready-made sample in the crucible, recycled from a previous casting, so that the mixture will take better. Beneath the workshop awning, not far from the furnace, he will wedge the lukewarm mould into a pit filled with sand, with the opening at the top, but in such a way that no particles will be able to get inside until the casting takes place. When the metal liquefying in the crucible has the right colour and texture, the metalworker will have only very little time to pour the metal into the mould: it will start to grow cold as soon as it leaves the furnace. The smith will then leave it to his apprentice to break the mould (the shake-out process), take out the item, check the casting, and he will help with polishing, sharpening the blade and riveting it on the bone hilt. For the moment, both master and apprentice need to concentrate on the helmet, nine of which have to be made in total, the same number as the breastplates. This is a variant of a similar type which the apprentice knows, and which also has prominent rivets that they have been manufacturing for some time. The apprentice is familiar with a helmet similar in its general shape, which he likes a lot because the rivets are extended, not unlike those he has just modelled in wax; these were cast using an alloy with a tin content of over 20%, resulting in a beautiful, very bright yellow colour, whilst the main part of the helmet, which is 6% tin, is orange-green. For the helmets, they have decided on a different way forward. The colour and aesthetic interest will be provided by the lateral fins, made by the lost wax technique, and riveted in place. These will then have feathers fixed in. As with the breastplates, it will be necessary to shape the two halves of the helmet and cut out the sheet to be sure of a triangular shape and that the top has a good pointed tip. Any unused material will go back into the crucible to be recycled for the other helmets. They are planning a system of folded sheet metal for the triangular part and an inverted section to round off the bottom, which will be riveted on and finished by the apprentice. The lower part will be edged in the same way as the breast plates, perhaps using the same type of ternary alloy made of tin (6%) and lead (4%), which will make it possible to guarantee a good degree of rigidity and resistance; this will also economise on tin and make casting easier.

In this workshop, as in all those of their colleagues, each part of every object is considered individually regarding choice of materials, use, manufacturing procedures and how the raw material is to be worked. Effective, high quality weapons have to be produced which will satisfy those bearing them, but without waste. The bronzesmith is the master of his workshop, but he has to think in terms of the warriors he is equipping and those who organise and control the society within which they live and work. A society which means war.

To declare war 'a call to arms' implies certain obligations. For example, one should have some knowledge of what 'arms' are. There are at least two levels of definition: generally speaking, a weapon is an object or apparatus used to attack or to defend; more precisely, the sole aim of this object or apparatus is to injure or kill an adversary, or on the other hand to defend oneself. For this second definition, greater nuances need to be introduced, categories involving how the object is to be used, exclusively or otherwise. In every case, weapons are linked with conflict and cannot be dissociated from war, understood as an organised confrontational activity. They are the tools of constructed violence. Studying war in the context of past societies includes the study of arms. You cannot have one without the other.

So, another set of questions arises: where should we, or must we, start: on the basis of what evidence, and with which object, which 'weapon'? Stories usually begin at the beginning, with the famous '*Once upon a time…*'. It would therefore seem appropriate to begin with the 'first' weapon in history. But this is a difficult challenge, at least put this way. Simply because I do not know, or rather, because it seems to me that the answer is not obvious. Besides, the question of the invention of 'war' depends on how we problematise the answer. I shall therefore not start at a 'beginning' and end up with an alleged 'end', but rather with a certainty, the undeniable existence of 'arms' in the sum total of data: objects with shapes and characteristics which make them specifically usable for combat, whether for injuring or killing, or else for protection.[176] We shall start with such objects, with what is (almost) obvious. In the following survey, we shall therefore explore such objects in their physicality, what constitutes them morphologically and technologically, until their identity can be arrived at, and we can see them as sources of information leading to an understanding of the most ancient forms of warfare.

The Sword extends the Arm…

There are thousands of examples of swords throughout Europe. In Scandinavia alone, most recent figures suggest that some 20,000 swords were placed in graves between 1500 and 1100 BC.[177] These easily identified objects have been collected ever since humans became interested in the past and started to come across them buried or submerged. Even before the beginnings of archaeology, swords from all periods were collected in curiosity cabinets. Such antiquarian collections highlighted differences in shape, length and even raw materials used, though this did not mean that they were well understood or accurately dated. For a long time, those considered to be the most ancient were associated with the beginning of the 1st millennium BC, the time of the Celts, periods mentioned by antique texts. Nowadays, though debates continue regarding detailed typological classifications, archaeologists have an overall grasp of the origins and evolution of this very individual object. The first examples from Central Europe can be dated to the 17th century BC and, a little further west, to the 16th century (between the end of the Early Bronze Age and the beginning of the Middle Bronze Age). The development of 'real' weapons intended for use rather than display started very early in Europe and followed a specific pattern. Let us dare, therefore, to claim that the sword as an individual war weapon has its origins in the mists of non-Mediterranean Europe. It did not make its way, slowly but surely, from the East following the *ex oriente lux* principle so dear to Gordon Childe.[178] It is the fruit of the inventiveness and skills of the bronzesmiths of temperate, Northern Europe, in the context of a society that needed swords.[179]

From a morphological point of view, the sword consists of two principal elements: a blade, the operational part, which is at least 30 centimetres long, with its effective aspect centred either at the point (for thrusting), or on the edges of the blade (for slashing) and a hilt which allows it to be wielded and which has to be well adapted to the combatant's hand. The most ancient metal objects, datable from the start of the 3rd millennium and the 2nd millennium BC (the Early Bronze Age), which most resemble the sword and could have been at the origins of its development, are triangular blades of two types. A blade fitted with a grip so that it can be wielded in a way similar to the sword is considered a dagger. When the triangular blade is fixed by rivets onto a vertical shaft, it is referred to as a halberd. These two morphological categories in which one can glimpse the beginnings of the sword also exist, in the 3rd millennium, in another material: stone, particularly flint.[180] These are found in many regions in Europe, from the centre of the continent as far as the British Isles, including present-day Brittany. The most remarkable examples have come to light in Scandinavia and in the Alps, regions where they have also been found depicted in rock art. This type of object is also represented on stelae and on some menhir statues depicting men, dating from between the end of the Neolithic and the start of the Bronze Age (the end of the 3rd millennium BC). The sword results from a lengthening of these triangular blades.

Technically, the advent of the sword is a little more complex. Stonework is scarcely comparable to metalcraft. The *chaînes opératoires* are different, as is the nature of the material. The common point which links together the manufacture of such items is that both require a specialised and skilled metalworker. Flint knappers produced extraordinary blades, very long and very sharp at the dawn of the Bronze Age, particularly in Northern Europe where the grip and blade are sometimes knapped from a single piece. As much as technologists may admire these objects, there is no getting round the fact that such long blades are extremely fragile so it seems improbable that they could have been used repeatedly without breaking. The metal blade is longer and, if one has mastered the technique, more solid when used: so, attacks can be made both with a stabbing and a slashing action. Here, the metal plays its role to the full: it makes possible a carefully designed form made of a resistant material that can be recycled if need be.

During the course of the Neolithic, copperwork was mastered, and axes made from this metal were produced alongside those still being made in stone. In the Alps, at the end of the 4th millennium BC Ötzi had a copper axe as part of his equipment.[181] In any case, non-alloyed copper is not suited for the manufacture of long objects if one wants to use them for attack, because it is too soft and yielding to be effective. A carefully judged alloy makes it possible to harden the material so long as certain principles are adhered to, both during manufacture and with respect to end-quality. A sword with an alloy containing 88-90% copper and 8-10% tin will work well. Below 5% the quantity of tin is insufficient. Above 15% the material is ill-suited, as it is too hard and breakable. Also, the cost will go up, tin being particularly rare. The presence of a small quantity of lead (less than 5%) can make the casting process easier, but the amount has to remain small because it is a soft metal which can cause problems after the casting process. On the other hand, the white colour of lead brightens the yellow of the mix, particularly in conjunction with tin, and it helps economise on the latter. Also, bronzesmiths could use different materials for different parts, since not all are required to act in the same way. Early Bronze Age daggers show that there was some experimentation with mixes, the addition of arsenic, then tin. This led to the appearance of bronzes, in the plural rather than in the singular as is usually assumed. All these technical evolutions in turn led to the first swords.

At first sight it might seem that this weapon's invention in the 2nd millennium BC does not constitute a real revolution, since it is made principally by casting, using techniques long since practised in Europe. Besides, all casting procedures were already in use, with or without permanent moulds. The sword is nevertheless a major innovation for several reasons – and it encapsulates the very question of what innovation means, how and why it comes about. From the point of view of the bronzesmith's workshop, it requires a mastery of many kinds of expertise. Firstly, alloying techniques, without which the sword would not be functional – a long copper sword could not operate as such. Then flawless casting: the metal has to be at the right temperature so that it can be poured without porosity, and without air pockets, both for the sake of its future stages of manufacture and for its eventual use. Though the initial shaping of the sword takes place during the casting process, it still has to be hammered when cold, the point and the blade-edge at the very least. Finishing phases (polishing and the fixing of the hilt) can also be compromised if the material does not have the required characteristics. In a word, casting is a strategic manufacturing phase and bad casting results in weaknesses (air pockets trapped in the metal) which can be right at the very heart of the object (not necessarily visible) causing the material to break on impact.[182] This is the last thing a combatant wants when facing an enemy, sword in hand...

Swords studied show that the bronzesmiths who made them possessed the skill necessary for their manufacture. The examples which have been discovered in archaeological contexts are finished objects that have seen use. They are well thought through and technically very accomplished. Nothing astonishing in this. There is no reason for us ever to come across any workshop rejects. These will have been recast. Between short blades and swords, both of which will have been functionally 'successful', there were no doubt intermediate stages, but physical evidence has not survived. This is very different from other non-recyclable materials which last well, like stone. In the latter case, if a mistake is made during a trial run, the work or at least the initial material will have to be abandoned and the failed item disposed of. An archaeologist is likely to come across such remnants. The craftman might well have made trial runs which turned out to be no good, but then the unsatisfactory object will just have ended up back in the crucible.

How did bronzesmiths make the move from short to long blades? No doubt they tried all sorts of solutions, ran various experiments, came up with many inventions and innovations. Not unlike cooking perhaps; putting the finishing touches to a new recipe. All crafters have a creative side which will make them want to surpass themselves, to find better solutions for their work, try out new methods, improve on current practice, thinking things through, working step by empirical step on the basis of what they already know, what they have thus far experienced, in the light of results that have been satisfactory so far and what they want to try out, bearing in mind the constraints imposed by the materials (or ingredients in cooking) and of course by their society. Then there is the question of where precedent stops and novelty starts, the dividing-line between innovation and tradition. What our societies come to regard as a good idea will not necessarily be universally obvious.[183] Keeping things as they are and avoiding change can be the key to maintaining an overall equilibrium, which a society might well seek to preserve. Innovation is a break, partial or total. It makes everything change, really change. The form, the content, ways of doing things, outcomes. To invent the sword was to introduce a totally new object, making long-term modifications to *chaînes opératoires* in the bronzesmiths' workshops. It involved alterations in the organisation of supply systems for raw material and the creation of the first weapon used exclusively as such.[184]

The bronzesmith was not alone in this sword-based revolution. Neither now nor 4000 years ago can manufacture be envisaged without an end-user. Between supply and demand, offer and need, who creates what, when? With only the finished product to start from, when it was already 'on the market', and in general circulation, who can tell who first really called a sword a 'sword'? The process, as we have suggested, is no doubt one of encounters: the metalworker's encounter with raw material (and its constraints), the manufacturer's with the end-user (and his needs), everyone in a society who has the right to say 'yes' or 'no': a complex interplay of technical possibilities, artisanal responses, and human expectations.

The sword evolves…

(As for words, whose greatness answers words, Let this my sword report what speech forbears) Shakespeare: Henry VI Part 2: Act 4, Scene 10)

The sword was highly successful and was to enjoy a great future. Both sections of the weapon changed over the years, in different ways and for various reasons linked to use. To begin with, they were made of bronze, then iron when this new metal was developed between the 9th and 8th centuries BC, then one or the other, depending on time and place, or sometimes both together, using a variety of alloys and shapes. Following morphological criteria, archaeologists have given names to different types of swords in a process referred to as typology taxonomy. The blade might be longer or shorter. At least 30 centimetres, sometimes 90 centimetres – for example the bronze swords of the 'Mindelheim' variety which date from the 8th century BC.[185] Iron swords of the Hallstatt type may have blades longer than 1 metre. The record is actually held by the Mindelheim sword from the Dutch Chieftain's grave of Oss (116.5 cm) and a sword found in grave 573 in the Hallstatt necropolis (Austria), whose blade is 115 centimetres long. Swords can also have various shapes, so their blades might be described as 'tapered', 'edged', 'pistilliform' or 'carp-tongued'. The cross-section also varies: it may be oval, lozenge-shaped, or thinned at the edges.

Morphological differences necessarily had an impact on the nature of fighting. Hilts could be made of various materials, metallic or otherwise – states of preservation depending on the materials used. The hilt of the short sword preserved in the Odescalchi collection still has attached to it the ivory which covered the metal part.[186] The hilt was the section of the sword which afforded the greatest liberty regarding shape and decorative details, the only technical consideration being that the grip should be a good one, so that it could be held in such a way that the sword might be brandished effectively. Beyond such formal constraints and general dimensions, everything else was a matter of taste, and indeed choice of manufacturing techniques, the prime considerations being linked to culture and identity.

The connexion between the blade and the hilt of the sword is essential, determining not only how the weapon is used, but also how solid and reliable it is. This becomes more complex over the course of the centuries. The form and the dimensions of the part attaching the hilt to the blade will depend on the nature of the hilt itself, which archaeological typology divides into three parts: the guard near the blade, the grip in the middle, and the pommel at the end. The join is made by an intermediate part, essentially invisible once the object is finished, the 'tongue' which is generally made at the same time as the blade and onto which the hilt will be fixed. This part can also be called the 'plaquette' for some types of sword (particularly in the Iron Age) or it can just be a finer 'tang' with other swords. The tongue can be referred to as simple, bipartite, or tripartite, depending on the kind of hilt and the way it is fitted. There are many options, and the number of sword types varies greatly in the European context over the two millennia of the Metal Ages.

Throughout this long period, numerous swords emerged from the workshops of bronzesmiths and ironsmiths. The many examples preserved make it possible not only to put forward hypotheses regarding the technical origins of this object, but also to get a more complete overview of the *chaînes opératoires* of such weapons' manufacture. The study of sword moulds is particularly interesting. The shape of the piece is simple and various technical solutions are possible, there being no problems with undercuts (a shape that is too complex and would therefore stop the mould from being opened without breaking) on removal. The use of permanent moulds (stone or fired clay) would be difficult since the object being made was long and thin. The technical difficulties for the manufacturer are, in principle, twofold: the metal has to reach the end of the mould rapidly, spreading well so that no porosity – or as little as possible – can form during the course of casting. For this reason, moulds usually have a casting aperture on the side of the sword's point. Another technical difficulty is the mould's capacity for mechanical resistance at the time of manufacture, whilst in use (the impact of molten metal), and when the crude piece of casting is removed from the mould. The bronzesmith cannot use a mould larger than a certain size because he would end up with a block of stone or fired clay which would be unwieldy, but without guaranteeing better resistance. Permanent moulds dating from European Protohistory are nearly always made of stone. Their shape echoes that of the sword. An aperture is made on one side for the metal to be poured into, variable according to type, and there are channels to ensure a better liquid metal flow into the mould's cavity. The mould is made carefully out of a material which is refined enough to ensure that the finished item has good surface definition, like sandstone, but it must not be too fragile.

A copper alloy sword can be made in a non-permanent mould for example by the lost wax method.[187] Such items' design and manufacture are different from those made by two-part mould casting, as are the available options. The mould has to be broken to extract the piece of cast bronze, the shape of which can be more complex, undercuts not being a problem since this casting technique means that the mould (though not necessarily the original model) has to be broken to remove the cast object (the 'shake-out' stage). This process gradually took over from about the 1st millennium BC, though it did not entirely replace the use of permanent moulds. This development can be explained by a process of spreading from one geographical area to another, at least from the 14th century BC in Europe, and probably earlier still in societies which had a good mastery of ceramic techniques and melting.[188] The procedure was developed initially for reasons of productivity rather than technological requirements.

In both types of casting, the desired outcome will be present in the mind of the metalworker before he sets to work. He will have planned the quantity of the metal to be cast at the very start of the operation. He knows in detail what the sword will look like: its length, any decoration, which assembly technique to use and the weapon's weight. He has to make sure the volume of the metal going into the crucible will be enough for the casting and he will include a little extra just to be on the safe side.

And a Scabbard…

We now need to look at the sword's companion, which came into being at the same time – the scabbard. Being sharp and pointed, the sword needs some kind of cover in order to avoid injury while it is being carried hands free, whether its bearer is mounted or not. The scabbard also serves to keep the sword's blade sharp. However, in Europe, fewer protective scabbards have been found by archaeologists than swords, and they are limited to certain periods and certain types. The majority of them were of course made from perishable materials like hides, which did not add much weight to equipment, so this remained manageable.[189] Making scabbards of other materials also helped save on metal which was not readily available in some parts of Europe and was therefore rare and expensive. More technical effort went into making swords than scabbards, although this was not so much the case in the Late Iron Age.

The metal part of the scabbard which most often survives from the Bronze Age and the beginning of the Iron Age is a small piece positioned at the very tip of the scabbard and which is called the chape. Its shape, its size, and the way it was fixed varied considerably. Its main functional purpose was to protect the tip of the sword, to which its shape was adapted: it was rounded so as to be broader than the sword's tip, thus avoiding too much rubbing. The fixing could take four forms: crimping, riveting, binding, and soldering.

There are some metal scabbards however, whole or broken, like the swords which go with them. They most commonly date from more recent times, from the 1st millennium BC, in Hallstatt as well as Mediterranean contexts. The development of iron metalcraft does not entirely replace the use of copper alloys. The partnership of bronze and iron is iconic, the two going alongside one another and alternating. Scabbards can also demonstrate high quality artistry and technical excellence. Scabbards intended for short swords (of a type called 'de Terni' or 'de Pontecagnano'), found in central and southern Italy, are decorated with animal and hunting scenes. Laboratory studies show that hammering played an important role in their manufacture: work on the 'blank' (the intermediate product that emerges from the first casting, subsequently to be reworked), can reduce a sheet's thickness by up to 90%.[190] Considerable technical investment went into such scabbards: flawless casting was required, a consistent level of malleability, and very fine decoration, not to mention fixing and finishing, all involving hours of work and exceptional skill.

From the start of the La Tène period, great care went into decorating iron scabbards with stylised vegetation motifs and fantastic animals typical of classic Celtic bestiary art. The skill deployed is exceptional, unequalled for centuries and still greatly admired by ironsmiths today.[191] Various composite materials went into the making of these scabbards, metallic or otherwise, and complex manufacturing procedures were deployed which required casting, hammering (cold or hot depending on the material) as well as fine decoration and assembly techniques. Since scabbard manufacture involves fewer functional constraints there is great scope for imagination and experimentation. Alongside the sword, scabbards are an important means of expression for the metalworker.

The Spear Thickens

'Spearheads' were first made in bronzesmiths' workshops in the 2nd millennium BC. A metal section is fixed to a wooden shaft, the other end of which can be reinforced by a metal cap (the spear-butt cover). Such weapons belong to a group of successful weapons including 'lances' and 'spears'. These were all thrusting and throwing weapons, relying on human strength alone. They all consist of a long shaft with a piece of pointed metal on one end whose role is to impale (and kill) an opponent; sometimes there is a counterweight on the other end for the sake of balance. 'Spears' and 'lances' are distinguished theoretically according to the relative sizes of the component parts and their function, though the state of archaeological material often makes it hard to get reliable measurements of the length of the shaft – a vital element in determining a weapon's range, since the wooden shaft will have been the first part to disappear.

The 'lance' is slender and fixed with a relatively small head that can be made of various materials (flint, metal). Its use requires limited movement, and the hand can remain on the shaft during use. The spear is generally weightier, both in terms of its metal head and its heel; it is designed to be thrown at a certain distance from the hand of its user in an intermediary phase, before reaching its target. This is the weapon that developed noticeably in Europe from the Bronze Age. In the Middle Ages it became emblematic of the knight and was designed to be used on horseback.

The use of the throwing spear follows the same principles because it is also thrown and loosed from the hand, but it is smaller. In the Middle Ages, the spear could be used by a foot soldier or by a horseman. Such subtleties of language also correspond to intellectual traditions: the 'spear' is used in the context of the Bronze Age in Northern Europe but the 'spear' (or 'javelin') is used in the middle-eastern Mediterranean for the same period and for antiquity.[192]

The very first models, like the sword, seem to have been inspired by the short triangular blades of the Early Bronze Age. This is attached to a shaft by a tang (just like that used for swords), and then, as the object grew more widespread, by a socket (a hollow part into which the wood is fixed and immobilised). Some English types ('Arreton Down') and Spanish varieties (called 'Palmela points') clearly illustrate the early stages of this development. In any case, it becomes possible to look at these items in different ways and broaden comparisons as to how we might consider their most ancient ancestry. We should probably not fail to mention the spears first used by humanity between Palaeolithic.[193] One of the most ancient and famous examples comes from the site of Lehringen in Germany, found fixed in an elephant carcass from some 250,000 years ago.[194] Though the principle of an active point held at a distance and manipulated by means of a long shaft might seem very ancient, the object which evolved during the Bronze Age is morphologically and technologically different.

The head itself consists, in addition to the part used to attach the shaft, of a blade or 'flame' which opens into two lateral fins. The spearhead is hard to fit into archaeological typo-chronologies, there being few variants in shape. Weapons of this nature are often dated by means of other objects found alongside them and the precise context of their discovery. They grow more frequent during the course of the middle Bronze Age, from the 14th to the 13th centuries BC, when they are often found well preserved; they are frequently present in the context of Late Bronze Age finds (the end of the 2nd millennium and the start of the 1st millennium BC). Usually they are present in hoards, more often than not deliberately broken, like most objects in such contexts. They continue to be used during the Iron Age, but turn up in graves, whole rather than broken, increasingly slender and more often made of iron as the centuries progress.

Technically, the spearhead is a less demanding object than the sword. The *chaîne opératoire* for copper alloy spearheads consists essentially of casting, either in permanent or non-permanent moulds, there being no particular problems with undercuts, and no details or curves which might get in the way of opening the mould in two sections. Risks during casting (mistakes, porosity) would be fewer for an experienced metalworker, the dimensions of the finished object being smaller and its geometry simpler. The metal therefore fills the mould rapidly. A core is fixed, corresponding to the hollow of the socket. The raw casting (blank) is not dissimilar to the final product, according to examples studied (the spearheads themselves or the moulds). This procedure fits in with contemporary technical skills and is time efficient. Finishing allows for the assembled unit to be polished and for the lateral wings to be fitted smoothly. Like the sword, the spear was a new development; it became indispensable in a warrior's equipment, and it was an integral part of the repertoire of a skilled metalworker, but its role in the history of technological innovation is quite different. Nor did it have the same function, either for the warrior, or on the battlefield.

Iron spears are a little more complicated to make to the extent that the casting stage – indispensable in bronze manufacture – does not exist. Sockets are nevertheless necessary for fitting the shaft; such sockets need to be rounded and of various sizes. For a skilled Iron Age metalworker this would be no obstacle. Such objects were practically mass-produced, following a standard pattern. In the Late Iron Age, some examples were very fine, with ornamentation rivalling those of scabbards from the same period, even though the surface offered less space for the metalworker's imagination to incorporate decorative patterns or designs from the repertoire of fantastical zoomorphic motifs.

Arrows of Outrageous Fortune…

Another object can be compared to the spear, that may well have inspired it. It had already been in existence for several millennia when metal weaponry arrived on the scene. This is the arrowhead, also fixed to one end of a wooden shaft, the other end being worked and weighted so as to control its trajectory as accurately as possible. There are analogies between spearheads and arrowheads, but considerable differences too. To begin with, the sizes of each have nothing in common. An arrowhead is never longer than 5 centimetres, whilst some spearheads can be as long as 40 centimetres. Most importantly, the two weapons are wielded in quite different ways. The spear, by use of appropriate movements, is propelled only by the strength of the warrior's arm, whether thrown or not. The arrow on the other hand is fired by a bow which is subject to maximum tension (drawn or primed) so that the arrowhead will strike its target accurately in terms of range, speed and precision.

The pair of items making up the bow and arrow came into being long before the Bronze Age. In the Upper Palaeolithic era, about 40,000 years ago, spear-throwers developed first. This was a kind of carved stick, with a notch from which the shafted projectile was thrown. Such items were sometimes decorated, usually with depictions of animals. It meant that the person using it had added strength at their disposal so the projectile could travel further. The bow, the use of which spread throughout the Mesolithic, consisted of at least two parts, one in supple wood to which a string of plant or animal material was attached, the other consisting of a pointed head designed to cut or pierce,[195] fixed to a straight piece of wood, at the other end of which a device (feather, weight and so on) was fitted to make sure the arrow would fly reliably. For millennia the point (also called 'the arrowhead'[196]) was made of various types of stone (or indeed bone/antler), with morphological and technical developments appropriate to the *chaînes opératoires* of each, mostly flint. These materials were still being used at the start of the Bronze Age in some European regions for the manufacture of spearheads. In Brittany particularly at the beginning of the 2nd millennium BC, examples of considerable refinement were made. The point was triangular in shape, with two well-designed lateral fins (barbs) and a stem (tang) in the middle, sometimes very long, which was used for attaching the shaft. Considerable use was made of the bow during the Mesolithic: whole populations seem to have been archers. The rock art in eastern Spain in which archers balletically confront one another date from this period.

Bows and arrows remained in use during the Neolithic. In the second half of the 3rd millennium, during the Beaker Culture period, an archer's equipment also included a small rectangular stone wristguard with two or more perforations. These have been identified as bracers to protect the archer's wrist. Often, only arrowheads have been discovered, but bows too have been found in a good state of preservation in suitably wet conditions. One of the oldest examples in France dates from the Cerny period (about 4500 BC) and was discovered on the banks of the Seine at Paris-Bercy.[197] Cut from yew, it has a simple shape and measured originally 145 centimetres. At the end of the 4th millennium BC in the Alps, Ötzi's equipment included a quiver, though it is incomplete. Gradually, during the course of the 2nd millennium, the production of flint arrowheads ceased, to be replaced by metal versions (barbed and tanged arrowheads), of low technical quality. These are often small pieces of copper alloy castings, sometimes in clusters (a central casting stream is used to produce several such items). When metal is first used, the form imitates its triangular stone precursors. Evolution happens by analogy, not by radical morphological breaks. Such arrowheads evolve alongside other technological developments without ever being a mainspring for innovation. Finishing work was summary and the number of such smaller objects was not very high during the Metal Ages, even though they do not disappear. Arrowheads are not easy to interpret.

Any interpretation has to be made not only in terms of technological history, but also in a broader societal context, including that of war. Arrowheads are polyvalent objects. In any study of war (by force of arms), they raise many questions. They do not follow the same patterns as subsequently fabricated metal weapons. Nor do they force us into particular interpretations. Generally speaking, the arrowhead can be used in many and varied circumstances: hunting animals and human combat. Comparisons can be made, up to a certain point, with the lance and the spear. If we look very closely at its morphology and technology, differences can be seen in the manufacture of arrowheads made for hunting and those made for combat. Ethnological studies confirm this. In addition to such variations in manufacture, poisons could be added to make sure an adversary would die (sooner or later) if the arrow failed to strike so as to kill directly. There seems to have been some experimentation with these technical options in the Upper Palaeolithic, coming to fruition in the Mesolithic period.[198]

The Ambiguity of the Hafted Axe...

Amongst the objects with multiple uses we should no doubt count hafted axes, which fall into two categories. The most common is single-edged and can be employed as a tool and as a weapon. This is very much a symbol of the European Neolithic in its polished version (knapped or flaked then polished at length). It could be fixed in two ways, depending on two distinct uses: with the blade parallel to the haft, that is to say as an axe; or with the blade at right angles to the haft, which then makes it an adze. The wooden haft is not usually found. The generic term used to designate this type of distal cutting blade (with its edge turned away from the socket) is 'axe'. We shall adopt this usage, other than in cases when the nature of the fitting is known.

This object with its relatively simple shape is the first to have existed both in stone (flint but also in many other rocks, like jadeite, serpentine, nephrite, and so on) and metallic material. In the 5th millennium BC, in the necropolis of Varna in Bulgaria, flat metallic axes with a single blade were buried next to bodies in some graves, for example number 43, which also contained ceramics and gold for classic ornamentation and decorations, and also, atypically, a small penis-shaped container associating the dead man's identity with the power attributed to metal.

A second, morphologically more complex type of hafted axe from the Neolithic is more difficult to interpret: it is an axe with one perforation in the centre so that it can be fixed vertically (also called transversally) with two blades, one on either side (often perpendicular to one another), or a sharp blade on one side and a flat or slightly rounded head on the other.[199] These have variously been referred to as 'double-axes', 'axe-adzes', and 'hammer-axes'. They were most often made of stone (a large variety of types), but they were also made of metal from the start of the 5th millennium BC in Central Europe, and in growing numbers in the 4th millennium. Those made of copper can be up to 20 centimetres long, massive cast objects which show just how early European metalcraft started in certain areas. The central position of the socket (which is created by fixing a core in the mould when casting) made it possible to balance the dimensions and the centres of gravity of the active parts.

These items are relatively rare in terms of overall Neolithic production and there is still debate about how they were used: some see them as combat-axes, but they are most often thought to have had a sceptre-like function, as symbols of power. They are found right up to the end of the Neolithic, particularly in continental and Northern Europe. Such stone axes seem to be linked, albeit in complex ways, with metal halberds.

In a fight you do not just have to attack. You also need to protect yourself. Protective materials and techniques are linked to modes of combat which are likely to evolve alongside one another, so one will yield information about the other. Personal equipment can therefore be divided into two principal groups: items which are mobile, and those which protect the body, extending the warrior and what he wears to cover weak points, real or considered as such.

A Shield to Protect the Body...

Individual protection is emblematically represented by the shield, at once a means of blocking blows and a mobile piece of equipment which can be used to repel an enemy. A shield might make warriors more likely to lose their balance and fall if struck, but it is less likely that they will be wounded or killed. There are no traces of shields before the Bronze Age in Europe though it is easy enough to imagine that archers would have found it advantageous to develop this kind of protection in a light and mobile form. There is nothing in finds or figurative representations to suggest that such a thing might have existed. Moreover, this piece of equipment seems to have come into being at the same time as the sword.

The earliest examples from the Bronze Age seem to have been made from organic materials, wood or leather which has been boiled and reworked. Since their state of preservation is poor, we know little about them, other than some exceptionally well preserved examples from bogs, particularly in the Britain and Ireland. Five of these (four wooden ones, each made from two different types of wood, and one made of leather) were discovered in Ireland.[200] Across Europe, remnants of such defensive weaponry are fragmentary, vanished or residual, consisting only of metal nails for example, or taking the form of metal fragments in Bronze Age hoards, sometimes difficult to identify because so little remains of them.

A general scheme becomes clear: European Bronze Age shields are circular or slightly oval in form, with an average diameter of 50 to 70 centimetres. Each has an internal grip which is necessary for it to be wielded and a sort of strap so that it can be carried over the shoulder whilst on the move and when there is no fighting. The majority of them are decorated with concentric circles and bosses, varying in type from one shield to another. Some, like the one from Beith (North Ayrshire, Scotland) have as many as 9000 bosses! The circular shape is emphasised by other circles and, with its representational stippling, belongs to a type of graphic and figurative decoration common to many Bronze Age artefacts. This is the same shape as the large burial mounds in the period, which could also comprise several concentric circles formed by alternating ditches and banks. No doubt there was a symbolic and spiritual meaning here going beyond the merely ornamental.

The circular shield is found everywhere in representations (pictograms) carved in Scandinavia like those in Tanum (Sweden). It is located between the belly and the bust on representations of men, sometimes clearly identifiable as such with their erect penises, whilst the rest of the body, including the head, is reduced to the simplest shapes, that of a single line. These men most often hold in one hand an axe, sometimes a spear, with a sword suspended at their side, the shaft and the end rivet or chape of the scabbard sometimes visible. They are very often associated with boats, and with various animals, on land or in the boat itself. During the 19th century, in Nackhälle near Varburg (Halland, Sweden), an extraordinary Bronze Age shield was discovered, in a context about which little is known, that in many ways brings together all these characteristics: it is a circular metal shield which has largely preserved its yellow sheen, through being buried in waterlogged sediments. It is decorated with water birds. Scenes involving two-wheeled chariots are also depicted, as at Frännharp (Sweden). Much has been written about these extraordinary figurative representations, though lists of objects and work done on them are not yet complete. It is interesting to see how the shield is depicted in such scenes and the place it occupies in relation to other equipment. Human silhouettes in pictures from the end of the Iberian Bronze Age become sexless and more stylised. Sometimes they are altogether absent.[201] Identity is implied by the objects, the shield always being present alongside the sword and the spear, and sometimes but less frequently one sees a chariot.

The bronze shield evolved starting from the 14th and 13th centuries BC, no doubt alongside leather shields that continued to be used.[202] High quality casting is required not only for final usage as a defensive weapon, but above all because its shape is arrived at mostly through alternate hammering and annealing, starting with a blank cast. The *chaîne opératoire* is therefore longer than that of a sword. Compositional analyses suggest that these bronzes have somewhere between 9-13% tin; the latter, higher figure results from the working of the material to reshape it, which also yields a fine yellow colour.[203] A level of around 9-10% would be quite consistent with a *chaîne opératoire* involving a large amount of hammering, whilst guaranteeing the right amount of mechanical resistance. The workmanship is that of an expert who has mastered the whole *chaîne opératoire*. The final result must have taken dozens of hours of work. All the elements appropriate to such bronze sheet assembly are present, the development of which clearly started in the second half of the 2nd millennium, as was the case for other items used in defensive armour or body protection.

Other shapes are made of other materials: the iron shield (at least for the Late Iron Age, for which there are good examples) is very different from its Bronze Age predecessor. Figurative representations give a good image of this item, whether on the Gundestrup cauldron (the procession section) or indeed antique statuary which depicts Celts, with whom the peoples of the Mediterranean basin came into conflict at various times. The shields themselves were not preserved. Wooden with an elongated shape, only the metal part has survived (the umbo), located to the right of the shield, ensuring its strength, and providing the means by which the internal grip was fixed and by which it was held. It still played a key role in combat equipment, though probably it did not have the same symbolic role as its Bronze Age equivalent.

The Metal Helmet reinforces the Warrior's Head…

The warrior's equipment would not be complete without protection for the most vulnerable parts of his body: the head and the torso, which contain vital organs, and legs. A foot soldier is worth little if he can no longer advance or take evasive action. Body armour evolves alongside combat weapons. Attack leads to defence. The function of body armour is different from that of offensive weapons and its nature depends partly on the type of combat. The three main items are the helmet, the breastplate, and leg protectors. Technologically too, a different logic applies to defensive as opposed to offensive weaponry. These objects were created especially for combat, like the sword, which came into being considerably later than the earliest developments in copper alloy metalcraft. Alongside the breastplate, they also fulfilled a social role to the extent that they were used to display identity, the power of the individual and that of the group to which one belonged. This is a third aspect to which ancient societies and their metalworkers paid sustained attention.

The helmet embodies the warrior who wore it and whose head was decorated and protected by it.[204] Though its primary importance was in combat, it could also have a representational role to frighten an enemy or display an individual's power. Its effectiveness came from its shape and the materials from which it was made. Leather was used for helmets and shields, but metal is more effective. Copper alloys were used for some shields from the second half of the 2nd millennium, though most date from the end of the period.

Making a helmet is a technical challenge. European Bronze Age examples are generally hammered (and annealed) starting with a cast blank. They are different in this way from later Greek helmets, Archaic, Corinthian or Chalcidian, where casting plays a more important role, particularly in older examples. Consequently, they are less heavy: from approximately 1.5 to 2 kilograms compared to 3.5 kilograms for the heaviest Chalcidian helmets.[205] Lighter, more able to withstand blows and highly functional when well made, these hammered helmets also saved on metal, probably an important consideration in terms of the production of a set of weaponry as a whole. They must have included an internal layer of leather or textile.

As with all such manufacture, flawless casting was needed for hammering to be effective. The precise proportions of the alloy and the final state of the material both play a vital role: all alloys are more malleable when annealed, and thus better able to withstand blows, but this means they lose their shape more easily; after hammering, sheet metal has better mechanical resistance, but in turn it can more easily be pierced rather than yielding if struck sharply. Let us look into the heart of the matter in order to see why. Metal is a crystal material in which atoms are arranged regularly in a three-dimensional network.[206] This crystalline structure forms while the metal cools down. In its solid state the metal consists of grains of variable sizes (from about 10 micrometres to 1 millimetre), each of them forming a polycrystalline ensemble. The grains are three-dimensional shapes, generally polyhedral, and they tend to be more regular in form the more isotropic (even) the cooling process is throughout the substance. The grains are adjacent to one another and the border between them is called the 'grain boundary'. On impact, a sword striking a helmet for example, the crystalline network shows signs of slippage at particular crystalline levels (areas referred to as 'plastic' or 'elastic') which the material can tolerate within certain limits. The resistance of the helmet at the material's microstructural level is vital for the combatant. For copper alloys, tin and lead levels make all the difference. A copper helmet, brilliant and shiny if well-polished, would remain 'soft' (too much plasticity/plastic domain) and would yield too much in case of impact, offering insufficient resistance, failing to play a protective role. On the other hand, too much tin would lead to the helmet being hard and more breakable. Manufacturing technique is vital regarding the final characteristics: if a helmet is cast it can in theory have a high tin level, but this does not mean to say it would be functional. On the other hand, if it is made by hammering, starting with a 'blank' looking little like the eventual product, the tin level has to be much reduced, theoretically below 15% tin added to copper, in practice 12-13% maximum.

Materials and manufacturing methods are all about decision-making and getting the alloy mix right; these decisions are made on the basis of the materials themselves, of which the metalworker has an empirical understanding. The main difficulty for the bronzesmith is to give shape, not just to simple and flat pieces of sheet metal, but to the shapes of the headpiece which will follow the lines of a skull. The *chaîne opératoire* is complex and the work difficult.

So, the metal helmet came into being in the context of a world which had a powerful mastery of what was needed for the creation of copper alloys and manufacturing objects from them by means of all techniques available. The earliest examples consist of two main pieces, not a single one. Scandinavia is again distinguished by its early arrival on the scene, and by the originality and skill of its metalworkers. The best known examples of helmets are probably those from Viskø (Denmark). These two very well preserved helmets from the start of the Late Bronze Age came to light in a bog in Brøns in north Zealand (Denmark) in 1942. Such helmets are depicted in rock art, not least worn on the heads of men playing the 'lur', a large war trumpet, and also worn by a figure in a rock art in Grevensvaenge (Denmark). The Viskø helmets consist of two semi-circular sections joined and held together by a central cast section, riveted on the level of two lateral extrusions at the top of the helmet. This central piece held the ensemble in place. It also contained a slot no doubt intended to contain feathers or a horse's mane (or a coloured equivalent) and a sort of hook reaching to the level of two large bosses, depicting two bulging eyes, themselves highlighted by arcs which clearly depict human eyebrows. The head piece as a whole bears bosses of various smaller sizes too. These Nordic helmets are particularly distinguished by the presence of two tall, bent horns made by the lost wax technique. These objects bear witness to the most accomplished metal skills and an astonishing imagination. They must have impressed or indeed terrified enemies. Again, the time needed to make these two helmets would have amounted to dozens of hours. They were deliberately and definitively abandoned in a bog. A powerful gesture, no doubt in the context of a specific ceremony.

There are far fewer helmets in the totality of Bronze Age finds than swords and offensive weapons in general. As objects, they essentially come to light in the context of hoards. Those from the very end of the Eastern and Central European Bronze Age do not usually have horns like those found in Scandinavia, but they are also made by fitting together two hemispheres, the bronze sheet being riveted, folded, and soldered, though in a different way. The majority of them must have included decorative elements and involved brilliant displays made both from metals and other materials, like coloured feathers, manes and plants, in a tradition which continued and took on a codified form in later helmets.

One of the most famous groups of helmets to come to light in France is that of Bernières-d'Ailly (Calvados). Discovered in 1832, this hoard consisted of nine almost identical helmets from the Late Bronze Age. They are typical of the kind of 'crested helmets' from the very end of the period, each example made from two main pieces of sheet metal folded one over the other from the front to the back of the helmet ('A' over 'B' and 'B' over 'A') meeting at the rear of the helmet's cap, where there are long-headed rivets to reinforce the fixing of the two pieces of sheet metal and also serving as decorative features. On both sides, a piece of cast metal has been added: its function would have been to hold decorative elements, presumably plumes. The upper part of the sheet metal (the triangular section and the point), is bent over, this time to one side. This kind of helmet in its general morphology continued widely throughout Europe until the Early Iron Age (the start of the 1st millennium BC). Variants are found in the Italian peninsula (Villanova), where they come to light in graves rather than hoards.[207] The helmets from Bernières-d'Ailly have received much attention since their discovery in the 19th century.

The example from the Odescalchi collection (Rome) is in a relatively good state though partially corroded. It weighs about 687 grams now and must have weighed at least 800 grams when 'new', as it left the workshop. A sample extracted from one of the pieces of sheet metal was selected for detailed laboratory study in order to analyse the metallic microstructure and carry out analyses of the alloy mix. The cap section consisted of an alloy of 9% tin.[208] Its final shape was the result of hammering rather than recrystallisation after annealing. This was an interesting choice for an alloy with less than 10% tin because tin gives greater mechanical resistance. It contains quite high levels of sulphur, which is quite common in such European bronzes of the period. These sulphur traces are useful from a technological point of view because they tell us how much the sheet metal was reshaped compared to the initial intermediate product (the blank) which came out of the furnace, here the reshaping was in the order of 70-80%. The analysis of its composition made with a scanning electron microscope indicated that the alloy was made of a bronze binary with approximately 8% tin, a level which fits in with other observations regarding the *chaîne opératoire* of the helmet's manufacture. Studies of the microstructure highlight the considerable degree of reshaping, as much as 50% compared to the original intermediary product. Particles of lead are present in very small quantities (and sometimes over 2-3%) as often in European bronzes of the period (including the Iron Age), though this is not so with Archaic Greek bronzes, for example. The purpose would have been to help with casting, but small amounts only would have been used to avoid problems at the hammering stage. This bronzesmith was an excellent metalworker who knew how to get the best out of his material and his own skills. It is not always possible to glean such information from what can be *seen* of such objects in their present state because of their wear and tear.

There has been a detailed study of a helmet approximately contemporary to those of Bernières-d'Ailly and very similar to it ('crested' but without lateral 'fin-holders'), the 'Helmet 358' (Musée d'archéologie nationale, Saint-Germain-en-Laye).[209] One metal sample was taken from the cap, and another from a rivet which also has a decorative rule in two places: at the front and at the back of the helmet. The sheet metal comprising the helmet was made of a ternary alloy of bronze, 5-6% tin and a significant amount (about 2%) of lead. They were hammered but not extensively. The rivet head was a piece of rough-cast, obtained from secondary casting (a casting involving an already existing piece of metal) fixed on a copper rod made of a bronze containing more than 20% tin – two very different materials for a small item. Again, the materials are entirely suited to their purpose, and their colour is an added bonus: the main part of the helmet was orange-yellow, whilst the visible part of the rivets was a much brighter colour, a pale yellow. So, this helmet has not only two *chaînes opératoires*, one for each of its two parts, but also an aesthetic dimension thanks to the two different alloys (not counting the visible copper), though the present state of conservation does not do this justice.

These ancient examples highlight the care taken with the manufacture and the real sense of imagination that went into creating various forms of helmet, though the *a priori* functional requirements remain considerable (the shape of the skull to be protected, resistance and so on). The helmet's shape, in the majority of types, goes beyond what is functionally necessary, so the warrior is made taller by the pointed and raised helmet, which is decorated with points to the front and rear, or even horns, with a boss on the upper part, not to mention a horse mane or coloured feathers on the top or to either side. Parading and cutting a dash seem to have been a constant preoccupation throughout the whole of the Metal Ages in Europe.

The helmet can also be considered the warrior's double. It extends the head, the sovereign part of the body, the home of reflection and thought. Perhaps some of the helmet's shapes or accessories have a symbolic role: they can 'hide' the warrior (Corinthian and also Chalcidian helmets in Greece); they can make him more agile and faster in combat (winged helmets or those with horses' manes), or stronger (decorative motifs depicting combat).[210]

The helmet remains part of the fighter's equipment from the Bronze Age on. Its morphology evolves in various ways. There is a development in the manufacture of the headpiece to become a single, semi-spherical piece, without riveting by the start of the Iron Age, and with a crest on the top. There is an attempt to give added protection by extending the headpiece to neck level, with a hollowed out shape so as not to restrict movement and sections are added to protect the face, as well as cheek-guards (paragnathides) which are sometimes hinged and often decorated. Iron helmets are manufactured alongside distinctive bronze ones, but some also use several metals in the same helmet (gold, bronze, iron) and other materials too, like amber, coral, and enamel, to produce a multi-coloured effect (yellow, white, and red). The most remarkable manufactured helmets (like the one from Agris in Charente, France – early 4th century – or the one from Amfreville-sous-les-Monts in l'Eure, France – late 4th/3rd century BC) probably never saw action on a battlefield, but were made rather for use in ceremonies linked to war.[211] These represent a high level of technical achievement from the metalworker's point of view. Of course, more sober objects, sometimes with just one distinguishing detail, were most often manufactured. Across Europe, including in Etruscan territory ('Negau' type helmets dating from the 5th century BC), there is some similarity between such helmets, with a predilection for simple shapes throughout the second part of the 1st century: one might almost talk of standardisation.

Though the number of known helmets in Europe for the first part of the 1st millennium BC is not high, they become more frequent, if not commonplace, from the start of the Middle Iron Age. Unlike Bronze Age helmets, they are regularly discovered in funerary contexts. They are also found in religious contexts: sanctuaries, alongside other pieces of equipment like those in Picardie (Gournay-sur-Aronde and Ribemont-sur-Ancre, France) or other regions (the oppidum at Corent, in le Puy-de-Dôme, France, and Mormont, Switzerland), in isolated hoards like those at Agris (the cave) or Amfreville-sous-les-Monts (Bras de la Seine, France), and in collections of objects not dissimilar to Bronze Age hoards and buried in a similar way.

Thus, at Tintignac (Corrèze, France) in 2004 weapons were discovered in the pit of an enclosure, some made of bronze and others of iron.[212] Alongside the offensive weapons (nine swords with their scabbards broken before burial), the iron central boss of a shield had also been buried alongside ten helmets, nine bronze and one iron. Six of the helmets had a simple, hemispherical morphology, typical of productions from the end of the La Tène period. One had a hemispherical headpiece with riveted neck guards, and two cheek guards which had been torn off and left inside the helmet. Another had a kind of bronze net exposed on either side of the crest-holder. The iron helmet contained pieces of bronze. The last helmet, found at the bottom of the pit, was shaped like a swan whose neck, in an elegant sweep, traced a movement forwards and then backwards so that its head almost touched its tail, coming to a point beyond the back of the helmet. In addition, there were sheet metal animals, including boars, and a collection of about 30 carnyxes, war trumpets whose bells also had pictures of animals, their mouths wide open, ready to terrify the enemy. The best preserved of these was about 1.6 metres in length. The items found in the Tintignac hoard are very much like those depicted in one of the scenes on the Gundestrup Cauldron (Denmark), also consecrated in a votive site and from the same period. War is about violence, fighting and technology, but it is also fully integrated into the religious rituals and practices which are inherent to it.

Metal to Embellish the Breast

As well as the helmet, another form of body armour evolved during the Bronze Age – the breastplate. It followed a similar logic and the same chronology. No doubt the first ones were made from organic material, reinforced if need be (with hard animal matter, metal pieces fixed over leather[213]), but then metal became the dominant material thanks to the development of high quality technical skills that combined casting techniques with reshaping by hammering. The number of European breastplates is very limited, only about 30 have been clearly identified at present,[214] to which we no doubt need to add some examples now lost,[215] and some unidentified fragments of sheet metal found in hoards. In terms of archaeological contexts, breastplates have come to light almost exclusively as whole pieces alongside groups of other objects, or isolated in watery conditions, or in the form of fragments in large metal hoards from the end of the Bronze Age.

Of all the available sources, it has been possible to study just three major groups of European protohistoric finds in detail using laboratory analysis, samples being taken *ad hoc*: the breastplates from the Marmesse hoard[216], the breastplate from Saint-Germain-du-Plain, and the breastplate referred to as 'from Grenoble'[217] as well as the Fillinges hoard.

The latter provides a good example of the characteristic way such hoards of emblematic weapons are arranged: they came to light during earthworks next to a village road in Savoie in 1901, visibly stacked inside one another according to first reports,[218] which mentioned that the soil around them was blackened by fire. Crude ceramics were also found, and a horse's jawbone. In other words, it was a ceremonial hoard, deliberately arranged, though details were not preserved.

It is just as challenging to make a breastplate as a helmet! So, from a technical point of view, it makes sense that the two evolved side by side. In some ways, making a breastplate was probably even more demanding because the surface had to be more even, and combatants had to be protected without being hindered in their movements or too weighed down by heavy equipment. The weight of a Greek hoplite's equipment in the 7th century BC is known: between 15 and 30 kilograms. Bearing such a burden, and relatively constrained in his movements, combatants had to remain in position, in close formation, for a combat time that was specific and limited.

Ancient Central Europe decided in favour of metal breastplates made from two main pieces. The best intact example of these, and one of the most ancient, is from Saint-Germain-du-Plain (Saône-et-Loire, France), contemporary with the Blainville helmet, dating from about 1000 BC according to recent chronological studies.[219] This breastplate was dredged up from the Saône, without any clear relationship to other objects, but in a context characteristic of the practice of abandoning hoards in boggy land in the Late Bronze Age.[220] It consists of two main pieces of sheet metal hammered out of a blank, the initial thickness of the blank being reduced to 90-95% so its original thickness would have been no more than a centimetre.[221] Traces of hammering are still clearly visible on the inside of the breastplate. Metallographic analyses (using an optical microscope) show that it was left in a deformed state, apparently original, since it was well preserved in the hoard environment of which it was part, and no serious restoration was needed before it was displayed in the museum. It is still quite shiny, and its colour is more golden yellow than green. The metal used is a bronze alloy with a 'small amount' of tin, 9%, and the raw material used was rich in sulphur content. The presence of this sulphur would surprise a present-day metalworker, but it was common in bronzes from this time and from this region – a residue from the ore reduction process. The metalworker 3000 years ago would have alternated phases of hammering and annealing with care and restraint. Decoration was achieved by resting what would be the outside of the breastplate on a soft mould during the hammering process. The final shape was achieved by edging with metal beading (also made by from rolled sheet metal rather than a flat piece) so the wearer would not cut himself on it; this also helped stiffen the sheet metal. The edging was made from an alloy identical to that used for the main sheets, with the same characteristics – probably a sample taken during the cutting process and then rolled into the final shape. The breastplate from Saint-Germain-du-Plain, France is older, but it corresponds to a type of technology typical of breastplate production as a whole that was carried out in two phases, front and back panels riveted on the left side and fixed with attachments on the right and at the shoulders so that it could be closed.

The Marmesse breastplates from Haute-Marne, France are probably the best known in Europe.[222] Each one consists of a front plate about 45 centimetres tall and a back section between 50 and 55 centimetres tall. Each piece weighs between 1-1.5 kilograms and is indented on the inside. These indentations are small, elongated marks, oval lens-like in shape and about 1 centimetre long. They are marks from hammering in places which were not supposed to have been seen. They would also have been hidden by an internal layer probably made of organic material (leather or textile). Each of the breastplates shows signs of later reworking (a crack which must have appeared at some stage filled by the addition of a small piece of metal riveted on) or repairs that indicate that they were worn in combat. Samples were taken from each of the breastplates. Some manufacturing decisions turned out to be surprising on close study. Thus, the initial blank (first casting) was different from current day practice.[223] The bronzesmith chose to use a thick initial piece (blank), well-casted (without any porosity which would have made hammering difficult), so more thorough hammering was needed than if the blank had been thinner.[224] At that time, metalworkers had the skills to cast very fine pieces, but not necessarily for large surface areas which then had to be thinned by hammering. This was vital in order to get an eventual thickness less than 0.5 millimetres which would guarantee a weight of less than 4.5 kilograms.[225] The fine-grained metallic microstructure matrix contained the usual amounts of sulphur (leftover from the reduction process) but also, in a way that was quite abnormal regarding all three samples, there were high levels of something known as alpha-beta eutectoids. Their morphology, which has a substructure (a bit like the veining of a decaying leaf which has become transparent), proves that their presence was related to the casting process, the point when the rough-cast cools. Analysis shows that these were present in parts where there was a high concentration of tin (over 20%) which makes the material harder but less easy to hammer, so this must have slowed the process down. Metalworkers must have compensated for these difficulties by precise and careful hammering work, and frequent annealing at temperatures around 600-650°C. The alloys used in the sheet metal contained 8-10% tin depending on the breastplate and the trimming with which the breastplates were edged so as not to cause injury was between 6-7% tin. From a technical point of view, this choice of materials is consistent with the *chaîne opératoire*, including the considerable reshaping of the sheet metal involved in the manufacture of the front and rear plates.[226] The front and rear plate of each piece had, ever since their manufacture, been kept permanently in place by rivets on the left hand side between the armpit and the waist. The number of these rivets varied from four to six in the pieces from Marmesse whilst there was a maximum of five in the Fillinges breastplates, these also being smaller. On the right hand side, they were rounded in a way that reflected the main decorative motifs. The Marmesse rivets had conical heads whilst the Fillinges examples were flattened. This was an aesthetic choice rather than a technical decision, maybe made by individual workshops. On the other side the edge is caulked and a ring or washer, more or less octagonal, had been slipped between the sheet metal and the top to facilitate maintenance. By way of contrast, on the right hand side, the closing system is not permanent but consists half way up of a sort of hook made from a tongue of cut-off sheet metal, bent and riveted into the back and which is hooked on the inside into a rectangular perforation cut into the front plate to keep the breastplate closed.

All breastplates of this type also show signs of repairs of various kinds, some big, some small. The first would have been carried out during manufacture when the metalworker thought it better to repair than start over. This would involve the careful addition and riveting of pieces in such a way that, after a good polish, they would have been practically invisible, other than at very close quarters. The second type of repair (functional repairs) would have been carried out after the breastplate had been used. If damaged by a blow, the breastplate would have been returned to the workshop for the bronzesmith to extend its life and maintain its lustre. The *chaîne opératoire* of these exceptional objects is therefore very long and complex. The investment in time and knowledge is evident in these objects, and more still would have been required for other equipment needed to protect the body, nowadays under-represented compared with what workshops must have produced.

Such two-piece metal breastplates were no longer made after the Bronze Age and in general there are few remnants of protective items for the upper body. Two kinds of reasons exist as to why manufacture of metal breastplates typical of the Bronze Age should have ceased: the economic investment in the manufacture of objects no longer used in combat would have been too high. The few examples of such items from the end of the Iron Age are made from moveable sections, probably leather, like the equipment worn by the statue of the man excavated in the Glauberg tumulus.[227] He is wearing a series of chevron-like shapes, apparently a system of leather clothing, with various sections superimposed, one partly covering another. The shoulders are protected by smooth plaques which are attached to the other pieces. This development would not have been the consequence of technical limitations but the result of changes in the warrior's needs. The rigid Bronze Age breastplates offered good protection, and they were relatively light, but to some extent they would have hindered movement, even though they were designed to be worn closer to the body than those more familiar to us nowadays. To improve mobility, the use of articulated sections had advantages, even though leather offers less protection than metal. Fighting techniques probably evolved, becoming more dynamic and mobile, on foot and also on horseback, for at this stage the horse was making its presence felt, suggesting that the characteristic warrior was now also a horseman. In the Middle Iron Age, the European ironsmith's solution was to invent chain mail.

There are very few examples of leg protectors in Northern Europe. No equivalent has been found of the Greek cnemides. Examples that are known are Mediterranean. The absence has nothing to do with technical know-how. Metalworkers would have been perfectly capable of manufacturing such items. There are Bronze Age leg pieces, but these are ornamentation for women's legs with decorated sheet metal on the front and a system of double spirals on the calf.[228] This is no doubt because of the requirements of different types of combat. The leg is not a vital part of the body, and a leg guard would hinder a warrior's movements, weighing him down. At this period, it seems that fighters favoured mobility, which makes sense in terms of movements required to wield a sword.

The pieces of equipment described here in detail are only small samples of what was a vast production, that these items have been chosen to represent. If one adds together the different categories of metal items, there are millions associated with violent confrontations and acts of violence between men. In their way, they are war. They are pieces of evidence connected to violence and they are essential sources in the history of craft. Studying them under a binocular or normal microscope reveals skills, hours of work and highly developed distribution systems. Far from leading us away from the subject of war, in fact they lead us straight back there. They are technological items, fruits of high level skills, combat weapons, objects specifically wanted by ancient societies. Organised and structured by society, these objects were also part of the means by which society was structured. André Leroi-Gourhan was right about (at least) one thing:

> "*Civilisation depends upon the craftsman [...] But his activities are the least valued in terms of official honours. Throughout all history and in all peoples, he stands in the background. Compared to the 'holiness' of the priest, the 'heroism' of the warrior, the 'courage' of the hunter, the 'prestige' of the orator, the 'nobility' even of the rural round, his actions are simply 'clever'. [...] His long history leaves one with the feeling that he represents only one of two opposite poles, that of t he hand.*"[229]

Of course, the metalworker does not explain war in isolation. But their actions do contribute to the phenomenon of war, including its physical aspects. By analysing the meaning of results obtained from technical data, we can seek explanations regarding the behaviour and decisions of people in societies when they are confronted with war.

V

OFF TO WAR

Taking up arms

Now it is time for our warrior to take up arms. He is a man of about 20 years old, vigorous, full of strength. He grew up knowing that one day he would receive his full panoply of weaponry, that he would bear a sword and that he would fight if ordered. He did not choose his own equipment this was done by his comrades-in-arms – but he followed the process of manufacture. He entered the warmth of the bronzesmith's workshop to watch the bronzesmith at work. He was fascinated by the way shapeless matter was transformed into yellow, brilliant, sparkling weaponry, and the reddening of the hot metal as the hammer struck home. The bronzesmith explained the work to him. To make sure the weapons would be right, the metalworker studied the young man carefully, thought about the size and shape of his body, and took his hand to make sure the grip of the future sword would be a good one.

Our youthful warrior did not go to the workshop every day, since this was not his place. The first time, his father was with him. Soon his equipment will be finished, like that of his eight comrades. During the course of a special ceremony, they will become full warriors. Nine crows will be killed, and their feathers will be displayed on the sides of their helmets. Then it will be their right to fight alongside the older men. Though they have learned some of the rudiments of fighting from a young age, they will still have a lot of training to do, relentless training, not least in the techniques of swordsmanship. The sword will be neither too long nor too heavy so it can be used both for stabbing and slashing – not something you can make up as you go along. In one-to-one combat at close quarters, the slightest error can be fatal. They will be together on the battlefield, but alone in each of their confrontations with individual enemies. The youthful warriors know this and though they have played at fighting and were taught basic techniques from a very young age, the sword itself is something quite different. It is their weapon, their double and perhaps their salvation.

The shape of their swords is different from those used by their distant ancestors who died many generations ago. They are longer and heavier. Each of the youthful warriors will first learn how to wield his sword, feet firmly on the ground. He will hold the weapon in one hand adding strength using two hands at critical moments. One day perhaps one of them will earn the right to fight on horseback. They already have the social status, but it will be their valour in combat that opens the way to this supreme honour. The horse has always been a companion of such young men, harnessed and ridden for centuries now. Their cousins in the north have long since been depicting them on windswept rocks, stars passing overhead like so many protective spirits. Where these warriors live, there are no such cave paintings. The presence of horses is more discreet. They are reserved for certain warriors. The most exceptional. Those who also have a role in command and in government. Alongside them, foot soldiers are, according to their place in society, swordsmen, spear bearers or archers. This specialisation of roles on the battlefield developed alongside the presence of the horse and the types of complete weapon sets that these youthful warriors are about to receive.

The sword, and weapons in general, are so redolent of power, so full of symbolism, that when a warrior dies, victorious or vanquished, such weapons meet a fate quite different from other, more ordinary objects. They are not returned to the bronzesmith's workshop to be recycled, though this would be technically possible. Our young warrior has learned that the custom has always been for some metal objects to be gathered together, sometimes broken by the bronzesmith during special ceremonies, and then buried or thrown into rivers or bogs. They mark the end of the life of whomever used them, so they are offerings to the gods of creation, associated with the most powerful elements: the earth which bears the rocks from which the metal is made; the water which extinguishes the fire and bears it away over the horizon to the depths where it comes to rest forever.

Archaeology gives no details about all this. It does, however, bear witness to the final acts of destruction, abandonment, and submersion to which we are trying to give meaning. If the sword is the double of the warrior, then when he leaves the world of the living, it makes sense that this weapon, associated with his person, his identity, and his actions, should do so too: his life is his weapon's. When our youthful warriors have been initiated, have each received their equipment, and if they are killed in battle, will society gather together the various components of their equipment and offer them to the world of the gods, in homage, and so that the gods will be merciful in the future? Such an action would indeed be religious in the broadest sense of the word. The sacrifice would certainly be an economic one. The nine sets together represent 35 kilograms of metal and countless months of work. Removing all this from the world of practical use, like the 14 kilograms of metal found in the Crundale hoard (Kent, England), can have nothing fanciful or spontaneous about it.

At the end of the period, hoards tend to be composite, with weapons being found alongside other items. Is there a link here to the social status of individuals, or traditions linked to the most important activities of the Bronze Age's agricultural societies? Were they a kind of weight measure, of a monetary nature, as was sometimes thought for more recent hafted axe hoards? Was the axe also sometimes used in combat alongside or instead of the sword if it broke in the tumult of action? There are more questions here for archaeologists than answers. Before these weapons were finally abandoned, what were the actions of the men who bore them? Where did they go to fight, how often and for what reasons? Again, the perilous road of hypothesis is the only one open to us if we are to explore the world which saw our young warrior first granted his weapons.

To wound, to kill and to protect. Such would appear to be the triple role of weapons. Yet archaeology suggests we should not restrict ourselves to these three objectives, which are real but insufficient. Weapons of war play these roles within a clearly defined framework, that of structured and organised combat. The Metal Ages, the Bronze Age and then the Iron Age, leave no room for doubt about the reality of such violence. The specific nature of objects manufactured in workshops bears witness to it. For more ancient periods, objects used for fighting had more than one use, so we cannot be absolutely sure about their function, how they were used on the ground, for hunting or for war, despite the desire of some researchers to see war as dating from at least at the very beginning of the Neolithic. The same goes for the Palaeolithic. But the evidence is slender, or rather, it points to violence taking place between men, but not necessarily in the form of *war*. Trying to see what happened means taking a new look at the data, following the thread of time backwards, and daring to imagine these people in their setting.

Violence is an ancient phenomenon. It is plural in nature. It is inherent in war, directly between combatants; it is visible on bodies themselves. It takes on less usual forms in European societies, not least during the Bronze Age. It has a bearing on objects, weapons being the most important of these, with entire hoards of them being gathered together, then broken. Far from being circumstantial or marginal, this behaviour speaks of war in terms of one of its most marked practices.

Violence in the Palaeolithic

The first period of European history, the Palaeolithic, covers the earliest hundreds of thousands of years of our history as *Homo sapiens*. What does it tell us about war? Archaeological data is inadequate. And it comes in limited forms: human remains and stone objects (flint for a large part) which diversify over the course of time; figurative representations can be added from the Later Palaeolithic (40,000-36,000 BC in the case of Chauvet Cave, France).

The evidence provided by archaeology for this period is terribly scant and frustrating. No one nowadays would deny that there is evidence of violence. Nor of its opposite: the care of the wounded (or injured) or the dead. Awareness of otherness, the relationship with the other – another component part of any social construction – is a very ancient phenomenon which brings together the dimensions of action and ritual: caring, feeding, consecrating a place of death, organising funerary ceremonies.[230] Yet it is difficult to go further. The existence of violence does not mean that a society constituted as such undertook it as a specific practice, acting accordingly when violence was present (in times of conflict) and when it ceased (times of peace). In other words, the existence of 'war' cannot be proven. The function of conflict seems rather to derive from empirical or pragmatic needs of those taking part in it. So, no doubt there was conflict hundreds of thousands of years ago. But there is no evidence to say how much violence or what form it took, or even how often it took place. Spaces were vast, so it was easy for social groups not to run into one another or find themselves in competition. Confrontations must have been episodic and linked to particular circumstances: settling differences, capturing game or even individuals. For the researcher, going any further would involve the risk of thinking in fictional terms, if not fantastically, but still going beyond the scope of history. We have mentioned how Joseph

Henri Rosny did this with talent and success. But it does not mean that the view of conflict as integral to social practices is illegitimate, not for the Palaeolithic or any other historical period. The difficulty is not in the formulation of the question, but in the proof required for an investigation to be conclusive. Here we have no mythical detective who, with little or no evidence, can reveal all. The archaeologist tracks down tiny pieces of evidence not to unmask some guilty party (or not necessarily) but to write history.

Archaeologists specialising in the Palaeolithic opened the way to the study of war because of the desire common to all historians to tackle each of the various aspects of human societies.[231] They were right to do so. But it did not mean that there would be clear-cut answers. Besides, they found themselves in a peculiar epistemological situation unavoidable in the 19th century, which was to do with the question of 'origins'. Such debates involved other areas too, not least the growing subjects of ethnology and 'Prehistory', which shared a fascination with primary comparative studies, this being a time when European colonisation was at its height. Archaeologists specialising in these early periods found themselves dealing with the subject in a very particular way. The mission entrusted to them, consciously or otherwise, was to find 'evidence', in the most ancient human remains, of the nature of mankind. Lines of descent from our predecessors to us were to be drawn up, biologically – the 'acceptable' *Homo sapiens* – as opposed to the 'unacceptable', as the Neanderthal was seen then, and beyond. It was not so much the archaeologists themselves, but rather the public, educated or provoked by writers and painters as we have seen, who appropriated the question. Human nature was understood, now as ferocious, now as peaceful, as if the ideas of Hobbes and Rousseau, thanks to eye-witness journalism, were being perpetuated or indeed given physical, human shape. The question of violence has never quite got away from that of origins though the question was no longer put in such terms. Rather, it has been seen (beyond the microcosm of specialists) as part of something whole and uniform, as Prehistory with a capital 'P'. The presence of violence since the earliest of times was recognised, though it was hard to give it any coherent shape in the context of such a long period, stretching over 800,000 years. Chronological sequences have been refined and Palaeolithic societies have been distinguished from those of the Mesolithic and Neolithic, though societies themselves were very heterogeneous within each of these three periods.

Violence cannot be envisaged as something simply autonomous. The topic makes no sense unless thought of as being at the heart of societies in their role as the organisers of relationships between members of the group (whatever their nature) and violence, the killing of others, the relationship with death itself, and the societies' taking ownership of all this in a framework or of rituals, codes, customs, and laws. These are not all identical and the rules that count in one place do not necessarily count elsewhere. Let us take a step back from the Palaeolithic world and look further forward to the modern world. The second amendment of the American Constitution authorises the free purchase and therefore the use, in certain circumstances, of firearms. France has absolutely no equivalent in her legal texts. The common rule is generally accepted (and such rules are not identical in all societies) on the level of a society seen as a whole, which does not mean that everyone goes along with it. Some Americans disagree profoundly with the legal provision regarding certain forms of violence, but the law of the land permits, enshrines and formalises it. The historian's job is to determine the nature of the social practice embodied and try to identify the rule or norm, whether or not this was integrated into rituals and however shocking these might seem from our point of view as human beings – as historians we have to look at them differently. Frenzied killing, cutting up bodies and even eating them might be normalised activities in some societies (perhaps this was so regarding the Neolithic pit found in Achenheim in Alsace, France) and we need therefore to try to understand the mechanisms involved. A particular find might of course have been linked to a 'criminal' act which has nothing to do with the rules, carried out by an individual acting outside the codes of the society which would therefore condemn him. Dividing lines are often fragile because social norms change. Contexts too. Rules are not fixed for all eternity. What was enshrined by law one day can be outside it another (the death penalty in France) or come to be within it (abortion). All societies have their shared laws (this is indeed a fundamental definition of what a society is), but not all laws are written down. It is not always easy for archaeologists to find their way. And it is not always easy for a paleoanthropologist to tell the difference, in a 6000 year old site, between a burial place presenting evidence of the actions of a 'serial killer', and that of a necropolis of a society where it is 'normal' to chop off heads or arms and to gather them together before burial…

Human violence is a long-term phenomenon. There is no doubt about it, though the amount of violence and its nature varies considerably, from one situation to another. What counts in historical analysis is to understand how human societies (and humans in society beyond their individuality) regulate the question of violence, in terms of scale and manner. In the case of the most ancient societies, the key question is to understand how – and by means of what kind of archaeological data – one can gain access to adequate levels of information regarding the existence, or otherwise, of rules providing a structure for violence, patterns by which violence might have been organised and decided upon at the highest level, so that such violence might be seen as an extension of politics, that is, an act of 'war'.

The importance of archers in figurative representations of human conflict during the Mesolithic (which followed the Palaeolithic round about 10,000 BC), gives us a way of seeing conflictual practices between groups in a social setting: forms of war – which would not be to prejudge the precise nature of the organising society (and even less so its unconscious hierarchies). Besides, technological specialists tell us that arrows can be seen in terms of specific *chaînes opératoires*. This is perhaps a clue. This kind of data can be compared to that which characterises the ethnologist's 'traditional' societies. The Clastres model would probably be appropriate for the Mesolithic.[232] Maybe even for the Neolithic.

Multiple-Use Technology in the Neolithic

The Neolithic is a period of multiple-use objects. The range of items usable as weapons can have other uses too. The inert and mute objects constituting the body of finds from this period raise many questions, but do not necessarily yield as many answers as one might wish. Evidence, continuing to some extent, from the Palaeolithic, consists essentially of the objects themselves and marks on bones. Figurative representations of violence are few and far between, limited to the beginning of the period and concentrated in some regions, particularly the Mediterranean.[233]

Arrows are used for hunting and for fighting. This does not mean that certain morphological details are reserved to one situation rather than another, but that there is a polyvalence in principle as well as an ambiguity in situations regarding such archaeological finds. Ethnological examples show the existence of cases where arrows made for human combat are not manufactured from exactly the same materials or in the same way. Then it does become possible to show that they were used in one way rather than another. This is known because there is direct information about differences in manufacture and use. But when such data is of an archaeological nature the question becomes more difficult. Cave paintings in eastern Spain from the eve of the Neolithic leave little room for doubt, clearly showing the phenomenon of fighting between archers. Men confront one another in groups, but such scenes are too few for us to be able to draw conclusions regarding the European Neolithic as a whole.

The data does show the presence of arrowheads in human remains, which have come to rest in places that could have caused death. A certain number of Neolithic funerary contexts prove that death must have been caused in this way, various parts of the body having been affected.[234] Ötzi himself seems to have died from an arrow shot into his back, still visible in x-rays. In any case, over the course of the millennia involved (five at least), that is hardly overwhelming evidence: no massacres with hundreds of bodies abandoned *in situ*; nothing to confirm regular outbreaks of archery battles over a long period which would fit in with the way societies then functioned. The lack of evidence no doubt explains why populations from this period have so long been considered as peaceful. An imbalance within the Neolithic adds to difficulties of interpretation, with a concentration of deaths by arrow after 3500 BC rather than before, but still the figures remain modest. The site of Baumes-Chaudes (Lozère, France) boasts the largest number of arrow wounds, though of the 300 to 400 individuals left in the cave in the 3rd millennium BC, only 17 had arrow injuries. During this period, though hunting was only a marginal source of food for populations, some graves had arrows positioned next to corpses. We could see in this an increase in the use of arrows as weapons. But it could also be interpreted as a status symbol in societies where everyone's place was defined and where hierarchies were clear, not least in modes of representation going beyond the strictly functional. So, there are mixed messages if we take arrowheads on their own: a number of deaths that does not make it possible to conclude that fighting broke out regularly; a type of weapon which could have been used in combat or hunting during the course of which deaths might have been accidental; but an undeniable existence of violence that can be shown to have taken place. So Neolithic man was not a virtuous pacifist, but the bows and arrows archaeologists find do not speak unequivocally of war. This does not preclude the notion that some objects might over the course of time have had a symbolic importance. Nor would such evidence contradict what we know from another important Neolithic object, the hafted axe.

This is incontestably also an object with many uses, like the arrowhead – following similar principles. There is evidence that these polished blades were used as tools (axe or adze according to the type of hafting) in dwelling places (including lacustrine areas where the cuff is often preserved) and they are also found in funerary contexts, which could broadly be referred to as religious (which included the funerary), associated with megalithic monuments, where they are found amongst foundations (for example Sweet Track in England[235]) and so on. These polished blades that are known throughout Europe could also have been used as combat weapons. This is technically feasible, at least for a number of them. Moreover, blows to some skeletons (like those found at Talheim, during the Late Neolithic) bear witness to the kind of frenzied attacks upon individuals which would have required a heavy, blunt instrument. Again, the analysis of archaeological data does not really mean we can conclude that any of these groups of weapons were specifically made for fighting. These iconic objects could be interpreted as being used for hunting, as tools, or perhaps even combat. Only the category of double blades with transversal perforations (double axes) could be viewed as having been manufactured for a purpose over and above hunting. Opinions are nevertheless divided between those who believe they were made for combat and those who see them as symbols of power.

The way these two types of potential weapons might have been used would correspond to two radically different types of combat: the bow and arrow is used in long-distance confrontations and is very fast and mobile, involving groups rather than isolated individuals; axes on the other hand require adversaries to be at close quarters. Nothing indicates that they were in fact used in this way, whilst arrows, at least at certain times and in certain places, definitely were – as shown by engravings from the start of the period. The disappearance of such representations over the centuries does not necessarily mean that combat ceased.

What Kind of Neolithic 'War'?

What conclusions can be drawn then about Neolithic 'war'? Can we go any further than with our hypotheses about the Palaeolithic? For a long while, there was a desire to see the Neolithic as a peaceful time when societies lived in an 'egalitarian' way.[236] The farmer was in his field and the cowherd was with his cattle and no one saw a need to introduce conflict into this fine pastoral postcard. But as archaeological studies began to develop over the course of the 20th century, anthropologists (in an ethnological sense) were not, as we have seen, really interested in warfare in traditional societies and tried rather to understand questions of kinship or modalities of gifting at the heart of societies identified as being 'primitive' or 'traditional', which for this reason did not seem to need hierarchies. In 1977 Pierre Clastres opened up new ways of thinking, but arrived in some ways too early on the scene. Nowadays, models put forward in the 1970s have been revised in two ways: on the one hand the presence of violence has been accepted in the light of new archaeological evidence (in particular studies of impacts in human remains), to the extent of being seen suddenly as omnipresent (war seemed to be everywhere); at the same time, the egalitarian model of society for the whole of the European Neolithic was subject to criticism and largely rejected. Let us return later to these two points.

Evidence of violence in Europe between the 6th and 4th millennia BC does exist, but not to the extent (in terms of objects and signs of violence) that we can draw any conclusions about whether 'war' existed amidst Neolithic populations. Violence did happen. But what sort? In what kind of society? The 'egalitarian' model is no longer convincing. Let us quote Maurice Godelier:

> *"In an egalitarian society, other than in relationships between men and women, no group making up the society has a sole right to exercise violence over other groups. This is equality. There can be no 'peasant' in primitive societies. Everyone is armed, everyone is a warrior and at the same time, a farmer, a hunter and so on. A farmer is not a peasant. A peasant is someone who lives in subjugation. A 'primitive' is a free person who, amongst other things, is a warrior, hunter and so on. So, there is no monopoly of violence in egalitarian societies. Violence is not concentrated. It is shared."*[237]

In this anthropological model there are no social divisions, or at least none that cannot be interchangeable. Could such a model be used to describe Neolithic societies?

Until the 1970s, this was indeed the kind of suggestion that archaeologists would make. Nowadays, no one – or almost no one – believes this anymore. The appearance of Marshall Sahlins' (1930-2021) work 1976 for the French version), *Âge de pierre, âge d'abondance*, signed the death warrant of any myth of some ideal (and idealised) Neolithic world allegedly synonymous with equality and peace: according to him, by inventing agriculture, humans had created their own degradation, subjecting themselves to hours of work far higher than those their Palaeolithic ancestors spent hunting and gathering. Agriculture therefore increased the constraints in which humans lived and reduced personal time.[238] The author's personal anti-capitalist convictions shine through. This work, which had a broad scope, did not completely settle the question of human equality, or the question of what the model of an egalitarian society should be. The large houses of the Linear Band Ceramic Culture (Early Neolithic) seem to have been fairly standardised, large enough for an extended family, and might therefore lead one to believe that the first farmers lived without dispute, sharing the fruits of their labours. However, increasing numbers of excavations and archaeological studies, diversification of sources (and therefore approaches), and progress made with work on technological issues, have revealed ever-increasing specialisation and long term *chaînes opératoires*.

This new data led to increased knowledge, but made questions about the nature of these societies more complex, including those related to conflict at their heart, according to various plausible models to which this knowledge gave rise. Let us take another look at possible scenarios and look at how archaeological data might fit in with a societal model. It is difficult to tell, using only physical data, whether humans at the start of the Neolithic were 'farmers' or 'peasants'. Agriculture, livestock farming, hunting, and fishing all went on. People adopted a relationship with time and space in accordance with these new preoccupations and requirements, since they knew that, when a field was sown, it would not provide nourishment the next day and that, when the crop was ready, there would be too much for a single meal, so stockpiling would be necessary. Such people lived in circumstances in which confrontation and violence must have played some role. Who does what and who decides? Do settling and new types of cultivated territory change everything forever? The sources are not enough to decide things one way or another. Even if we take into account the fact that neolithization was an arhythmic, stop-and-start phenomenon, something that happened over a long period rather than as a one-off, it still led to a profound change in ways of life, subsistence and beliefs as well as social organisation. It is by no means 'just' a movement from hunter-gathering to production according to a simplistic economic model, but a far more profound change at the heart of societies.[239] What is more, the Neolithic was not one uniform and continuous state of affairs, but a long period of time throughout the course of which there were many breaks and continuities, as the physical data makes clear.

Throughout Europe raw material processing grew more intense during the Middle Neolithic (the 4th millennium BC). The increase in raw materials (types of stone as well as copper working), the spread of exchange systems, the cultivation of new lands, and a growth in funerary practices and religious monuments, are signs of considerable change. Can we advance further hypotheses about these societies on the basis of this? Or perhaps find clues regarding the question of inequality in Western societies? This topic, well known to philosophers and further pursued by anthropologists, has its roots in the question of natural human dispositions and therefore the original state of man and changes brought about by agriculture.

Grave goods from the Late Neolithic have often been interpreted as early manifestations of inequality. This is only partially accurate since such funerary hoards were also buried in the Upper Palaeolithic (for example the young man in the cave of Arene Candide in Italy dating from the end of the period – between 20,000 and 10,000 BC[240]). Let us say rather that necropolises, sites dedicated to the dead, became the places where such funerary practices involving the deposition of objects took place, thereby also giving expression to the esteem in which particular dead people were held. At the same time, signs of human violence also become more evident in source data. Combining these two elements, we could see here tangible signs in favour of the hypothesis that Neolithic societies were non-egalitarian. Such a view gains in credence if we think in terms of divisions of labour and the increasing specialisation of tasks, starting with the activities of metalworkers and the raw materials being used. Ethnological studies of societies analogous to Neolithic European societies can help here: the long blades of New Guinea demonstrate a powerful codification of production modes and times.[241] If we accept this notion of constitutive inequality, what kind of societies would this imply? Ethnologists have shown in detail that, everywhere on the planet, there are many possibilities, at least in some respects. Kinship is one of the phenomena that shows the least degree of variation, a topic that archaeology is currently not in a position to study.[242]

As for war, Pierre Clastres' suggestion that warfare might be present in societies like those of the Neolithic is plausible, but unprovable. It has the merit of giving a sense of reality to the notion of what warfare might have been like, in a way compatible with archaeological finds and ethnographic models. It fits in with the ambivalence of weapons that might have been used for war until the dawn of the Bronze Age. It also fits in with the establishment and the regular redefinition of territories in the context of agricultural Europe. And it enables us to envisage conflicts of a different nature, more regular, motivated by the desire to possess and conquer, to control territories, motivations which are more economic than social. It also becomes possible to combine the notion of 'territorial' war, at the time when territories were first established (in the Late Neolithic), with wars of 'balance' such as they are set out by Pierre Clastres, which would fit in better with the idea of already established societies wanting, from the start of the Middle Neolithic, to maintain their territorial and social integrity. Regular conflict then would be a component part of activities regulated by a society for the sake of its own continued survival. This model also makes sense in terms of large the architectural spaces and enclosures present in Europe from the start of the 5th and 4th millennia BC. It remains difficult to define accurately the nature of 'war' in the Neolithic. In order to do so we would need a better knowledge of details that physical archaeology on its own does not really permit. A plausible case could be made on the basis of 'traditional' societies which exist (or existed) in other parts of the world and are similar to early European agricultural periods. We would then need to see war as a way of integrating violence (and combat) into society (with models that no doubt vary over time), without having to deny the multiple use of objects used in fighting, in organisations which Europeans have called 'tribal' or 'chiefdoms'.

The Bronze Age no doubt evolved towards different ways of being, and the notion of state should certainly not be precluded, this being just, as Maurice Godelier reminds us, a change of scale in a system where the *"same functions (religious, military and so on) are concentrated in the hand of a fraction of society"*.[243] Besides, there is nothing anodyne about the definition of a state, as we shall see. Now, in the light of manufactured objects, and the expertise needed to make them, there can be no doubt. War is a phenomenon in the Metal Ages which the new weapon inaugurated and embodied. A symbolic frontier had been crossed.

Declaring War in the Bronze Age

The Bronze Age declared, by means of the sword, the advent of war.[244] 'War' understood as behaviour which was isolated to the extent that it was a specific area of activity but also integrated, with society dedicating to it 'extraordinary' resources in the original sense of the word. War as 'total social fact'.[245]

Technological studies demonstrate the enormous investment in weapons manufacture. In the name of war, society mobilised a great swathe of itself which in turn comprised men, goods, economic organisation, social status and so on. This kind of war makes its presence felt increasingly over the course of the millennium. Somewhere around 1200 BC, the development of bronze defensive armour came to enshrine the existence of a specific kind of war. The greatest development was the increased number of metal items in the warrior's equipment, which grew finer and more ostentatious. Now perhaps, the social dimension of being a warrior had become as important as his role as a combatant.

Combat is effective if weapons are, and those who wield them do so skilfully, doing the very best they can to wound and kill. Weapons are effective if they are designed in a considered manner and adapted to suit the type of combat for which they are to be used, or even to go further still in terms of their of 'performance'. In a word, though there can be spontaneity in the context of man-to-man confrontation in a street brawl, during combat in the context of war there can be no such thing. Even though the chance nature of combat makes the outcome just as uncertain. The study of weapons tells us nothing about the frequency of combat, nor reasons for it. Nor even the idea of peace. But there is no way round it: war was a driving force in technical innovation and copper alloy metallurgy made possible the invention of the first weapons used exclusively for war. This process, in the form of arms races, has never since ceased: the greatest battles seem to have been won not only because strategists and tacticians got things right, but because the most fearfully high-performance technology had been deployed.

The European Bronze Age marked the start of a new type of war. And of a new type of warrior. Technology and society combine to create the 'swordsman'. There is no single word for this in French (other than '*épéiste*' in the realm of fencing), whilst archers, spearmen, and later the fusilier and even the hoplite (with reference to the shield) are all designated by means of the weapon they use in combat. The absence of such terminology for one type of warrior could be seen as reinforcing the idea that the sword had – and still has – a specific status, that it is an integral part of the individual masculinity of its bearer, his double. He becomes a tangible reality, though we cannot judge his precise social status any more than that of the metalworker (who also played a front-line role) in the general organisation of things. On the battlefield, at the heart of the action, the swordsman confronted his adversary individually. The fighter was a man, and we see here a shift in values, for in combat the individual male becomes more important than the group. This category of warrior must have involved small numbers when the sword first came into being. As the centuries went on and populations grew, their numbers must have grown too. It is possible that from the very start there were various kinds of warriors: swordsmen and spearmen. Or perhaps this subdivision of roles and modes of combat at the end of the 2nd millennium arose alongside the specialisation in types of equipment, in particular metal defensive armoury. The warrior's gear required considerable investment (means, time, skills). It necessarily had a cost in the context of a hierarchised society in which everyone had a role assigned to them which was neither ambiguous nor interchangeable.[246] It seems inconceivable that poorer members of a society might have been fighters in this kind of war, even in an army comprising several categories of fighters all grouped according to the nature of their weapons. The numbers must have remained limited, even if today we can count thousands of such objects. The Bronze Age sword covers at least eight centuries of history… In terms of the total number of swords found, this does not add up to a vast number of fighters per generation. The latest studies give estimates for the north of Europe where finds have been numerous: in Denmark there would have been about 2000 warriors per generation in a population of approximately 300,000 in about 1100 BC, that is a 0.6% of the total, or 2% if one only counts adults.[247] Globally however, there must have been a larger number of combatants if we include all the various categories. By the end of the Bronze Age, at least in some areas of Europe, we probably need also to take into account horses and horsemen alongside foot soldiers. The general movement is one of a growth in numbers against a backdrop of increasing specialisation.

The Revolution in Fighting in 1700 BC

As far as fighting is concerned, the sword represents a radical change in equipment that took place between 1700 and 1600 BC.[248] The morphology of the weapon committed the warrior to a form of confrontation, a face-to-face combat between enemies, that the arrows of previous periods made it possible to avoid. Western swords are long. They are wielded in person-to-person confrontation by 'swordsmen'.[249] The pattern is different from combat between organised groups, the final form of which came into being in the fighting techniques of the classic Greek hoplite.[250] The European Bronze Age encouraged one-on-one fighting, even when groups of individuals were involved. Over distances of thousands of kilometres, in different chronologies and in different societies, analogies can be seen with the Mycenaean world where there is also combat in the form of duels.[251] By way of contrast, in other Mediterranean regions, such as Mesopotamia, the swordsman is not a privileged combatant.[252] In the tip of Eurasia, a particular type and model of combat was invented. Warriors approached one another individually, at least some of them, those whom one might refer to as 'sword-bearers'. These are seen in painted representations of the time. In these fights, the role of hafted axes is ambiguous. The representation on Scandinavian carvings of combatants armed with metal axes (rounded and very broad slicing weapons), and the sword hanging at their side, shows that both these weapons could have been used under certain circumstances. The most ancient examples of swords are shorter than those of the Late Bronze Age. The weapon could be held in one hand, its action reinforced by using two hands at the height of action. The dimensions of the hilt made this possible. The length of the blade meant that it could be used in a stabbing action (using the point to pierce the opponent) as well as cutting (using the blade-edge to slice and cut).

The growing importance of hammered sheet metal is part and parcel of the new technical developments, growing sophistication of *chaînes opératoires*, greater specialisation and improved workshop skills, and an increased amount of time dedicated to weapon manufacture. Changes in the warrior's equipment might well be a sign of change on the battlefield. Breastplate and helmet offered extra protection to the body. They weighed the combatant down, foot soldiers in particular, and somewhat hindered movement, even though European Bronze Age items were not as cumbersome as those of the hoplite. They could still have been used in a fast and highly mobile form of combat. At the same time, sword blades grew in length. This change in shape over the course of the centuries might suggest slashing rather than stabbing was the favoured action for combat. Besides, the longer the sword, the more advantageous speed and height would apparently also be. Such a development in the shape of weapons would then beg the question about fighting on horseback, the presence of horsemen and not just foot soldiers – even charioteers.

Human connection with the horse is very ancient in Europe, going back to the Palaeolithic, growing ever stronger over the millennia. The animal is depicted on the walls of the caves of Chauvet almost 40,000 years ago and at Lascaux about 20,000 years ago. The horse was domesticated in the Neolithic, then harnessed and mounted in the Bronze Age, as can be shown by bone and metal horse-bits from this period. The wheel had existed from the Neolithic and carts enabled men and goods to criss-cross Europe's exchange routes from at least the 4th millennium BC. It is not possible to fight a battle on a heavy cart, but a fast two-wheeled chariot could be a strategic advantage in some kinds of fighting. Copper alloy metalcraft made it possible to hollow out the wheel, making it lighter and more resistant. Besides, so long as the wheel was entirely wooden and the cart too heavy, only oxen had the power to pull it. The lighter metal wheel, invented in the Bronze Age, made it possible to harness horses to chariots. The war chariot was first adopted in ancient Egypt or the Near East. It could be used in the context of group fighting with a privileged place accorded to archers. In Scandinavia, depictions of two-wheeled chariots with a man at the back first appear in the 16th century BC.[253] In the 14th century, in the tomb of Kivik (Sweden), the chariot depicted on one of the orthostats (a decorated slab connected to cave walls) has two wheels and is drawn by a horse. A man, sword at his side, holds the reins. The metal Trundholm sun chariot (Denmark) has six wheels and is drawn by a horse, with no human presence to guide it. In Spain, on stelae from the Late Bronze Age, two-wheeled chariots are regularly depicted alongside men and their weapons.[254] In France, in Coulon (Deux-Sèvres), a wheel made from copper alloy (1000-900 BC) manufactured by the lost wax technique was part of a religious hoard typical of this period. It was buried intact and not broken, as was often the case for the most prestigious weapons then. From the same period, other metal hoards like the one at Vaudrevanges in the Sarre (9th to 8th centuries), included horse-bits, pieces of harnessing (including a *tintinnabulum* hung round a horse's neck), of chariot, ornamentation, and arms. The bronze sword found there had been broken. There are many more examples. They highlight the fact that the horse, and the chariot to a lesser extent, must have been an integral part of the life of a Bronze Age warrior. There is still much debate about this. The mode of combat for a swordsman would have favoured a face-to-face approach, stressing individualism. He might have been a foot soldier or a horseman. The presence of chariots cannot be excluded, but the evidence is still too lean for us to be able to define clearly their precise role in fighting. Were they used to transport various warriors, to get them to where combat was taking place, or to display their status on various occasions? Or were they really used on the battlefield? At present, it is hard to tell. The presence of the horse, the chariot, and their links with weapons and war are proven facts. For us to know how each was positioned and deployed, more data and work would be needed with regard to horses: there are relatively few studies of Bronze Age horses, far fewer than on horses in the Iron Age.[255]

The growing presence of horses in the second half of the 2nd millennium BC, parallel to the development of defensive weaponry, allows us to glimpse a second revolution in fighting, the first having been the advent of the sword. Sources in the form of archaeological objects, though lacunary, suggest that the fighting horseman arrived on the scene at the end of the Bronze Age, no doubt alongside the establishment of various categories of combatant with a specialisation in different types of combat according to role. Let us look again at the data. The objects are, literally, inanimate and immobile, wherever they are discovered. They are groups, lists. In Scandinavia, we see them depicted in action, but in a way that would be impossible if wielded as the scenes suggest. All that equipment could never be deployed by a single man: you would need at least four active hands (right or left depending on the individual) and two other supporting hands in order to carry out complementary actions (drawing the bow or seizing the sword in two hands and so on) to operate a shield, a sword, an axe, a spear, a quiver of arrows and a bow all at the same time. Everything – too much – is depicted in detail on these rock faces (archaeology can attest to all the component parts), but they are put together in a way that leaves room for only two interpretations: these either represent different phases of combat, the weapons being used successively by the same individual over various time spans; or each man here embodies a synthesised representation of a warrior, including several categories of warrior seen fighting at the same time, but with different weapons according to the modes of combat specific to each of them.

The only potential Bronze Age battlefield found so far, that of Tollense, in north Germany, has not yet yielded technological details regarding how the battle might have been fought or how weapons might have been divided between warriors.[256] The study has not yet been completed and we will have more results in the future. Human remains have been found over an area of several square kilometres in conjunction with spearpoints and arrows. The latest discoveries include swords and horses too, but in smaller numbers. There seems to be no evidence of chariots. Studies of the finds do not currently make it possible to identify different sectors corresponding to different modes of combat. What can we deduce?

There are two categories of weapons, and therefore probably of combatants. On the one hand there are the swordsmen, most of whose weapons have been found close to those who bore them. If there were metal helmets and breastplates (the development of which coincides approximately with the start of the battle, about 1200 BC), this armour does not seem to have remained on site. On the other hand, there were the archers and spearmen, who used weapons that were not essential to their individual identity: the value of their equipment was not high enough to justify collecting them when they had dispersed. From Tollense we can see two ways in which weapons might have been used on the same battlefield, but it is impossible to say how the various kinds of warrior were positioned during the course of the action. The role of horses is also unclear as yet. The obvious move would be to place this important and still rare animal alongside the most eminent and wealthiest of the combatants, since there was a real cost in keeping them. The hierarchy of weapons coincides with the status of those present at the scene of the battle and their respective weaponry. These categories reflect the position of individuals in society, not just in combat.

Multifaceted War in the Iron Age

Iron Age war has many contrasting faces. Again, the sword was the driving force of technological innovation: large iron swords were made at the start of the period, produced by processes quite different from those used to make copper alloy swords. The raw material was more widely available and more evenly spread throughout Europe. A new network of exchange and production came into being. Ironsmiths were soon found alongside bronzesmiths, in different places and with different skills, the former still working hot metal whilst the latter hammered metals when they were cold.[257] Such skills grew richer and more diversified. The means of metal supply became more complex. The need for copper and tin remained strong, soon also involving the Mediterranean world, likewise greedy for metal weapons.

No new weapons came into being and modes of combat do not seem to have been profoundly upset in any way. Such changes had already taken place in the Bronze Age. The sword still played a key role. The long blades suggest that it was primarily a slashing weapon. The disappearance of breastplates can be explained by the need for the warrior to be highly mobile, and cost must have played a role too given the number of hours work needed for the manufacture of each of them. The metal helmet, on the other hand, continued to be used in a more standardised form, now equipping another category of warrior, those who fought with spears and arrows and who can already be glimpsed at Tollense.

The wagon and the mounted horse play an increasingly important role and are found alongside armed men in their final resting places. Some members of the 'aristocracy' are indeed buried alongside whole or dismantled wagons. Such wagons had four wheels at first, then two. Between the end of the 6th and the start of the 5th centuries BC, men and then also women, were given extraordinary tombs found in the context of the Hallstatt Culture (from the eponymous site of Hallstatt, Austria), as in Hochdorf, Vix (Côte d'Or, France), Lavau (Aube, France), and so on.[258] Such social recognition went beyond war. None of the women were laid to rest anywhere near weaponry.

During the 7th century BC there was a change in funerary practices. The grand, rich graves typical of the end of the Eary Iron Age contained weapons (those of men) but such items were no longer the most numerous. Metal dishes, drinking vessels and ornaments began to adorn the last resting places of the dead (men or women) much more strikingly than weaponry. Should we see in this a reduction in conflict during a period of intense exchange between different regions of Europe and the Mediterranean? This is possible, even if it seems rather unlikely that human conflict should have ceased entirely. There are changes in societies' priorities and in the values that support and structure them: at the same time there is less physical evidence of conflict. It is difficult to evaluate war that does not display itself as such. This situation does not last!

During the Middle and Late Iron Age (from 475 BC) archaeological finds start again to give us strong evidence of warfare: objects, places, images and human remains. Narratives we have from antique authors at the very end of the period echo this. The data is exhaustive. The horse occupies a privileged place, and this role continues into following centuries. Some practices are nevertheless astonishing. At Gondole in the Puy-de-Dôme (France), eight young horsemen were buried together in about 50 BC, carefully laid on their right-hand sides, each with a hand on the shoulder of his neighbour, all looking in the same direction towards the east, horses as well as men. The skeletons do not bear marks that would suggest violent death during combat. These young men have therefore been interpreted as horsemen who fell in battle or as sacrifices made following their leader's defeat…[259] At the end of the La Tène period, the warriors' weaponry is complete, again benefitting from new material and from technical innovation. There is even a new type of body armour, chain mail, made patiently by a blacksmith, one iron ring after another. Is this growth in the number of weapons a sign of an increase in warfare? It is difficult to give an unequivocal answer. It is clear that war seems to have a very strong and widespread presence in the second half of the 2nd millennium, from one end to the other of the Mediterranean basin and across the greater part of Europe. Again, antique texts inform us that societies depended on its warriors, embodied as citizens. On the 'barbarian' side there was no equivalent of the city state such as the literary sources describe, but they had their own forms of social and political organisation that institutionalised the warrior. Their number increased noticeably, and their status grew increasingly elevated. The notion of the swordsman alongside the archer and spearman is probably inadequate to describe armies at the end of the Iron Age.[260] There were increasing numbers of weapons. Some of them became standardised, almost serially produced. The individual, isolated and dominant swordsman disappeared. Troops consisted of foot soldiers, and cavalry, with leaders and internal subdivisions of various kinds. Armies now combined individualised units and fighters organised in large groups. The ironsmith joined the bronzesmith not only in semi-industrial manufacture, but also the creation of specialised and exceptional items.

Violence upon violence

The archaeological proof is unequivocal: human remains linked to brutal deaths and objects used for killing are characterised by marks of additional violence. These all bear witness to such redoubled violence, destruction or abandonment (the latter a sweeter, symbolic death, perhaps, but very real in the human world). Bones show marks from blows inflicted during fits of frenzied destruction, body parts are cut up, reassembled in different ways (like the extra arms in the Neolithic pit in Achenheim). Skulls are sometimes inserted into buildings (as in Roquepertuse in central Gaul in the 4th century BC[261]) or buried away from bodies. Bronze, then later iron swords, are bent, twisted, broken, and carefully arranged in hoards. Bronze helmets and breastplates are gathered to be deliberately buried. Swords and helmets are thrown into water and bogs. Collections of broken weapons are gathered with ingots, parts of some objects are forced into parts of others, and then all this is arranged deliberately for burial. Crazy 'primitive' folk!

But these actions cannot all be anarchic, incoherent or the result of chance. There is a kind of logic to them. The difficulty is to find out what kind of logic, bearing in mind variations in such practices, over time and from one society to another. Our task is to conceive of them as part of a coherent phenomenon whilst trying to isolate specific acts and see how they can be linked to violence in general and war in particular.

Natural, powerful elements play a role in all societies and particularly those which have a strong link with their environment: agricultural or maritime. The sky, the stars, water, fire and earth are all at the same time fundamental references in the unfurling of everyday life, in calendars (continuous or cyclic) and more broadly in the domain that one might refer to as 'religious', the world of belief and spirituality, a world which is at once irrational ('believing' is accepting without 'proof'), yet often rooted in realities that are rational and tangible in themselves, even if they are not always understood as such. It is possible to observe the movement of the heavens or the cycles of the seasons without understanding the rotation of the earth or the way it tilts on its axis. And one's own observations can easily be seen as resulting from the intervention of divine powers.

The history of humans in society is that of their relationship to otherness, their relationships with one another, their environment (their fellows and the heavens that have power over them), and their organisations (which codify such relationships). Such a vast system involves beliefs which forge links between humans and a world that surpasses them: religion, as an organising principle, transforms such links into rules at the heart of society. These relationships can be very varied and result in practices of many kinds, rituals that seem 'strange' because the deeper meaning escapes the observer, even in very well-known religions, like the Christian religion in which one eats the body and drinks the blood of Christ – metaphorical cannibalism – during the Eucharist…[262] These acts always have a logic, sometimes complex, for those participating in them. Natural elements are never far away, and they are sometimes even indispensable for the completion of the ritual. The water of baptism cleanses and therefore purifies. The link is relatively easy to establish in such actions, and might be simple in itself, relating to something common to all humans. It cannot be denied that water cleanses. The link between cause and effect is direct. What can change from one religious belief to another is the symbolic and spiritual scope of factual phenomena. In short, the meaning attributed to it beyond what can be seen and translated into action.

Farewell to Arms

Let us get back to our archaeological data. At the same time as weapons specifically made for combat came into being, through the development of copper alloy working, metal objects also began to be buried in hoards. Weapons form the majority of such objects in hoards, but there are others too. So, we have the manufacture of new objects in a material that could be recycled, but at the same time such items were deliberately abandoned, often after being disfigured. This seems, to say the least, strange to the modern Western observer.

Let us try to untangle the complex skein of threads of a phenomenon that is longstanding and has its own historiography. The deliberate burial of objects and materials in hoards (ochre was amongst the very first) is a very ancient activity. It goes back to the earliest Palaeolithic graves and formed a part of funerary rituals. Thereafter, it never ceased. Grave goods grew more diverse as raw materials also became more varied. For archaeologists, these funerary hoards represent an essential source of data. The first role of such actions was to exclude the buried objects from any functional use in the world of the living, though physically they were still in a good state of repair. They were being consecrated. Secondly, a gift – or present – was being offered to the dead by means of such actions. The motivation for this could vary, from attempts to relieve the pain of losing loved ones, to fear of what the dead might do if they were not given due gifts, including contributions of appropriate items to accompany the dead to wherever they were going. One might think of many other reasons and variations. Thirdly, by means of such actions, another world was being addressed, one that was beyond the human world and involved various powers, 'the gods' in the broadest sense. It is hard to know on what level Palaeolithic and proto-historical people were acting, since thought leaves the least archaeological traces.

Two comments, nevertheless. Acting in this way, the living definitely deprived themselves of goods that could have been useful to them. The second observation explains the first: people acted in such a way because the burial deposit was more important than keeping objects for their own use. The motivation went over and above the material and symbolic value of what was being buried.

Arranging goods in the context of funerary rites is an activity common to a number of societies, past and present. Such actions have never seemed incomprehensible or strange to archaeologists even though certain details regarding the nature of burials or the way they were conducted might sometimes raise questions. The first metal objects found in graves go back to the 5th millennium; they are made of copper and gold, constituting presents of considerable economic value at a time when metal was very rare. Why should they have been abandoned when they could, technically, have been recycled? But there are few examples of this until the beginning of the 2nd millennium BC. Then, during the course of the Bronze Age, such behaviour grew ever more complex.

Various kinds of copper alloys were developed. These alloys, thanks to the metalworker's skills, were used not least in the manufacture of weapons of war. The societies in which the bronzesmiths worked, and in which warriors wielded weapons, organised production and provided a structure for war. The number of copper alloy items, according to archaeological finds, grew over time. As soon as weapons of war began to be manufactured, though people continued to have such objects placed in tombs, some items were also buried or thrown into water – a new phenomenon. In this, there is a double logic which runs in parallel or in succession: what counted for burials also had a place in religious practices, at the heart of which the forces of nature, particularly water and earth, came into play.[263]

The more such hoards are discovered – there are now thousands of them throughout Europe – the harder it is to interpret them. This is partly because of their nature: intact or fragmented objects collected together – sometimes in ceramic containers or in organic matter – or in isolated groups unrelated to burials. This is the key. A man buried with his sword makes sense. Even if we may not understand everything about the situation, we can say we are in the presence of a warrior's grave. A sword dredged up from the Seine however is less clear: an accidental loss? Death in combat? A weapon taken by the enemy? The weapon of a victor paying homage to his gods? The possible scenarios are endless because the link between the weapon and its owner has not been plainly established. The logic of a perfectly functional sword ending up in a river is hard to explain rationally at all. So, the action of placing it there seems to lose its meaning.

The case of the undamaged sword submerged underwater is nevertheless (almost) the most straightforward. Even though there can be no certainty, hypotheses have been advanced since the 19th century.[264] An offering to the gods (the sword of the victor or of the vanquished) is the most frequent. Since its invention, the sword, in various forms, has always been part of a warrior's equipment. One can see in it the double of the combatant, the warrior, his soul. It is a real and symbolic weapon, and there is no lack of real and symbolic swords in medieval and more recent literature. Everyone knows about Excalibur, King Arthur's sword. It is at the heart of two legends: in one, it is imprisoned in a rock and can only be set free by King Arthur; in the other it is a present from the Lady of the Lake who promises to protect it. When the King is dying, and the sword is returned to the lake, a hand reaches out of the water to take it. The emblematic weapon here is a gift to the waters, which is taken back by a superior force. Of course, if we extrapolate too much from this, we can get ourselves lost and force the data to tell us more than it possibly can. It is nevertheless interesting here to see the analogies between this and the treatment of swords in very distant times. The role of water is extremely important. Very many weapon hoards are associated with water, fords and bogs. The suggestion of an act linked to a world which reaches beyond the ordinary world of man cannot be excluded. Europe could have developed its own model of this without other societies ordinarily observed by ethnologists being in any way analogous – fairies, gods, superior forces of a different nature.[265] We also need to consider the objects concerned, swords first of all, and defensive armour too for the most recent phases of the Late Bronze Age. Weapons whose power and ability to resist – even if they are not invincible like Excalibur – are nevertheless essential in combat.

In a grave or in a hoard a sword can have no life as a weapon in the human world. It dies a symbolic death. It accompanies the person buried or meets another fate. From a technological point of view, the submersion of a metal object is also a form of destruction, of killing, which can be seen against the backdrop of its coming into being through fire. There is no archaeological proof of this possible symbolic juxtaposition of two opposite elements.

Nevertheless, it makes sense in terms of practices relating to the disposal of weaponry in water during the European Bronze Age and the role that might have been attributed to natural powers. One fact remains: the importance of fire in the metallurgist's workshop. For anyone who has experienced this, and for the metalworker, fire is the heart of the place, where the success or otherwise of the manufacture is played out, where there are intense smells, colours, and an air of solemnity. At strategic moments of casting, everyone falls silent, and the stillness is broken only by the crackling of the metal as it melts. Time stands still in the workshop, taking on an almost magical, sacred quality, even for the most convinced disbeliever. Without allowing ourselves to drift off into wild imaginings, we might reasonably maintain that such places, like the objects produced during the Bronze Age, had an extraordinary quality which opened a path to possible beliefs and rituals. If it was important to get rid of an object, appropriate ways to do so had to be found. Submersion in water was one. The fire is definitively extinguished. Recycling the metal would be to reactivate the cycle of creation by relighting the furnace flame.

One might dare take a further step in a technological interpretation of earth-buried hoards. Let us go back to the example of Excalibur. One of the legends, no doubt the most popular, is that of the rock. The sword comes out of it and returns to it by the hand of Arthur who is its double. The advent of the sword, its link with original matter is even more direct here if we bear in mind that the metal comes from ore found primarily in the form of rocks before being transformed into a material that can be worked by the bronzesmith. Planting the sword in the rock is symbolic: causing it to return to its place of birth, indeed the place before its birth, and therefore destroying the object in the form of its present function. Again, there is nothing of this in archaeological data, certainly nothing to suggest that Bronze Age people had any ability to plant swords in rocks! On the other hand, close to the rock, below the world of plants and living things, there is the earth, a place where metal hoards are found in large numbers.

Over the course of time, these groups of objects in their various and complex forms evolve. There is something cyclic about the state in which they are abandoned. Though left intact at the start of the Bronze Age, by the end they are usually abandoned after having been broken into many pieces, though this varies from one category of object to another. The lack of consistency is hard to interpret. Water and earth, intact and broken objects, large hoards and isolated items... with such a mishmash, how can one hope to find any coherent pattern at all, other than one that is perhaps *sui generis*?

Metal Hoards

Consequently, metal hoards have caused the spilling of much ink from scholars' pens for over 150 years, and there is no reason to think this might soon stop. There are those who doubt that there is any logic at all to be found in these hoards or isolated objects, at least as far as the majority of them are concerned. Such is the thinking of the most rational minds, the most inclined to be suspicious of over-interpretations. They are no doubt right in a way, at least in their desire to exercise due care. On the other hand, there are so many objects like this, found in so many places, that it is hard to believe that they were all just the results of fortuitous loss (and discovery). There are different forms of logic, and one has to take the risk of trying to find them. Arthur Conan Doyle has his hero say: *"When you have eliminated the impossible, whatever remains, improbable though it might be, must necessarily be the truth.*"[266] This is a saying one would rather like to see applied to the study of metal hoards!

Ever since the 19th century, though unbroken buried weapons have sometimes been poorly interpreted (like the helmets at Bernières-d'Ailly, France), hoards were often explained in terms of votive offerings. This interpretation was intellectually acceptable. Ancient populations had their beliefs and gods: they sacrificed to them, like other peoples during antiquity.[267] Places where hoards were found were not necessarily as clearly defined as specially constructed sanctuaries, but since these peoples' connection to nature was greater, it made some kind of sense. On the other hand, broken items in hoards, fragments (and even ingots) caused problems. If it was broken it must have been scrap – such was the binary logic. It would have been no use in its present state. The logic was economic, as one might expect from Europe then. This is how the notion of 'founders hoards' came into being: a bric-a-brac of random pieces which could only have been there for one reason, to be returned to the bronzeworker's crucible. Such groups of objects consist sometimes only of weapons, but not always. Since the 1990s, re-evaluation work has gone on regarding hoards, and a certain logic has been seen in the way these groups of objects are constituted.[268] Again, the sword has an important place. Objects placed in hoards were first deliberately broken, sometimes in several places, or bent in the case of sheet metal or iron, often in a way that suggests that the actions were performed in a kind of frenzy. Though some hoard burials might have been accidental, it seems most probable that these assembled objects were linked to certain *sui generis* rituals which have no equivalent in other points of history or other societies. Given the marks they bear, some deliberate processes of destruction and disfigurement must have been involved. What meaning can we give to such actions? A symbolic death of the objects and those to whom they belonged? In each case they fall into the category of 'reinforced or redoubled violence'. This seems also to apply for human remains which were likewise mutilated, torn to pieces, cut up, and put back together again in pits.

These are the first signs of tangible violence associated with a form of deliberate ownership being taken of that violence by means of actions performed *a posteriori*, mostly upon bodies of the newly dead. The brutal end of these people's lives is real and then re-multiplied. As soon as people become attached to possessions it makes sense to include goods in such processes of destruction, not only of individuals, but their possessions too. It is a way of killing them a second time.

It is interesting that this violent relationship towards others is associated very early on with rituals of disfigurement, firstly bodies, then goods too. The phenomenon intensifies and grows more complex following the pattern of development of societies themselves. Besides, this cannot be envisaged other than within some kind of framework for structuring such practices adopted by the societies themselves. Here, we find ourselves in the domain of religious acts in the broadest sense, the societal aspect of religion. As we have discussed, the very foundation of a society is its ordering of relationships between people, their place and their deaths. The way they took ownership of violence therefore tells us something about people in such societies, their relationships to others and more broadly to death and their religions. The Palaeolithic paved the way for this. This does not mean to say that 'war' as such featured in such contexts, but rather that forms of belief existed, and that these led to ritualised practices at least in some cases, and that these involved death and violence. Of course, this does not really settle the question of cannibalism, which could be interpreted either as a religious act or simply as a mode of food consumption.

In such circumstances, environments and their powers, including animal powers, also play a role in the pantheons of gods, as soon as something of their presence can be identified. The link between humans and animals in the Upper Palaeolithic is clear, as cave paintings demonstrate. These are complex relationships, combining violence and fear. Nor are these relationships entirely settled during the Neolithic when animals were increasingly domesticated. Firstly, a large number of species remained beyond human control, even though hunting in part extended this human domination. And then, the animal world was a component part of the broader conceptual framework of the world and the universe, which in turn justified their presence in the realm of religion, with specific attributes linked to violence, then war in some cases. In the Bronze Age, the relationship settled. Animals linked to travel were given a privileged place: birds and horses. They had real roles to play, but also symbolic roles in systems of belief. This double dimension continued into the Iron Age. In the second half of the Iron Age the repertoire grew richer, sometimes fantastical, including the combination of men and animals in the form or of chimeras. The Gundestrup Cauldron from the 1st century BC was not alone in displaying representations of this nature, but it was a remarkable example to the extent that war was very much present in this dream-world where the fantastic and the real rub shoulders[269] – like the horses in the procession panel. Horses had already won their place alongside warriors in the Bronze Age and for some, this continued, in the form of horsemen and their swords, into the Iron Age. At Gondole, the careful burial of men and horses together reinforces this sense of complicity.[270]

Disfigurement, ritual practices related to violence and war, are activities which took root gradually, and were performed at particular times and places. For ancient periods it seems that clues regarding such acts are most visible in the case of dead bodies (mutilation) and objects (breaking and abandoning); sometimes these were assembled in deliberately designated places in the landscape (sanctuaries); but sometimes the process was more discreet (hoards buried with no monument). Though these activities can be related to combat (certainly real enough given the real presence of weapons), this does not necessarily imply the early stages of warfare. Such actions took place either after conflict or between confrontations. In their material aspect, they are a form of construction of the image of war, but not war in all its aspects. Large swathes of these activities and their direct consequences are beyond us. Vestiges are of necessity neither numerous nor obvious. We might look at our own contemporary societies in which war has been very present over the last two centuries. As an archaeologist, what can I see of these conflicts? Some structures are very striking, and some places were so powerfully affected at the start of the 20th century that they still define landscapes, as in Flanders and the north and east of France. But elsewhere, even if excavations reveal places of battle, the discoveries could never show us the extent of combat, particularly in sites further from the action, or where fighting was not so heavy; nor would we necessarily find buildings related to war away from the battlefields, and so on. Of course, there are sites that have been preserved as places of memory, which have become sanctuaries of sorts: Oradour-sur-Glane, Auschwitz, First World War trenches… There are also buildings erected specifically to mark places where wars were fought, like monuments to the dead. These are lists of names, lists of the dead, lists of those who are no more. All these remnants talk to us of war, both directly and indirectly. In ancient societies, constructions are of a different type (just as the wars and the societies were). They involved manipulating corpses and objects to reinforce or redouble violence, as well as other important actions and traces of action which, visibly, tell us something about such peoples' belief systems, their religions, their relationship with death, with violence, with the items themselves and their status, what they embodied. Gathering together objects, human remains, and then disfiguring them relates to a particular kind of ritual: a concentration of violence with respect to beings and objects. It is a demonstrative manifestation of war directed as much towards self as other witnesses. It can be interpreted in various ways: to frighten an enemy, to remind people of the rules, or to ward off something (the vengeance of man or of the gods). Finally, exposing corpses is also a warning about the fragility of life; it can be interpreted as a way of coping with the fear of death in some violent situations, also involving a resolution of relationships with others, either negatively (enemies or traitors) or positively (ancestors). Such disfiguring does not just bear witness to war, to marks of violence. It also bears witness to belief in 'something' that is part of what it is to be a warrior. It is a sacred, religious, and social act, as are all ritualised practices in a society. Archaeological accounts of extremely ancient conflicts can speak only indirectly of war as it happened. Archaeological evidence operates in a timescale quite different from immediate actions, that of what one might call the instrumentalization of activity, of retrospective monuments and various ceremonies. It offers a panorama of incomplete sets of circumstances displaced in time, by means of which the researcher has to reconstruct actions, those who took part in them and their societies.

Warfare is a phenomenon that is clearly manifest in the Bronze Age. Archaeological data makes it possible to demonstrate this because it can offer unambiguous proof. There is evidence. The evidence does not tell us everything, but it does oblige us to consider the fact that 'war', understood as such, existed in Europe from the 2nd millennium BC. Regarding the most ancient periods, the Neolithic and the Palaeolithic, the question becomes more complex because of the ambiguity of object use. This does not preclude the possibility of forms of conflict being part of societies, but it is more difficult for the archaeologist to be certain. On the other hand, the evidence of violence is unambiguous. It can be seen. The sources make the conclusion clear. They either tell us directly, provide evidence or, by contrast, allow doubts and questions to persist. In any case, they cannot be divorced from the contexts within which they come to light and acquire meaning, the societies themselves.

VI

WAR IN ALL ITS STATES

The 1000 BC warrior on the Normandy coast

We have located our bronzesmith in a substantially sized village, with an administrative, structuring role in the context of the local territory and where different spaces are given over to various functions: dwelling, funerary, agricultural areas organised in plots, and communication routes. Archaeology indicates that an advanced and well-organised agricultural world existed in the year 1000 BC which was open to the outside world. What were its limits and how did links with neighbouring societies function? The question of frontiers is crucial but difficult in the case of vanished oral societies. This is one of the reasons for typo-chronologies in investigations. Archaeologists rely on the fact that groups of humans forge their identity through the materials they use for production, which are themselves significant in terms of social practices. A type of pot, a type of sword or helmet is therefore an identity-marker which can be related to individuals and territories. Some objects are more significant than others, for two almost opposite reasons. Very ordinary everyday objects produced locally are specific to human groups on a household level. Domestic pottery vessels would be an example of this. By contrast, there are exceptional objects which define the way such societies are seen beyond the frontiers of the village, and which literally embody individuals. This is the case with weapons and, most of all, the sword. Archaeological typologies are able to divide these into geographical groups that one might call 'families', and then into regional sub-groups. Thus, our Ewart Park type sword is typical of a sub-group at the heart of a larger group referred to as 'Atlantic' which reaches from the Iberian coast to the North Sea.

We are not used to seeing a coherent geographical pattern here. To get a change of perspective, we might turn a map of Europe 90 degrees anti-clockwise – so that north would now be west. We become aware then of the long maritime corridor of which Bronze Age sailors would have made great use. We are now less used to thinking of the sea as a normal way to move from one part of a coast to another, seeing it only as a frontier. Our Normandy helmets fit in with this geography, though they are a little older. Our breastplates are probably rather more continental given where they were discovered, even taking into account the way imports would have circulated. As we have seen, our set of weaponry can help us get a glimpse of human beings in action: the bronzesmith, the warrior and their society.

One thing is certain: for the society to which he belonged it was essential for a warrior to be properly equipped, as essential as warfare would have been for that society, the phenomenon that this man embodied. This means not only that such an individual had a place and played a role, but also that resources were mobilised to create a military way of life. If our village were somewhere near the town of present-day Le Havre, the first need would be to supply raw materials for the manufacture of weaponry. Locally there was neither copper, nor tin, nor lead which are the three metals which have been shown to make up our weapons in various percentages. They had therefore to be fetched from elsewhere, if there were indeed workshops in the village. It seems hard at this period, in the context of an ever-growing production of such objects that were both strategic and linked to identity, to imagine a scenario in which such objects were exclusively imported in one piece. Metal was trafficked in the form of ingots, even though we cannot preclude the occasional circulation of finished pieces. There is evidence of this from the beginning of the Bronze Age just as there is evidence of boats, roads, wagons, and carts. Tin could have come from England, and copper from central France or the Alps, as well as lead.

Our bronzesmith would therefore have received the materials to which he devoted his talents, skills, and work hours directly into his workshop. It is impossible to find direct proof that metalcraft was his sole activity and that, in the context of a highly specialised organisation which divided everyone's tasks (or at least the tasks of some categories of people), his society fed him because of what he produced. But this is something that can be deduced. The objects manufactured were so specific, and required so much individual skill, that it seems difficult to conceive of our metalworker spending one day in the field and another in the workshop. He needed time and a sense of continuity in his work, which would scarcely be possible if it were an occasional or marginal activity. The number of workshops in a place must have depended on the amount of production. It is probable that they were grouped in certain habitats of a considerable size, perhaps in places where other kinds of activities were pursued. But who would have made decisions about the supply and movement of the raw materials and the distribution of the products? Again, we have no lists of accounts, travellers'tales, sales prices with names, job descriptions or titles. Arms manufacture is an encounter between maker and user. Our youthful warrior and his father visiting the workshop every now and then would not have seemed too out of place.

Someone must have orchestrated all these processes, either from within or at the top of the social organisation, or alongside those in it: groups of individuals who controlled exchanges and probably society as a whole. The problem is to find a name to designate such a way of life, which can be deduced rather than proven and which has never yet been described with words using a precise set of vocabulary.

The warrior of the year 1000 BC would have been so costly, such a logistical investment, that it is impossible to see him anywhere other than in a hierarchical and specialised society with war as a structuring and legitimising activity for those in control. If these populations occupied identifiable territories with defined borders, we need take only one more step to see these societies as hierarchised and state-like (whatever its precise nature might have been), with populations subject to a mode of government entrusted to the hands of a small number of people. But then, over what kind of territory or realm did those with power reign? What role was given to women who had no part in the things of war? Who was our young warrior? Were armed men, as in other societal models, those who commanded and controlled? Did men of war hold the reins of power? It is possible. The physical data suggests we should see military activity in the context of a social model of this nature, with war literally at its heart, even if it is difficult to go into any further detail.

It is certain in any case that these Bronze Age societies created, albeit in diverse ways, a societal model which is neither that of civilisations of the written word and cities (taken as a whole), nor that of populations in a world where metalcraft had not developed. Weapons reflect and embody this social model. In order to see them, we have to look at them for what they were.

Let us then retain this hypothesis of a third way in the Europe of our 1000 BC warrior and the world he lived in. There is still one component missing from his story: why, when he lived on the coast 3000 years ago, near the mouth of the Seine, would anyone have wanted to go to war? Against whom? And in what way? Studies of the environment, houses, types of agriculture, the growth in the varieties and quantities of produce, all rather give the impression that the world of the Bronze Age was an age of farmers peasants. And the world of the peasant is scarcely one of warmongering. The peasant needs time, stability, and energy to dedicate to his fields and animals. So, there is a stark contrast between weapon finds which provide evidence of war as such and the even greater sum of evidence on the ground suggesting rather that these were peaceful times. Probably we shall have to see the second as a result of the first, in terms of warfare that has been successful or that has acted as a successful deterrent. Fear generated by the possession of arms may sometimes avoid having to use them. This apparently paradoxical situation can be vouched for over and again during the course of human history. If the European Bronze Age is indeed the time when 'real' war was invented, it is logical that there must have been a role for deterrence. Our warrior from the year 1000 BC seems in fact to have lived in quite a prosperous world, characterised by regular exchanges between different regions, by sea in particular. Weapons had never been so numerous or metal hoards so abundant. There was a time in the 1970s when it was thought that these burials of weapons were linked to a period of insecurity. But nowadays it is tempting rather to interpret this abundance of weapons as a sign of wealth, linked to times of peace, or at least partial peace, rather than continuous warfare. This does not mean to say that our warrior would have had no reason to take up arms. It is sometimes necessary, in order to preserve balance, or because of the pressures of demographic and economic growth, to resort to conflict, offensive or defensive. Nor does this mean that the whole of the Bronze Age was a long period of peace… It was probably all a question of cycles and rhythms. This is perhaps best understood from the perspective of what happened 25 generations earlier, the moment when the warrior and the sword which became his inheritance both came into being. Since then, over the 37 centuries that have passed in Europe, this emblematic figure has never disappeared, whatever political and social models have evolved, bringing and legitimising warfare in the name of the common good.

At this point of the enquiry a little more order is called for. I have no doubt given the impression – deliberately – of leading the reader up the garden path. A few human remains, lots of objects, technology (sometimes pointy) at the heart of the topic, historiography, ethnology, histories of primitive people and a prehistory that existed without existing... 'And now what?' This is what I would like to ask those who are asking themselves that question, but who are not holding the pen to write it. Now we need to review the evidence to try to make sense of it. Like pieces of a vast jigsaw no longer in their box but tipped out over a large wooden table and waiting to be fitted together to form a picture. With the difference that a (real) puzzle is made from a real picture, which has been deconstructed in such a way that only one solution is possible (no two pieces being interchangeable), whilst here the picture will be a suggestion, a thesis that does not preclude others.

Let us take these pieces, clues, finds. Archaeological data are rich in objects and remnants that inform us increasingly about forms of violence in very early times. The manifestations of such violence are not uniform. Objects change as do the societies in which they are produced.

The data indicates a growing phenomenon, and then a sudden break between 1700 BC and 1600 BC, in a development linked to metalcraft technology and the production of specific weapons. However, the notion of the possibility of very ancient warfare has been doubly conditioned epistemologically, leaving scarcely any space for us to talk of 'real' warfare at the heart of such oral societies which are neither 'primitive' nor 'civilised' according to the meanings of these words we have inherited from the 19th century. Studies of European Bronze Age weapons suggest we should look towards the creation of a different kind of model, unlike any that have come down to us. The failure to understand European oral societies results from a failure to see them as a page of history written on the basis of data from under the ground. War was conceived of erroneously because it had been looked at through lenses that distort and cause blindness. Europeans made mistakes about their own wars, and the men and governments who brought them into being, because they did not make use of available data. This came from a world which is not ours, which for a long while did not even have a place in human chronology. The significant role played by the sudden arrival of metal war-weapons, and the technical and societal implications of this, has not been fully ascertained. To do so, there has been a need to combine detailed technical studies, archaeological data from the periods involved, and to seek out new and specific models to explain what was happening. Let us begin again therefore with individuals and attempt again to see them and warfare in the context of the societies to which they belonged.

The Bronze Age warrior certainly existed. Is he in any way similar to the hero of archaic Greece? This has sometimes been suggested. Is he one of the two antithetical warrior-figures described by Homer in the *Iliad* and the *Odyssey?* Is he Ulysses the strategist deploying ruse and cunning to the extent of having himself tied to the mast of a ship to avoid succumbing to the sirens? Or rather the valiant Achilles whose courage in combat remained unbridled whatever the chance of an ineluctable 'noble' death?[271] Unless he were a combination of the two. In the light of weaponry used, it is not entirely incongruous to draw parallels, even if the societies, centuries apart, are not identical.

At the end of the 1980s, after decades of typo-chronological classification of weapons, researchers considered them to have been 'prestige goods' and their possessors to have been part of an 'elite'.[272] But such a definition is not enough. Weapons do not just show that their possessor was rich, but that he was a legitimate killer acting in the name of the society to which he belonged. He was a component part of this society, mandated by the 'government', a form of power which directed and organised the framework in which he lived and worked. We need then to spend a little time considering these individuals and what they were, as persons and as participants in their society. More broadly, the question of war should lead us to ponder the social and economic roles of each, their respective power, including links between war and gender.

Women: Goddesses or Sinners?

Studying the situation of women and men on the basis of archaeology is not straightforward. Of course, there are indicators and clues relating to one sex or another beyond mere biological identification made on the basis of skeletal remains. Nevertheless, the move from observation to identification is often difficult, generally controversial, and influenced by ethnological models of archaeological data. The process is not without risk.

In the most ancient representations dating from the Palaeolithic, animals were depicted before humans, and women before men. In the Upper Palaeolithic, feminine statuettes represented women as nudes with their sexual features very prominent: buttocks, breasts, and vulvas.[273] This continued into the Neolithic. Much has been written about the reasons for these representations and their meaning. It is worth retaining two principal interpretations linked to the power and therefore the possible role of women in society and thus in relation to war. The first (and most common) interpretation is that they were 'goddesses' or 'Venuses'. This is a symbolic representation linked to feminine forces or powers, associating female fertility with abundance and wealth, not least in the context of agricultural development. Women in their role as birth-givers possess, through the function of procreation, a form of power. The accentuation of sexual characteristics is the physical manifestation of this. Amongst those who defend this thesis, let us cite Marija Gimbutas (1921-1994), whose text adopts a feminist slant,[274] and of course Jacques Cauvin (1930-2001) who associated the Neolithic revolution with a revolution in symbols, attributing to birth-giving woman a new and divine status, associated with fertility needed for agricultural production to succeed.[275] The second hypothesis is very different, practically the opposite of the first: the representation of women's nudity is not a homage to power and fecundity, but instead has to be understood sexually, from the point of view of men who dominate her. This thesis is based on sexuality as illustrated by present-day comparisons and representations of naked women, where buttocks and breasts are no less absent, and which have little enough to do with fertility in the way men look at them... Beyond the image, each of these explanations is rooted in physiology and its consequences: human sexual activity is thought of as less constrained, less interrupted by pauses. Indeed, the human species experienced the disappearance of visible signs of the oestrus (probably at the time of becoming bipeds) and so sexuality was practised outside periods of rut, quite differently from the norm in the animal kingdom. No longer strictly linked to reproduction, sexuality can then be seen in terms of desire and expressed in terms of pleasure. Moreover, the biological evolution of the human body (becoming bipeds, loss of hair) makes certain parts of the body more prominent, which in turn become erogenous zones, suggesting sensual excitement in the practice of sexuality. Seen in this way, women represent a form of risk, of freer sexuality. And therefore a danger to the social order. Such questions of sexuality play a key role in all narratives and religions in societies, in which sexuality is framed and indeed repressed. In general, the role of women is not great, since they are often accused of being at the root of all evil. Women as temptresses and sinners populate many narratives (written by men) regarding original sin. Ulysses' sirens are themselves an incarnation of feminine temptation in maritime form... Confronted with this risk, men, those who have the greater strength, are placed in a position where they need to dominate and therefore control these alleged dangers. The representation of female nudity may therefore be regarded as one of the first manifestations of such masculine domination. This more recent thesis has been defended by archaeologists like Jean-Paul Demoule and anthropologist like Alain Testart.[276] The fact that, of the thousands of societies known and listed (about 10,000[277]), none seem to have been matriarchal in nature, would validate this theory of early masculine domination transposed into iconography.

It is clear that in a broader vision of the history of societies women are not given roles of pre-eminence or decision-making, or even independence. The role of women is often restricted to their ability to procreate, their role being linked to birth-giving and spheres of activity that concern them directly. Women are not absent but consigned principally to guaranteeing offspring and lines of transmission, not least in what one might call a 'biological'[278] sense. The evolution of the uses to which the body is put goes alongside the positioning of everyone in a society. The development of 'sex for pleasure' which goes beyond physiological functionality has a simultaneous effect on the organisation of men (*Homo*) in society. Rules are necessary to avoid chaos. So, everyone has to have a role in this, and to accomplish the tasks allotted to them, both in their social and sexual identity.

Archaeology, by studying the way such roles are depicted, can only reply partially to such questions which are largely non-material, outside the world of writing, by means of which rules are fixed. There is nothing unreasonable in hypotheses suggesting that regularised couples were established and made legitimate by continued but socially controlled sexuality, thereby creating more stable family cells for the sake of reproduction. Such arrangements organise relationships between groups and between men and women. The themes of kinship, of alliances and marriages is a very rich one in ethnology.[279] It is far more complicated – impossible? – for archaeology to deal with. If one accepts that masculine domination was an early phenomenon, we have also to suppose that it was men who determined everyone's place in society and the roles allotted to them. Including participation in war.

The depiction of women is one of the main pieces of evidence on the basis of which hypotheses can be formulated regarding the organisation of societies, and therefore the relationships between its members. This is because the underlying principle of relationships between people in a society is based upon rules which organise the status of various individuals as persons, socially and so on. Power is held by those who determine common norms and take specific decisions about events which punctuate people's lives, including warfare. One thing is certain regarding all the images of women in the Palaeolithic and Neolithic: they were never depicted in a combat situation. They are not represented as participants in violence. What can we deduce from this?

Masculine Domination

The hypothesis that masculine domination is very ancient, dating from the very first social organisation of *Homo sapiens*, is plausible. It is reasonable. Yet this does not mean that these pictures are a demonstrative (and eroticised) manifestation of such masculine domination, any more than the representation of women is a proof of some power as 'goddesses'. Perhaps we should see in these images of women an iconography of the wealth and fertility embodied in female figures, because they give life and therefore embody the future, what is to come. This is fact. It is a physiological fact with which men, being males who have no such opportunities, had to come to terms. It is implied by pictures of women with exaggerated sexual characteristics. A form of recognition, through fear (if we can talk of fear) not of a feminine power, but rather of a divine world which makes sure the course of events centred upon these activities will be benign. It is clear, on the other hand, that the way men and women are seen changes during the course of the Neolithic, and that this was linked to developments in the societies themselves.

Let us move forward in time. Ancient pictures, in chronological order, are of animals, women, men, then composite beings, chimeras and various hybrids. Women, so present at the end of the Palaeolithic and at the beginning of the Neolithic, become far more discreet from the 4th millennium. Very few are depicted during the course of the 3rd millennium, and they disappear almost completely from the iconographic repertoire of the European Bronze Age, in favour of men. One might be tempted, making a rapid and rather feminist judgment, to imagine that we have here an inversion of the sexual theme advanced for the feminine figures: now we would have dominating women contemplating the nudity of men... It is certain that this was not the case. Besides, the men are not naked. They are armed. They bear shields, spears, and swords. Their masculinity is conveyed by their erect penises, a sign of their strength and virility. Such scenes, which are very numerous in Scandinavia, where the sword came into being at a very early stage, are not found throughout the whole of Europe. But they are no less significant in what they tell us of the changes that went on beyond the image.

The advent of the sword is like a signature to the declaration of war as total social fact, to the extent that everyone in the system is assigned a role, a task. Alongside the sword, close combat, and war, logically the warrior also came into being. Was the latter necessarily a man? In absolute terms, a woman can fight just as well as a man. No doubt physical strength needs to be taken into account, but only in some forms of conflict. Besides, there are feeble men and strong women. Of course, there is a myth of fighting women – Amazons. It is true that according to this legend they amputated one of their breasts and thus mutilated their femininity. Beyond the myth, a recent thesis has attempted to demonstrate that Amazons did exist in some regions of Eastern Europe and on the edges of Asia (Scythian lands for the most part) from the 8th century BC.[280] Tombs of horsewomen in particular have been found to contain weapons (essentially arrows, but also some helmets, and even swords), which would tend to demonstrate that they were not excluded from combat.[281] Again, the presence of arrows does not settle the matter because arrows can be used for more than one purpose: hunting is not the preserve of female Scythians. On the other hand, the presence of spears and swords in women's tombs, alongside the fact that their remains show signs of sustained horse-riding and corresponding bone deformation, means that we should not preclude an early presence of women fighting in this particular context. Like the men, they share very rich tombs.[282] At present, this is a far from typical phenomenon, as atypical as the life led by populations on the vast, windswept planes, having nothing to do with what went on further to the west.

In Central and Western Europe, archaeological data and ethnological studies suggest things were quite different. In addition to pictures on cave walls and rock faces, the question of gender and social divisions can be approached archaeologically, not only on the basis of human remains (with sexual identification if possible), but also through grave goods, if there are any, which are associated with the individuals buried. Certain categories of objects are found either primarily or exclusively in the graves of men and/or women. Jewellery is mixed, but not always. Ceramics are largely divided evenly between the sexes. But tools and weapons of war are not mixed at all.

Rich women without weapons

If burials do indeed reflect social phenomena, it cannot be said that women are excluded from rituals reserved for personages of a certain rank, whose status is translated materially into tombs. And yet, of all the thousands of women's tombs found, not one, when anthropological study has been able to identify the sex of the dead person and the nature of the funerary rites, has been found to contain a sword. In this domain, there is no homogeneity in the European Bronze Age, either geographically or chronologically. Whilst the last part of the Neolithic in the West was characterised largely by collective graves poor in grave goods, the emergence of individual burials is characteristic of the end of the 3rd millennium BC, becoming more marked at the start of the 2nd millennium. Particularly lavish, large tumuli (underground architectural graves) are offered to individuals, not least in areas rich in copper and tin ore, and along exchange routes. The tomb of Leubingen (Saxony-Thuringia), dating from the beginnings of the Early Bronze Age (20th-19th centuries BC) has given rise to debates about the respective places of men and women. An old man was buried with metal axes and daggers. A young woman was literally placed on top of him, at a right angle, on his pelvis. The scenario of an old man making sure he has the company of a young woman for eternity has of course been suggested. This cannot be proven from the two bodies. It is nevertheless troubling, and no doubt relevant, to note that there were such exceptional tombs for men at the very time when bronzesmiths were producing the immediate ancestors of the sword. The situation of women in Bronze Age graves was not always so wretched. On the contrary, in the Middle Bronze Age, between the 16th and 14th centuries, some were granted funerary rituals which included rich hoards of objects. Thus, in continental Europe and in Scandinavia, the burials from this period contain metal jewellery of exceptional quality. And yet not a single woman was laid to rest with a weapon. They were rich but they were not warriors.

It seems that same phenomenon – the same roles played by each sex – continued into the Iron Age. Some women have a preeminent place at the end of the 6th century BC.[283] The tomb of the woman buried at Vix (Burgundy) is a very wealthy one: a four-wheeled chariot, a large bronze drinking vessel, imported Greek ceramics, a golden torc, and so on. But no weapons were found alongside this rich 'princess' (or any woman like her). Neither defensive, nor offensive. Not the least trace of a sword, which no doubt embodied this new form, of war and the values associated with it.

If one wished to err on the side of prudence, one might say that this was not true for 100% of graves with swords (and that some were excavated before systematic analysis of sex took place), but rather 100% of known burials. This might mean we are not talking about an absolute truth, but still a significant archaeological fact. Besides, if a counter-example were to be discovered tomorrow, we would need to understand why, because it would be outside the norm, such as it exists. Amongst the human remains discovered in possible sites of war, including Tollense, there are no traces of women according to data analysed so far. If we are to be particularly vigilant regarding all vestiges of the past, we should stress that metal hoards are richer in weapons than any other form of find and that in these there are no human remains and therefore no evidence of any warrior's sex.

During Protohistory, women do not seem to have been totally excluded from the higher spheres of society, indeed power. In any case, nothing in the finds suggests any connection between women and combat. In iconography and statuary, they might be present alongside armed men, but they never bear arms themselves. For thousands of years, at least in Central and Western Europe, women were excluded from participating in combat and in war. One might wish to find or maybe seek a world that was more equal in some respects. But here the opposite is true. Europe in the Bronze Age instigated a warrior with a sword who was male, not female – a masculine figure.

Anthropological narratives and models are nowadays moving in the same direction even if, on certain points, nuances have to be introduced. For a long while it was thought that divisions between tasks and roles were very simple: men went hunting, women went gathering and stayed at home with the children; men fetched provisions for the home and women cooked, turning these provisions into food. But more detailed research, involving less such *a priori* thinking, shows that societies sometimes did adopt less simplistic, binary systems. The divisions between such tasks were in reality more fluid, more subtle, time spent on an activity often being divided up, so women could, for example, beat game but not kill it: or kill it, but then not proceed to cut it up in certain ways, and so on. In any case it is certain that women were not always excluded from hunting in societies where this activity played a key role.[284]

The question, in reality, is just as much about what is prohibited as what is allowed – the former also being part of a society's norms. There are prohibitions for men and prohibitions for women. Sexuality, usually seen as key, is important, but it certainly does not explain everything. The question of menstrual blood, which gives rise to taboos in many societies, has been important, sometimes very much so, in the role assigned to women. And that of power. It seems that something common to all societies – in particular 'traditional' ones – is that women are prohibited from taking up arms. Here we need again to define what we mean by 'arms'. The prohibition no doubt goes beyond the object itself. Those who give life to human beings cannot take it away. Here though we are going beyond prohibition and entering the realm of that which simply cannot be imagined. But from an archaeological point of view, we still have the problem of distinguishing 'weapons' (arrows made for combat) and hunting equipment (hunting arrows). Nothing in the material we have available to us, nothing in data from archaeological finds (not least funerary contexts) regarding European Protohistory, gives us any information about any possible relationship between women and arrows. The data indicates rather an association between arrows and men, on painted cave walls and in burials. The fact that arrows are only found in Middle Neolithic tombs for men makes this link seem stronger. There are no graves that might allow us to see any connection between Neolithic multiple-use weapons and women. Perhaps, looking at this the other way round, we should see here an early prohibition regarding all forms of combat which became more powerful still when war became a social phenomenon.

Transgressing Norms

The question of prohibition leads to that of transgression, by men or women: the former acting in a way that their status does not allow or behaving in a way that society does not permit: the latter, though *a priori* excluded from war, bursting in on the scene.[285] Archaeology has a partial answer.

The symbolism of the sword is powerful. One might think of Excalibur. Amongst 'historic' and famous swords, Brennus' too deserves a mention. We have already glimpsed this bold Gallic chief who dared defeat Rome in 390 BC. Though there is nothing to indicate that he was anything like the man painted by Paul Jamin in the 19th century, with cruel features and ready to resort to the worst deeds of violence with regard to innocent young women, he nevertheless was, (according to Livy's Roman History, book V, chapter 48) the man who spoke the words: "*Vae victis!*" The scene took place at the moment of the surrender of the Romans, who were made to pay for their defeat with a tribute of 1000 pounds of gold, that is more than 300 kilograms of precious metal. When the vanquished Romans complained about the weights being used, Brennus made the ransom heavier still by throwing his sword onto the scales, pronouncing the words that have since become famous: "*Woe to the vanquished!*" We do not know the precise model of sword that Brennus used for this. It was probably made of iron (even if there were still bronze swords in existence then, mostly for shorter models), probably about 80-100 centimetres long and weighing about 1.5-2 kilograms maximum, unless it was an exceptional sword. A derisory difference in weight in the overall scale of things. And an absolute humiliation embodied by the victor's weapon. Few examples are as famous as this.

The symbolism linked to the sword and the dishonour it can embody as well as recognition and glory is illustrated by an example far more recent than the Bronze Age. On the 5th of January 1895, captain Dreyfus' sword was broken publicly during his degradation in the court of honour of the *École Militaire*. To exclude a soldier from military life, you had only to take away his sword. Destroying the sword amounts to destroying the man by means of his double. The event's dramatic intensity is palpable

This breaking of a sword is reminiscent of what happened in the case of some hoards from the Late Bronze Age. The data is a little different (there are other broken objects, sometimes in large numbers) and it is difficult to know if the damage inflicted on swords was, in such cases, to the dishonour or honour of the weapon's bearer.

Though the sword was the weapon *par excellence* (and has been for more than 3500 years), and the physical double of the masculine warrior, the interdictions that accompany it are comprehensive. The question of the transgression of interdictions related to arms-bearing – not least the sword – in the context of various social categories including women, can be traced through the social history of women themselves and the societies to which they belonged. One of the first and most famous transgressions involving weapons in the western world – with the myths and fantasies that went with it – was Joan of Arc's. Officially, for women to have access to weapons and their use in a real and accepted way, they had to be part the world of weaponry and acknowledged as combatants. This happened belatedly and to a limited extent in the 20th century, thanks no doubt to the two World Wars, but only hesitantly and in a way by no means accepted in all societies. The bench of the princely Early Iron Age tomb of Hochdorf reminds us elegantly of this: fighting with swords is a dynamic face-to-face confrontation which is vigorous and dance-like. It is both an act of extreme violence, so long as the objective is the death of the other, and a form of physical challenge, a 'game' which forms part of the rules of honour and of combat.[286] In the original Olympic games, those of Ancient Greece, there was no competition involving the sword. The west introduced fencing into the programme of the Olympic games in 1896. In 1924, women were allowed to participate in the foil event, but it was not until 1996 that they were allowed access to the *épée* event, and 2004 for admission to the individual *sabre* event.

As for the symbolism of the sword, it remains powerful. A French example, just as symbolic of the sword itself, shows a belated form of transgression regarding women and sword-bearing, which was not really a sword as such by the time the institution involved recognised and used it as part of its ceremonies. Created in 1795, in the former building of the *Quatre-Nations*, the *Institut de France* grouped together five academies of wise men, 'immortals', to form the *Académie française*. Every academician who is solemnly admitted into that place during the course of the ceremony at *la Coupole* receives academic dress and chooses a sword. None of them ever draws the sword whilst the *Académie* is sitting! It is a symbol of recognition of the power that these academicians demonstrate in their intellectual combats. A battlefield that can indeed involve risk at times... This costume, and the symbolism it represents, was designed by and for men, at the time of the 'gentleman', as an extension of themselves just as it had been when it came into being some 3500 years earlier. Only ecclesiastics wear the costume without a sword, also for symbolic reasons connected to the sword's function. This tradition was long upheld with the belated entry of women into the *Coupole*. The first to be invited to join (*Académie des sciences*) was Marie Curie (1867-1934) in 1910, though Édouard Branly (1844-1940) pipped her at the post when it came to the voting. It was not until the 1970's that women were elected as members rather than just correspondents: Suzanne Bastid (1906-1995) in 1971, to the *Académie des sciences morales et politiques*, Jaqueline de Romilly (1913-2010) to the *Académie des inscriptions et belles-lettres* in 1975 (then to the *Académie française* in 1988), Yvonne Choquet-Bruhat (born in 1923) to the *Académie française* in 1979, and Marguerite Yourcenar (1903-1987) to the *Académie française* in 1980. The latter's election caused a degree of turmoil. One of those opposed to her election was none other than Claude Lévi-Strauss. His arguments did not include any particular reference to swords, but to the stability of societies. Women should not be admitted because the 'rules of the tribe' should not be changed. To do so would be to threaten an 'endangered species'. The *Académie française* had to be protected from women just as British clubs were. This assembly had to be considered as the last rampart of a world which could become extinct, like primitive societies.[287] This *affaire* caused quite a stir just as feminism was really finding its feet. From the point of view of women's liberation in France at the time it was an unacceptable position. But from the point of view of an ethnologist watching his objects of study gradually disappear, the logic is understandable. Through this instructive episode one can get a perspective on the impact of major changes in past societies: the sword strengthened the position of men. It was also to play a role in the end of the 'tribe' (in the metaphorical sense) such as the Final Neolithic had constituted it.

Reasons for War

Since war happened, and is evidenced in many ways, evolving over the course of time to become a military phenomenon from the Bronze Age onwards, we must now ask why this should have been. For what reasons did people fight? It is difficult for archaeology to enter into the intimate thoughts of people, but it can sometimes offer possibilities.[288] In the 17th century, Hobbes suggested three main reasons:

> "In human nature we find three principal causes of quarrel. First, competition; secondly, diffidence; thirdly glory. The first, maketh men invade for gain; the second, for safety and the third, for reputation."[289]

What might this have looked like in the most ancient periods of European history? No doubt several motives can be envisaged, with variations over time.

The first is linked to this rather painful question about human nature, also raised by Hobbes: do humans fight because they are naturally violent? This would mean that instinct causes us to fight, to attack or defend depending on the situation. It would explain the most ancient forms of human violence, as witnessed by human remains from Palaeolithic times. This kind of explanation is biological. Every *Homo, sapiens* though he might be, bears within him this form of aggression. This is hard to deny… Nevertheless, two observations need to be made: firstly, individual fighting is not enough to make a war. The two phenomena are of a quite different order. Secondly, humans in society are people living according to rules which require self-control, not least in their relations with others. Breaking rules, including those regarding acts of violence, results in exposure to the consequences and sanctions that society applies, depending on the case. The instinct for violence, though it might explain individual physical and psychological dispositions leading to confrontation, cannot be confused with conflict as a social or societal act. It is not a motivation in and of itself.

The second reason for confrontation is economic in the broadest sense of the word. People fight to have more, to take from others what they covet, but do not have. The Hobbesian notion of competition covers this in part. Such economic interests can take on several forms: movable physical objects or chattels (various items including money); immovable goods including lands; and persons (women, slaves). This kind of motive is generally evoked in many conflicts as one of the fundamental driving forces of war, perhaps one of the most ancient for organised human groups. For the Late Neolithic, given the value attached to lands and settlements, the question of the control of territories and spaces becomes central. Perhaps this has a place in the explanation of conflicts that can now be seen to have happened in various places. The need for defence is sometimes advanced to explain the development of Neolithic and some more recent enclosures.[290] The consequences of new means of production should also be considered, the creation of surplus brought about by the development of agriculture, the increase in production and the ever-growing diversification of foodstuffs and raw materials in circulation. The latter, in a complex economic system, would be an attractive enticement, if not a reason for war as such. In such circumstances, an ability to dominate exchange systems and the territories over which strategic materials are exchanged – metal first and foremost – would be a major advantage. The economy as a driving force for war would occupy a role growing over time alongside increasing wealth.

Parallel to this economic and territorial component, there is the question of population size. Archaeologists are not too happy to be drawn regarding numbers and demography.[291] During the Palaeolithic, Europe was thinly populated. Neolithization, the development of agriculture, was accompanied by population growth. The pressure was no doubt not very strong at first, but there might well have been strategic areas, key agricultural areas, where this did play a role. This is a 'classic' argument to explain ancient conflicts. During the Bronze Age, the population of Europe grew exponentially. Some researchers think that it doubled between 2000 and 1500 BC and that, during these key five centuries, reached about 14 million people.[292] Agricultural practices and the choice of new kinds of cereals largely explains this demographic increase. No doubt better ways of storing food, and better living conditions, such as we see in clothes that became more elaborate and comfortable, should also be taken into account. Such pressures might be considered to have played a role, but not so as to constitute a sufficient reason for going to war.

This corresponds to another set of factors of a political and religious nature, the two being closely linked in many societies. Here the question *why* is associated with the question *how*. Those who have power, those who govern, decide to go to war for many and varied reasons, including glory and the display of power – such reasons may be combined with more 'acceptable' motives (and materials) like the need to extend one's jurisdiction over other lands for economic reasons, or reasons of security. There may also be religious reasons: imposing one's own beliefs and getting rid of those who fail to go along with them. The dividing line between political and religious power is sometimes permeable. Étienne de la Boétie, theorising in the 16th century about the mechanisms by which the dominated accept domination, saw this as a key explanation.[293] In its most extreme manifestations, the religious justification was invoked in war to eradicate races, political positions, sexual practices, and various forms of behaviour and activity. As far as more ancient periods are concerned, there is nothing to allow archaeologists to go so far. On the other hand, it is certain that war from the Bronze Age onward must in some ways have fitted in with this kind of structure, and that it would have been conducted, justified, and decided upon by men holding political and religious power.

It is possible, amongst these various motivations, to make out a kind of divide between war experienced and understood as a form of 'necessity' (defending oneself, and also providing food for one's own people) and war desired and decided upon *a priori* without such constraints. The various motivations are closely linked to different kinds of war and thus to the models of society in the heart of which they are organised.

State, Primitives, the Written Word: Terms of Power

War is anticipated before it takes place. It is prepared and organised. It is unleashed as a political act, dressed up with various motivations. Those who have power may decide to use armed force for many and varied reasons, the most often being when peaceful means are no longer effective. The decision to go to war commits all segments of a society to warfare in a variety of ways according to the nature of the society itself: its composition, the nature and the origins of its power, its political regimes, and its modes of governance.

Words are never value-free. Those used to designate most ancient European societies are borrowed from two groups of vocabulary formalised in the 19th century to describe two practically opposite versions of reality – in line with a view that societies can be more or less 'advanced': on the one hand, the vocabulary used to designate regimes exerting power in modern and contemporary Europe; and on the other hand ethnological language invented in the 19th century (and sometimes even specifically archaeological terms, like 'culture', for example). Archaeologists have, consciously or unconsciously, used this framework (and straitjacket) in their thinking about societies, and in doing so have accepted a divide, intellectual barriers in fact, not least between the world of 'states' ('civilised' societies) which were literate and worthy of a 'history' – and those of 'primitive' 'traditional' societies (those of 'barbarians'), with 'chiefdoms', and 'tribes' described in terms of 'customs'.[294] But how much do these inherited 'catch-all' words really mean? Are they sufficient to describe the societies in Central and Northern Europe in the middle of the 2nd millennium BC where war came into being? Are they not, paradoxically, rather Eurocentric whilst at the same time being ill-equipped to describe the truth about the Europe of 'pre-antique' periods? Do they not force us to use mistaken and anachronistic concepts in our dealings with the societies of the last millennia BC in Europe, when what we really need is to invent a new and appropriate model?

The exercise is not straightforward. Between a constricting heritage and archaeological data which is abundant but, in this respect, not very eloquent, where might one find a form of truth and explanation for the structural foundations of war? Epistemology seems to lead us down tangled paths, but it is indispensable if we are to see how our understanding of European oral societies falls between two stools: such societies have not been understood so much in terms of what remains of them as how they were perceived in the context of a European construction of history and ethnology. Perhaps we should look again at these terms, their meaning and their history, seeing them in perspective so that we can get a better understanding of these societies that brought about and sustained war.

The first key word is 'State'. The term has a history and meanings that evolved over the course of time. It was fixed in the 19th century, describing an entity that was not quite what it is today, nor what it was when first debated in the 17th and 18th centuries, at the point when its definition drifted from notions of territory to those of power. The State is, in terms of a more general definition, a political entity delimited by a territory contained within frontiers, a population and institutionalised power. The term can cover regimes of various kinds depending on the nature of the sovereignty of the power, which has classically been of an aristocratic, monarchic, oligarchic, or democratic nature. The means by which power is legitimised and means of access to various functions of government vary from case to case. A key difference is found in the extent to which the individual who embodies power is associated, or not, with its function. In a democracy, public power is sovereign, over and above differences between the people who embody its exercise (including that of the Head of State), whilst in a monarchy the king or queen are themselves, and individually, the power which is inherited and transmitted. The State can be broken down into various components – political, sociological, juridical, and organisational. This entity has a power of authority and collective constraint in the context of the general interest (in the preservation of the coherence of the ensemble) over and above individual interests (even those of the individual who embodies it, so deposing a king can be justified). In the sphere of war, the State (whatever its precise nature) claims for itself (and has done so for a long while) the monopoly and use of legitimate violence. A key notion for Max Weber, in particular in *Le savant et le politique*. It was not by chance that this text appeared in 1919, directly after the First World War.[295] The subject has been debated and has given rise to much thought amongst lawyers as well as historians and philosophers.[296] Approaches and perspectives change according to specialisms and periods. The most complete study of this notion of the State – or the 'non-State' in so-called 'primitive' societies as we still call them, is found in Pierre Clastres' *La société contre l'État. Recherches d'anthropologie politique*.[297] Questions of power had been obfuscated in the works of ethnologists from the very beginnings of the discipline, but not in an obviously one-sided way. The author's objective is also political: to show the workings and the weaknesses of coercive power, which is denounced as representing not so much progress as rather a failure to maintain a balance in the mechanisms of the control of power. According to this model, certain, more prestigious men play more prominent roles, but die or disappear from the scene before they have quite taken control of everything and everyone, they die. Great warriors in particular can be seen in these terms. This is the essence of the 1977 text.[298]

In many societies, there is a formal link between those who make war and those who have a social role, and this is reflected in their positions on the battlefield.[299] Somewhat as if the latter extended, or more broadly echoed, a society's organisation. The individual is not to be entirely forgotten, but individual identity is not what interests us here. It is individuals' status as representative of a social category, and the position they legitimately occupied in the overall social context, not least because of their role in war. It is not human beings of flesh and blood, but social beings in the context of the State, be this an antique city-state, a monarchy, or more recent political and national systems, in each case involving the practice of writing, the notion of the State not having been envisaged in oral societies.

What all these have in common is the privileged – if not exclusive – use of a particular kind of source, written rather than any other. Here, the nature of the evidence has determined the enquiry, caused researchers to think in certain kinds of ways and to impose societal and political models over and above real human beings.

What consequences and questions arise out of these lexical and historicised constraints? Firstly, is the State inevitably bound to the practice of writing or could there be societies worthy to be called 'state-like' with a centralised government, but which do not use writing? In the former case no oral society in the world, present or past, could be referred to as 'state-like'. Epistemology highlights just how central this question has been to the theorisation of the State, and how this opened the way to talk of 'civilisations' in the context of the most ancient societies. Secondly, for specialists in the subject of certain forms of European societies who are aware that weaponry yields proof of violence used in an organised (if not necessarily 'legitimate') way, there is a need to know just how much, without falling prey to anachronism and contradiction, can be retained of the notion of 'State' to describe very much more ancient periods than those for which the term is generally used. Finally, what kind of societal and political models can one use if these are not to be referred to as 'States'? Do we have to adhere to terminologies inherited from the 19th century to designate 'exotic' worlds and apply them to ancient societies that have disappeared from Eurasia? Do these really take into account local situations not imported from different times and places? What kind of criteria do we need in order to decide? And again, what is the role of writing if it is allowed to dominate such criteria and intellectual hierarchies, at least with regard to Eurocentric models?

No doubt there are many more questions here than answers, at least for the present. Perhaps we should free ourselves from such words, break out of the boxes that shut them in and invent new ones. Let us start again from what seems to form a block as well as a reference-point: writing. Writing was used in recent societies considered to have been state-like, whatever the name used to designate them, including antiquity, like 'city-states', 'republics', or 'empires'. The origination of the term, such as it is applied to governments, seems to be linked not so much to questions regarding the nature of power as to number. Beyond a certain threshold, the accounting of income, taxes, and populations can no longer be mastered just by individuals. Besides, the latter are mortal, so facts, figures, and ways of doing things might well disappear with them. A possible solution is to create a physical system of notation that records such data for the future. Writing organises memory and the future in a way that goes beyond those who are in the know.[300] This creates a new kind of proof. The use of writing is therefore an organisational and utilitarian tool, indispensable as soon as there are enough people, even more so if they are concentrated in such new places as 'towns'. The correspondence between the advent of population concentrations (including urban centres) and the development of writing seems quite clear.[301] As soon as writing was adopted, various developments took place, but not really in such a way as to undermine underlying principles. Broader uses of writing developed involving words to record stories, which then gave rise to different forms of literature. Writing was adopted because of the need to keep accounts but then a taste was acquired for written words which could outlast human memory.[302]

What Sort of Society?

In what kinds of societies was war invented in Europe? If we want to capture these human phenomena, what pictures and words can we use, given that those available to us are inadequate? Protohistory, according to what archaeological excavations tell us, appears to involve a landscape more rural than urban, but with some concentrations of population, even though such places cannot yet be called 'towns', at least not before the Middle Iron Age. By the Bronze Age, such societies had largely taken charge of the landscape, and had deforested the countryside, not least for the sake of metalcraft, which is nothing if not fuel-hungry.[303] We have no exhaustive maps regarding land-occupation. We can make out fields, isolated houses, and also some large town-like areas. There are many routes and means for communication. Human mobility is a constant in European history. The advent of the agricultural world at the beginning of the Neolithic (between the 7th and 5th millennia according to the regions of Europe) led to a reorganisation of human movement, not to its cessation. Just as humans chose to settle in one place and began to see time differently, they also constructed roads, transport-wagons, and boats. As we have seen, the Bronze Age and the development of metalcraft expanded and reinforced this way of life.

With the Iron Age, in the first half of the 1st millennium BC, areas of population concentration seem to have grown more marked in some regions, with a predilection for high places. Throughout the Metal Ages, the specialisation in tasks and in production grew, so we might suppose that exchange and trade took place between various people following patterns established in the Neolithic.

The bronzesmith who dedicated himself to hours of work in his workshop could not have toiled in the fields and looked after his needs in an independent way, any more than the peasant dedicated to increasing cereal-agriculture crop-yields could necessarily have seen to his. Almost a millennium earlier, during the Bronze Age, societies lived within a different kind of spatial structure. But with what sort of power, and with what mode of government?

The invention of the sword – and that of war, which went with it – has to be understood as a key moment, with something sudden about it, like a chemical reaction. Material productions indicate organised manufacture, the control of raw material supply routes and the involvement of a military dimension. It is difficult to see here, in the light of archaeological evidence, how these systems might have been just 'cobbled together'.[304] It required at least some anticipation and organisation, even though we should not pre-judge the precise modes of government. We do need, however, to concede that there were centralised forms of power and a government concentrated in the hands of a small number of people, a consolidation of social hierarchies and divisions of labour, a place set aside for men of arms, and so on. Writing played no role here because the need had not made itself felt. Europe was not uniform in every aspect of its development. The north was not 'behind' or more 'primitive'. It opted for different modes of life and ways of working in which writing did not prove necessary. This does not mean that Bronze Age societies can be called 'primitive' or 'traditional', if indeed these words still have any meaning.

What then shall we call them? They must once have had words to call themselves by, using terms and concepts of which no trace remains. All we can do is draw parallels and make comparisons, if need be with different times and places: so, in southern Africa, between 1450 and 1629 Monomotapa was an 'empire' without writing and without towns...[305] But mentioning other places where power was centralised does not totally settle the problem of a Europe that has vanished. What words can we use? Do we not have here forms of state, according to the notion of a gathering of people in a given territory within frontiers (yes, they exist and can be seen through archaeology), endowed with a government in which some individuals have powers and specific functions of a political, religious or economic nature? No doubt rules and norms dictated behaviour and practices in all domains of life. This phenomenon, for which it is so hard to find a name or even to portray in any detail, is best glimpsed through war, almost in the manner of the negative of a photograph: archaeological data show that war could not have existed without this kind of society. So, this kind of society must have existed.

Modes of conflict tell us about societies, and vice versa. Society is the key to understanding war. In a word, one cannot be envisaged without the other. It is not enough just to count weapons: we have to go beyond objects. We need to draw up not just a typology of weapons, but also a typology of societies. Though archaeology allows us to draw up lists of objects in a relatively straightforward way, the matter is a little more complicated for societies. Or rather, getting closer to the identity of past oral societies is made possible by grouping data and various analysis together (typological, dating, technological, contextualisation, comparative and so on) in a kind of synergy. The interpretation of archaeological data makes it possible to insert them into an explanatory schema which should be at the same time technological, economic, cultural, and religious – in a word: societal. If we return to the question as it was put, that of violence and war to be looked at in terms of weapons, some kinds of coherent sense, groups and possible types of society begin to take shape.

Three Ages of War?

Let us go back in time and dare to propose societal typologies for European oral societies, those of prehistory and Protohistory, in their connection with war.

Let us start with the most ancient times, globally understood as the Palaeolithic, in order to follow such processes over the long term. People lived together but we cannot enter into the intimacy of what went on. Evidence of violence has been found, as has evidence of caring for the sick and wounded and accepting responsibility for others. As soon as otherness is recognised and adopted as part of frequent practices (and therefore normed), it can be said that people are living in society. This says nothing of precise modalities, of choices and details of social organisation. Probably, without making any positive or negative judgment, we are talking here about a kind of society similar to what has been termed 'traditional' (might one dare use the expression 'society based on otherness'?). Sources do not allow us to prejudge any degree of specialisation in carrying out tasks (or even to claim that such specialisation even existed, as objects from the time prove), nor can we prejudge how tasks might have been shared between individuals or what forms of equality or inequality there might have been. As for violence, the marks of impact on some bones show that it occurred. This aspect of what it is to be human was part of Palaeolithic society. It does not resolve the initially attractive question as to when violence between humans started, which contrasts violent and peaceful views of man in a way which is too simplistic for us even to be able to envisage the notion of violence. As such, it offers no comfort to the Hobbesian model, nor does it do much to undermine Rousseau's. Violence is simply present. No specific means are available to it. It is not part of a fully-fledged social system. In hunting and gathering societies it can be understood as a means used to acquire goods and to protect oneself. To the extent that death is owned and ritualised, we have to admit that killing others was part of a mental logic which meant that a minimum of violence was 'acceptable' even if it was not legitimate. If I were to try to be Christian Jürgensen Thomsen two centuries after him, and I were setting myself up as a typo-chronologist of war relating to different periods, then I would call this first period 'The Age of Empirical Violence'. No doubt one would have to introduce nuances in order to account for variations (including those of a technological nature) over the very long millennia of the Palaeolithic.

The second grouping is characterised by items which in theory could have been used in multiple ways, though this was probably not the case. At least not for all of them. Here, two types of phenomena appear to emerge if we look from 'weapons' in the broader sense, to societies themselves, and back again. The first is that of archers at the heart of hunting and gathering peoples. The polyvalence seen by archaeology here is convincing, even though specialisation of *chaînes opératoires* suggests diversification in use. Depictions of archers in combat validate this hypothesis. But it still leaves uncertainties about details of combat organisation, who the participants might have been, and the question of whether or not such societies were egalitarian according to Godelier's definition.[306] The second type arises out of the fundamental break constituted by neolithization.[307] Societies which brought about and lived in the context of neolithization are different from those of preceding periods. Such profound changes go beyond the economic, that is a movement from hunter-gatherer to producer. A far broader set of references and practices arises in these new types of societies (societies of the 'sectorised' type, with poles of activities?).[308] Under these circumstances, violence continues to make its presence felt through multiple-use weapons (therefore with a certain continuing ambiguity) but with a use of larger numbers of materials and involving different shapes of weapon. In this context, I would find it hard to believe in an equal distribution of wealth and status, unless this could truly be seen in terms of an organisation of tasks and status. At the heart of this neolithized Europe, there would also be a need to distinguish between at least two time-scales: one that marks the beginnings of the Late Neolithic, and another which applies to societies from the 4th millennium and to some extent also the 3rd millennium. Investment in technology and exchanges is more marked. Societies now more clearly display signs of integrating instruments of violence (functionally and symbolically) into their modes of organisation. It is a component part of a whole regularly making its presence felt. It is no doubt at this point that the ideas of Clastres most clearly find their echo. If I were to allow myself to be Thomsen again, I would dare to talk of an 'Age of Integrated Conflict', even though I would have to acknowledge the heterogeneity of these forms of conflict.

Over time, there is a growth in archaeological data and chronologies become more precise. Contours of societies seem clearer. With the sword, the 2nd millennium marks the birth of a weapon that one might call 'military': an object used only on the battlefield, and in the social and symbolic functions attached to it. This phenomenon can only be conceived of in the context of a society which has achieved the means to create it. It cannot be reduced simply to economic and technological components. It is a whole. It is a phenomenon that can be isolated in terms of a specific activity, and at the same time one that structures society. The organisation and logistics necessary for warfare imply a hierarchised society, where power is concentrated in the hands of a limited number of individuals who have the authority to take decisions of a political nature. As such, war is to some extent institutionalised, even if we have no details regarding the modalities of this process. How might we designate this type of society which has no writing, but which is framed by a certain number of codes, values, and modes of behaviour? Maurice Godelier uses the term "centralised chiefdoms".[309] Godelier's definition criteria regarding organisation, beliefs and political functions, correspond to the Bronze Age societies which invented a kind of war. Only the territorial aspect, the concentration of the bulk of political and religious functions, does not come to light in archaeology, which tends to reveal farms and villages rather than urban centres, at least in the case of earlier phases. Perhaps metal hoards are also an atypical kind of religious practice in non-urbanised territories. The

Bronze Age escapes the kind of classification that fits into a binary opposition between a 'primitive' or 'traditional' world (which can be applied to the Neolithic world to the extent that it is possible for specialists in the Neolithic to draw parallels with ethnology) and a world of writing and states. This difficulty with classification, with generating criteria that are not 'simple' (cave paintings, settling, agriculture, and so on), perhaps explains to some extent the somewhat marginalised status of the Bronze Age in the higher reaches of academia. In order to get an answer to the question as to what truly characterises the Bronze Age, perhaps one might reply that it was the advent of 'war' as a total, social fact. This phenomenon makes its presence felt so powerfully in the implications of how military equipment developed that I would call this time 'the Age of War as Structuring Principle.'

In some ways the Iron Age is distinctive, not least in its territorial forms of centralisation. It is characterised by a growth in specialisation in all domains of society including the way war is conceived. But this, archaeology indicates, is more a change in scale than a fundamental, underlying transformation suggesting a truly new type of society and war. Perhaps one might call this an 'inclusive' society (or indeed an 'Age of inclusive War') in which different sectors are articulated independently of one another.

Words and functions for all

There is nothing anodyne about daring to use new words ('other-based', 'sectorised', 'inclusive') to designate societies à la Thomsen, audaciously defining whole periods in terms of war (the 'Age of Empirical Violence', 'the Age of Integrated Conflict' and 'the Age of inclusive War). Intellectually, it shows just how difficult it is to create words for past realities that do not have (or no longer have) words of their own but are already designated by a vocabulary that is unhelpful, thanks to former (and indeed outmoded) connotations. These terms are based on data and archaeological knowledge and then placed in the context of broader theoretical models. They have something to say but they are quite inadequate. In any case they make clear the need to leave behind former categories which restrict present thought.

The phenomenon of the warrior grew ever more in magnitude and significance from the Bronze Age onwards. Worse, from the moment writing became central to state-like societies, war was the first subject of narratives. This gives the impression that war is part of a society's history. Yet this was a preoccupation present well before it was told by means of the (written) word. Typologies of war tell us as much about societies as organised modes of violence do. Moreover, they are reflected in (chronological) divisions globally established by archaeologists, even though the latter did not, alas, always see conflict as a component part of the human species, at least since the advent of *Homo sapiens*. 'Alas', because *Homo sapiens* are us, and he (we) has (have) never ceased from using our intelligence and certain cognitive faculties for the purpose of a particular objective – killing others.

Debates about how very ancient societies were organised, the parts played by individuals within them and the original attribution of roles and functions within them have themselves had a long history. We should give due mention to Georges Dumézil who saw the foundation principles of organised societies in Europe in terms of three key functions: the sacred and sovereignty, the warrior, and production and reproduction.[310]

This trifunctionality was linked to Indo-European foundation myths, mythologies, and religions. His ideas have been debated at length,[311] but this is not the place to go into detail. Here though it is worth highlighting the importance he ascribed to the warrior.[312] Whether or not Indo-Europeans are a phenomenon that might explain large-scale evolutions in European history, it is still clearly the case that the warrior-function is an important marker in European history. Though one might not want to see this in terms of some vast epic, seductive but reductionist, it certainly still makes sense to study specific aspects of this, and its complexities, based on data coming directly from the societies themselves.

The West in the Dynamics of Warfare

Let us go back to our starting point: the appearance of the sword in the west round about 1700 BC. Can it be maintained that, in the Eurasian context and even beyond, this event came late compared to the rest of the world, or at least close neighbours? For many decades the northwest of Europe was seen as a place to which innovations, all of which came from the Near East, simply spread. This notion of *ex oriente lux* was largely conditioned by studies of ancient periods up to the 1950s and the invention of radiocarbon dating. [313] Nowadays this has largely been revised in the light of facts but the idea of some regions being more 'advanced' than others persists, in a conscious or unconscious way, according to an intellectual model inherited from the evolutionism of the 19th century.

What does the sword have to tell us about this? When the sword came into being in Western Europe, metalcraft was already going on in other Mediterranean regions. In the Near East, in Egypt and in the Greek world, metal objects were already being manufactured for other aspects of life.[314] In the 2nd millennium, and sometimes even beforehand, copper alloy metalcraft was known. In these various regions there were regular conflicts between people, but the models and dynamics of war were rather the opposite of the European pattern. In Mesopotamia, forms of centralised states were organised very early, and concentrated human populations were big enough to result in the development of writing for administrative purposes. Conflicts between sovereigns broke out and armed men became involved in confrontations. These wars were directed by states and centred on the use of armed combatants wielding clubs, bows and so on. The iconography of such periods shows scarcely any long swords which could be used in face-to-face combat such as we see in Scandinavian pictograms for example.[315] Archaeological data as well as figurative representations show the existence of short swords that fit in with this kind of combat. War requires groups. The warrior is a soldier, a component part of an army.[316] The town-based world as a form of State and government involved a military organisation that we might refer to as 'downward'.

In Western Europe, when the sword came into being, the situation was radically different. There was no such thing as a state structured and administered by writing, and there were no towns. Though we are not sure about the precise alchemy of what happened, war-weapons arrived on the scene as part of a story involving raw materials, metalworkers, and individuals. Technology gave rise to the warrior. One can see him as the successor of 'proto-warriors' from the end of the Neolithic, that is to say individuals in pre-eminent positions, elites, chiefs. [317] Archaeology shows, particularly in the context of funerary practices, an evolution towards more marked individualism, but nothing in weaponry demonstrates this clearly before the advent of the sword. The sword represents a powerful break in terms of objects and practices too. Metalcraft therefore disseminated not only a category of object, on an individual level, but also a form of combat and of war.[318] And, beyond this, social and political organisation.

No doubt one should go further. Since the bronzesmith is literally the creator of this mushrooming effect, in the context of a non-egalitarian and non-urbanised society, the invention of the sword can be seen as causing this society to evolve following what one might call an 'upward' movement, from the sword to the State, in some ways the opposite of what happened in Mesopotamia. The weapons might have issued from the bronzesmith's workshop, but metalcraft made such demands that its development cannot be envisaged unless society, not least men in power and governments, took responsibility for and organised it. Technology created not only the sword and individualised combat but also the forms of State which provided a structure for war and legitimised it in the full sense of the word. Seen in this light, the west was neither ahead of other societies nor behind. It created a system in which technology drove social and political change, without any need for writing. The life cycle of weapons, including their ritualised abandonment ('metal hoards'), and the way they were sometimes deliberately broken, plays a key role in the understanding of how such societies functioned. This is a combination of the technological and the symbolic, again in a model specific to the European Bronze Age, for which words are sometimes lacking. We need therefore to invent them, to study over and again the archaeological evidence, enquire ever more deeply and to be clear that the relationship of Bronze Age men to metal weaponry was intense and committed. The process brought about involved manufacture, individuals, usage (including breaking), types of wars, forms of power and social organisation. On our hypothetical date of 21 April 1688 BC 'war' was probably not invented as such, but rather a form of war and a form of society that are a constitutive part of European history.

VII

THE HUMAN LEVEL

The sword tells us of weapons. Weapons embody the warrior. Warriors are a sign of war. War pre-supposes war-like societies. So, Bronze Age society declares that it invented the most comprehensive form of war...

Our talk of Bronze Age society does not mean it is impossible to talk of various forms of conflict during previous periods and in different societies (some of which have been referred to as 'primitive'), but the Bronze Age does clearly does mark a change in the nature and scale of what was going on in these new societies – this can be seen through the development of metallic weaponry clearly evidenced by archaeology. The point here is not refute other possibilities but to assert something which really took place as a result of the advent of the sword and the weaponry developed at the same time, adding to its effectiveness.

The logic of these connections is unavoidable. But however obvious this might seem now, it was for a long time disregarded: firstly because of lack of awareness regarding source-evidence pointing to war so long ago, and ignorance regarding the 'Bronze Age' as such; and then because the societies in question did not conform to models conceived and understood by the West. Instead, there were the 'boxes' into which history is generally tidied away and which turn into the slices (*'tranches'*) or periods of which Jacques le Goff (1924-2014) talks.[319] Sometimes breaches have to be made or walls knocked down, and 'slices' of history have to be rearranged or nibbled away at.

There is no way round this if we want to see what war really was in the 2nd millennium BC and investigate it as a long term phenomenon. Just as we need to analyse closely the particular kinds of evidence offered by the 'book' of archaeology. Then it does become possible to glimpse the bronzesmith, the warrior and their society. At the end of this voyage into the Bronze Age, two questions nevertheless remain.

Questions of Scale

I am committed to the physicality of archaeology and convinced by what it has to tell and teach us about past societies. Very committed. For at this point, the very foundations of archaeology are at stake. If archaeology cannot speak to us in this way, then it has no reason to exist – it has no legitimacy. It would be just a collection of objects sitting in museum showcases and not one inch of intellectual progress would have been made over the last two centuries, which would be unthinkable. Nevertheless, though I attempt to see things as they are, I still have to wonder what might be escaping me in this connection between archaeology and war. If I take a long view of the subject, not just the distant past, but recent periods too, then I have to admit that much of what happens in war, over shorter or longer periods of time, leaves no obvious, physical or tangible traces. As a specialist in ancient oral societies, I am well aware of the lacunary nature of my data, and I have to cope with this on a daily basis. But then, what do I not have? What am I missing in this grave and weighty subject? By basing my enquiries on existing archaeological evidence, what am I trying to focus the subject on? Am I not perhaps inflating or distorting it, perhaps forgetting something important? I have looked carefully at a category of items, metal weapons of war. I have opened up the range of other archaeological evidence bearing witness to violence. This physical data has led me to become aware of a particular type of technological and societal change between 1700 and 1600 BC. The common thread here seems clear, up to the beginning of the 1st millennium. 'Afterwards', weapons seem at the same time to say not enough and too much. They are there, but now the fundamental key to understanding societies seems to go beyond them. 'Before' is an ambiguity about using weaponry as a sign and marker of violence, and in certain respects, this is inadequate from a strictly archaeological point of view. No doubt we should therefore try to get a broader perspective by seeing violence in the context of more general archaeological data. This has been suggested, but surely the analysis can be taken further. Rethinking the potential presence of war (that is conflict organised by a society) in the European Neolithic, is to look again at the way we synthesise data about Neolithic societies even down to the level of the finest subdivisions ('cultures' or 'facies' in specialist language) making links between archaeological data and population phenomena. This means reviewing, even more comprehensively than we have done so far, data regarding the economy (subsistence, exchanges, raw materials, and so on), beliefs and social organisations, as far as we can reconstitute it. In terms of archaeological evidence, it means looking at the way people lived away from places where violence occurred, to places where life went on, and seeing how such activities also developed, grew, or indeed disappeared, following various fluctuations over time and their demographic effects. This enlarged vision, this sideways look which means seeing society in terms of war – and vice versa – should no doubt also apply to the study of war for all periods.

War is made through fighting, (of this we can have evidence), but it is present too beyond the battlefield, in everyday life, in the organisation of society economically and politically. A 'war' which is chosen, organised, and declared, is a political act in the broadest sense of the word, beyond the precise nature of a society and its mode of government. It is the leader, whoever he might be (and by whatever name he might be designated), who has the task of thinking about war, making decisions in the sense of who does what, what should happen when, and making sure various sectors concerned work together in response to the decision; he also has to decide how to fight and means to deploy. There is every reason to believe that our so-called 'primitive barbarians' did indeed practise war.

Weapons and forms of combat change over time and from one society to another. Societies at the beginning of the Bronze Age developed a model of war in conformity with their values, the way they were organised and the way they worked, with a government (a power structure) that was in some way centralised and in the hands of a limited number of individuals – and all this was in the context of a clear hierarchy no doubt overtly displayed as such. Societies at the end of the Bronze Age had taken matter further. In any case, the increase in metal hoards involving weapons alongside other objects seems to suggest real economic prosperity. It is not clear that this would have been compatible with very marked or numerous occurrences of conflict. On the other hand, displaying one's wealth and one's power as a warrior (real in his case) is an activity we can make sense of. Such behaviour was very marked until the end of the 5th century BC, but this does not mean war had disappeared. Dating from the Late Iron Age and particularly the 3rd century BC large numbers of weapons have come to light in archaeological contexts. Does this mean that there were more wars? This was a time of extraordinary developments in all areas of manufacture and major economic changes. Could this really have been compatible with ongoing warfare?

We clearly do not know in sufficient detail when wars took place and for how long. The First World War lasted a little more than four years. It was appallingly destructive, and it was hell for those who went through it at the front. And yet it was 'only' four years. War as experienced by men, war as related in words and war as seen by archaeologists embody three quite different phenomena and three quite different timescales. The long term view means we can talk of some processes taking place over a period of time, but this deprives us of a direct and tangible feeling, which is cruelly lacking if we wish to understand what war was really like. The fact that some 'snap-shots' might have been taken on battlefields, in trenches or in sanctuaries, does not wholly make up for what we lack. We have to accept this and cope with what we know to be impossible. Archaeology means we can show that war took place and give information about some practices (fighting and rituals linked to war or violence). It nevertheless remains on a certain level and within a restricted discourse: at once general and at the same time very specific, literally on the level of an object which is never seen in movement, or being made, or being used, other than at the moment of its abandonment. We lack a certain intermediate level to the narrative, and a way of relating the different scales of analysis and discourse offered by very diverse sources. In the 19th century, when very ancient periods were beginning to emerge from the depths of time, people began to dream, to fantasise about our very ancient ancestors who both fascinated and frightened us. Archaeology was just beginning. Some dared to go beyond the ill-defined borderlines. Narratives were constructed and there were depictions of men and women typical of those huge 'prehistoric' periods, at least as they were imagined. This was a time when people were unreserved about going beyond what they knew, so they gave life to such individuals, never mind archaeological evidence and methodology, and what would have been strictly legitimate in the light of these. No matter: they came into being. They became creatures who made an impression on the public. Since then, research has evolved considerably, grown richer in data and means of analysis. Two new forms of discourse have been acquired, one on a micro- and macroscopic level, and another on a level that gives us an almost birds-eye view.

A view from the human level, however, is what we would really like to pursue. The 19th century dreamed of it, and the 20th century reacted against it, though without really offering a new kind of narrative in its place. On the one hand we have the kind of stone and the basic qualities of wood used to make houses, their layout, details of what people ate, what they ate with – this is the kind of thing we have on the one hand – and on the other, a village's long-term evolution and that of the environment in the valley where it was situated. But it remains hard to get a glimpse of the people who lived there, one fine summer's day, setting about their business.

What actually exists, as well as the gaps in between – this is the starting point for archaeology as it rediscovers, reconstitutes and gives speech back to men and women who have fallen silent, leaving behind only the physical traces of their existence. The archaeological imagination can make up for some of what has been lost, enabling us to see physical remnants back in action (and context). Scales and levels of analysis create difficulties and constraints, so that certain degrees of subtlety can never be achieved, not least when it comes to detailed timescales. Every historian has to cope with such problems of scale and deal with the frustrations caused.[320] The nature of the evidence clearly determines some of the rules. When they are studying a site that helps them understand a society or period more globally, archaeologists are, in a way, practising micro-history. The interest of a site is not the number of finds it yields but their representative quality. In the context of the Late Palaeolithic, much pioneering work was done on the site of Pincevent (Seine-et-Marne, France), excavated over a long period when it was also a school for field archaeology.[321] At the time, and still today, lacustrine and riparian sites have played a major role in our understanding of the Neolithic and the Bronze Age. Recently, the British site of Must Farm has had much to teach us about the Late Bronze Age, going beyond this remarkably well-conserved habitat itself; just as the Dover boat dated 1550 BC, in itself and in conjunction with nearby discoveries, has proved an extraordinary source of information from a technological point of view and in the study of coast-dwelling peoples. One site or one group of objects can provide an explanatory model. Archaeologists do not work and cannot work otherwise. The path is not straightforward, neither for historians of the written word nor indeed for those who work with physical evidence.[322] From a micro-historical perspective, the focus on a type of material, like weaponry, is illuminating, yielding information about groups of practices, in workshops, in combat and indeed in the societies where people lived and moved.

War and Peace

War is therefore an ancient phenomenon but probably, then as now, not a continuous one. It is cyclic. At some times and in some places, it was at the centre of everyone's life, but not others. Different types of war came into being, but we cannot talk of a Europe of ancient oral societies in which war was uninterrupted over a period of thousands of years. Tolstoy summed it up in the title of his first novel: war and peace go together. But following a rhythm of alternation which follows very irregular intervals and modalities. If we talk about one, we cannot remain silent about the other. The majority of people aspire to live in peace. And this is indeed how, for a long while, people wanted to see the Neolithic peasant, thinking only about growing his crops and the wellbeing of his livestock. If we want to go further in our understanding of the most ancient conflicts, we need to take these rhythms into account, try to see what kinds of consequences war had for peaceful societies and how such societies might have prepared for possible future wars. Can we see demographic changes in the form of population reductions that might be explained in terms of war? Or at the very least through territorial changes associated with atypical mortality rates or abandoned conflict zones? Or the construction of monuments to mark peace, or which aim to frighten enemies to avoid future conflict? Though such questions are legitimate and useful, they rapidly run into problems of information accuracy and vocabulary. We should perhaps bear these questions in mind, at least regarding some kinds of data, particularly when time seems to close in round the Bronze Age. La Tène sanctuaries are marked by war. Battles did take place and warriors did die. Perhaps one might also envisage them as places of commemoration in times of peace? And looking back again from this, can we introduce such kinds of ideas in our analyses of Bronze Age weapon metal hoards?

So many questions for a conclusion. I would like to think that other researchers will continue to work on them. I dream of being able to convince myself that, as a historian, I have done my duty and can now move on to pastures new. However, unless I give up being an archaeo-metallurgist specialising in the Bronze Age, I fear that I shall keep on running into the world of weapons, of war, people who kill, those who equip them to do so, and indeed their victims. For anyone interested in human history, it is hard to get away from organised violence.

A Trip to a Bronze Age Kitchen

Bronzesmiths did not only make swords, helmets, and other weaponry to equip warriors and pander to the human thirst for power. They used their skills to make other items too. We have rather neglected such objects here in order to highlight others, but they had an important place in the production carried out in workshops. They also required time, means and an understanding of needs. The Bronze Age and its exceptional workmanship were not, fortunately, exclusively about violence. Some things they made can be seen as belonging to less momentous categories.

The comparisons between the work of the bronzesmith and that of the cook makes sense because both deal with mixing things, correct temperatures, and heating. The difference is that one is tasted and consumed whilst the other is not, or at least the consumption is of a different nature. Besides, the metalworker also directly serves the interests of the cook and in a rather distinctive way. Real cooking this time, not the kind that simmers in a crucible, but in an actual cooking pot. In the bronzesmith's workshop metal vessels were made during the Late Bronze Age, evolving alongside defensive weaponry. In both cases, on a technical level, flawless casting had to be combined with high quality beating, reshaping and assembly work. Manufacture in itself is very similar – only the end-use and the consequences of failure are different. A cooking pot with flaws does not endanger someone's life in the way a breastplate does, but it is still useless if cracked or badly designed. And, as objects, both combine excellence and an element of luxury in their use and appearance.

Various manufactured objects have been successful, sometimes over unexpectedly long periods. In 2007 I travelled to Hungary to study various metal objects in the national museum of Budapest and in other museums. In the context of collaboration with the university and the national Museum, a tour was organised across the country with stops in different towns where metal objects were kept. We set off in a little group in a minibus driven by a Hungarian colleague. We crossed the vastness of the Great Plain of Puszta as far as Debrecen, before heading northeast, until we reached the hills of Tokai, the town of Miskolc, that of Mezőkövesd, with various stops. It might seem strange for a French researcher, a specialist in Bronze Age metalcraft, to travel so far. And yet present-day Hungary covers an area where the Bronze Age was particularly rich, with metal productions of exceptional quality. The metal hoards there are numerous and remarkable, and the swords date from a very early period – from a technical point of view, their manufacture is very fine. As such, it is legitimate (if a researcher really needs to justify every intellectual exploration) to travel hundreds of miles to see the hundreds and hundreds of objects preserved in the city museums, some quite modest. Besides, these past ages can only be understood from a European perspective – certainly not from a point of view limited to present-day national frontiers which have no meaning or reality.

On the edge of the roads of the Great Plain at various intervals we came across metal pots hanging from hooks and fixed to tripods. I asked our colleague what they were for. We stopped and looked; he explained. This was a traditional pot for making the national dish, goulash. He himself had one. The most astonishing thing was no doubt to discover amongst them pots whose shape and decoration were practically identical to Bronze Age pots made in this same area some three thousand years ago. The very ones that we had come to study. Ten years on, I still have a powerful memory of a traditional stew that we were offered to celebrate the end of the trip, a dish with an extremely delicious sauce, and the incredibly delicate texture of meat which had been cooked for 24 hours over a wood-fire burning beneath this round-bottomed pot, attached by two handles to a hook hanging from a tripod in a sheltered corner of the garden. Here, metalcraft really did join hands with cooking and finally moved beyond the sphere of war (even though, on these very lands, fighters and local people involved in conflict must have been fed). So, sitting round the table, we made the most of the time we had together, an unusual one for archaeologists, since we were living in the present amidst direct testimonies of the past. Of course, we were not really transported back in time over 3000 years. But then, I had a fleeting glimpse of what a Bronze Age meal might have been like, this time in terms of something I was doing on a human level.

This experience marked me. The journey into incredible landscapes, the study of numerous items kept in places that were often quite astonishing, and that extraordinary dinner in the gentle heat of a June evening. It reminded me that objects of archaeological study have to be seen, both intellectually and in reality, in action, doing what they were intended to do, if we are to understand them. It reminded me too that historical knowledge results from a process whereby evidence, traces and objects of study, are gathered and compared, and that by sifting through various levels, and processes of comparison, we researchers have a slightly better chance of at least some understanding of the evidence that has come down to us, slender though it might be. It is possible to engage in the study of handicraft to see how it fits in with a whole period, to work on jewellery and ornamentation in order to understand war better, and then return to the study of ceramics whilst at the same time raising questions about the nature of hoards. Societies studied from a particular perspective can nevertheless only be understood as a whole. Oral societies which lived thousands of years ago in Europe still have much to tell us about our history, peaceful or otherwise.

Acknowledgements

This is my book, but the English version is the result of collective endeavour. I should like to thank Karsten Wentink, Sasja van der Vaar-Verschoof, the team at Sidestone Press, and Tim Armstrong for his tremendous and careful work on the the text, as well as Rebecca Peake for her help.

Notes

Dedication

1 *To the memory of Peter Clark who passed away suddenly and far too young while we were working on this manuscript in the Spring of 2021. Peter was an archaeologist at the Canterbury Archaeological Trust, deeply involved in work on the 'Dover Boat', which was excavated at Dover in 1992. No one did more to make this discovery and its implications widely known. In 2011 we set up a European project focussing on this boat as a means to increase understanding about the Bronze Age, sea-faring and cross-channel relationships, showing just how close we are as neighbours on either side of this stretch of water. The project 'BOAT 1550 BC' was a magnificent opportunity for people to work together as a team. Peter loved sharing his work, his time, his enthusiasm and his music with everyone. With friends, colleagues and new acquaintances; with grown-ups and with children. He had a tremendous ability for striking up positive relationships with people, in a straightforward, kindly manner, with great openness of mind and warmth of heart. We worked together uninterruptedly for five years, often in fits of laughter, drinking beer and talking about the essence of 'true' fish and chips (complete with mushy peas!); we drank many a liqueur coffee, which he adored. Whenever problems arose, he never lost his habitual cool. He would always do what he could to find a solution or reach the best possible compromise. He was proud of what he had achieved, grateful, always smiling. He was very sensitive to the feelings of those around him, and he was always full of enthusiasm. He was a true professional and a remarkable man.I wish therefore to dedicate this book to him, though it can scarcely compensate for his loss, and to include this dedication in French, a language of which he was very fond.*
On the Dover Boat : Peter Clark (ed.), *The Dover Bronze Age Boat*, English Heritage, 2004; id., *The Bronze Age connections. Cultural contact in Prehistoric Europe*,1, Oxford, Oxbow Books, 2004; *The Bronze Age connections. Cultural contact in Prehistoric Europe*, 2, Oxford, Oxbow Books, 2009; and his ultimate book with Grand Shand and Jake Weekes, *Chalk Hill. Neolithic and Bronze Age discoveries at Ramsgate, Kent*, Sidestone Press, 2019; On BOAT 1550 BC, Anne Lehoërff (dir.), [with the collaboration of Jean Bourgeois, Peter Clark, Marc Talon], *Beyond the Horizon. Societies of the Channel and North Sea 3,500 years Ago*, Paris, Somogy, 2012; Anne Lehoërff, Marc Talon (ed.), *Movement, Exchange and Identity in Europe in the 2nd and 1st Millenia BC : Beyond Frontiers*, Oxford, Oxbow Books, 2017.

Encountering War

2 "I hate travel and I hate explorers"; this is the famous first sentence of Claude Lévi-Strauss' (1908-2009) *Tristes Tropiques (Sad Tropics)* – he was forced to adopt a methodology, out of a sense of duty and necessity.

3 Marc Bloch, *Apologie pour l'histoire ou métier d'historien*, Paris, Armand Colin, 1949, seventh edition, 1974, p. 37.

4 Bronze Age specialists agree nowadays that the sword came into being around 1700 BC in Central Europe and slightly later in Western Europe. For example, in the specialised chronologies of 'Bronze A2'. See Antony Harding, *Warriors and weapons in Bronze Age Europe*, Budapest, Archaeolingua, 2007, p. 73.

5   This notion comes from the title of Umberto Eco's *A passo di gambero. Guerre calde e populismo mediatico*, Bompiani, Milan, 2006 – English translation: *Turning Back the Clock: Hot Wars and Media Populism*, 2007, Alastair McEwen. The volume consists of a collection of texts all of which shed light upon 'new' forms of war (modern terrorism in particular, which is referred to as neo-war). This illustrates the notion that we often step back in order to move forward, in the manner of a crayfish which proceeds forwards by walking backwards. The image is strikingly appropriate, making us think again about the notion that progress always moves 'forward' in a straight line. The metaphor seemed appropriate to my own work which did not initially address the subject of war. I also arrived at it by a backwards form of walking forwards.

6   François Hartog, *Régimes d'historicités*, Paris Seuil, 'La Librairie du XXIe siècle', 2003.

7   Stéphane Audouin-Rouzeau, *Une initiation. Rwanda (1994-2016)*, Paris, Seuil, 2016.

8   By the same author: *1914-1918. Les combattants des tranchées*, Paris, Armand Colin 1986; *La Grande Guerre. 1914-1918*, Paris, Gallimard, 2013; *1914-1918. La violence de guerre*, Paris, Gallimard, 2014.

9   For a definition of this period see: Anne Lehoërff, 'Les paradoxes de la Protohistoire française', *Annales HSS*, septembre-octobre 2009, n° 5, p. 1107-1134; Anne Lehoërff 2011: 'L'Âge du bronze est-il une période historique ?', in Dominique Garcia (eds.), *L'Âge du bronze en Méditerranée. Recherches récentes*, Paris, Errance, 2011, p. 13-26.

10 Anne Lehoërff, 'Dire sans les mots', dans Anne Lehoërff (eds), 'Dossier Préhistoire', *Nouvelle revue française*, 622, janvier 2017, p. 125-152, part. p. 125-129.

11 An insight into the reversal of this principle is offered (whereby the 'other' is seen as the European written tradition) by the debates surrounding the use of 'other' at the time of the opening of the Musée du Quai Branly in 2006, which was styled 'the Museum of the other'. Here, the pronoun 'we' meant the European tradition. The neo-colonial attitude implied by this simple term was criticised alongside other assumptions made in the context of this project. See in particular Françoise Choay, 'Branly : un nouveau Luna Park était-il nécessaire?', in *Le Débat* 147, 2007, p. 57-64; André Desvallées, *Quai Branly: un Miroir aux alouettes ?* On the subject of ethnography and 'primitive crafts' see:', l'Harmattan, Paris, 2007; Benoît de L'Estoile, *Le goût des Autres. De l'exposition coloniale aux Arts premiers*, Paris, Flammarion, 2007.

12 Christophe Delage, 'Once upon a time…the (hi)story of the concept of the '*chaîne opératoire*', in French prehistory', in *World Archaeology* 49-2, 2017, p. 158-173.

13 In particular: André Leroi-Gourhan, *L'homme et la matière*, Paris [1943], 1992 and *Milieu et technique*, Paris [1945], 1992; id. *Le geste et la parole, I. Technique et langage, II. La mémoire et les rythmes*, Paris [1964], new edition, 2022 (coll. Espaces Libres Albin Michel). On the man: Audouze Françoise, Schlanger Nathan (eds), *Autour de l'homme. Contexte et actualité d'André Leroi-Gourhan*, Antibes, Éditions APDCA, 2004; Lehoërff Anne, "Préfaces" 1 & 2, *ibid Le geste et la parole*, t. 1 & 2, 2022, p. 7-17 & 7-17.

14 Anne Lehoërff, 'Les cuirasses de Marmesse (Haute-Marne), un artisanat d'exception', *Antiquités nationales* 39, 2008, p. 95-106.

15 Anne Lehoërff: *Les armes anciennes de la collection Odescalchi* (Palais de Venise, Rome), in *Jahrbuch des RGZM* 55, 2008, 2011, p. 43-79.

16 Hélène Dumas, *Le génocide au village. Le massacre des Tutsi au Rwanda*, Paris, Seuil, 2014.

17 Christian Ingrao, *Croire et détruire. Les intellectuels dans la machine de guerre*, Paris, Fayard, 2010.

18 In France, a commission working on museum collections, led by Michel van Praët, submitted a report in 2015. The study was extended in 2016 to include human remains in university faculties. Also, a dialogue was opened with archaeologists, the primary 'producers' of human remains in the context of archaeological excavations. The debates remain complicated; archaeologists regularly run into such difficulties during the course of their work, difficulties that legislation is not really designed to help with, at least not with respect to associated scientific and ethical questions. Anne Lehoërff, '*Rencontre avec nous-mêmes. Les restes humains en contexte archéologique*', in *Esprit*, 457, September 2019, p. 131-142.

19 Jean Guilaine, *Caïn, Abel, Ötzi. L'héritage néolithique*, Paris, Gallimard, 2011. Anne Lehoërff, 'Ötzi, l'homme des Alpes', in Anne Lehoërff, *Préhistoires d'Europe*, Paris, Belin 2016, chapter 7, p. 290-297.

20 Mention has been made of Rwanda. One might also mention, in the context of recent conflicts, the former Yugoslavia and the Second World War, for example Christian Ingrao's studies on Nazi torturers *op. cit.* 2010.

21. If we really want to keep Herodotus as the founding father of an Eurocentric vision of history, we need at the very least to reconsider the usual analysis (and the scope) of the first sentence of the Preface, bearing in mind that Herodotus himself makes no reference to sources of any kind but only to his own objectives: *"I, Herodotus of Halicarnassus, here present the results of my enquiries, so that time should not be able to destroy the works of man, and so that the great exploits accomplished by the Greeks and by the Barbarians, should not be forgotten..."*

22. For information about the methodological considerations of its founders see: Marc Bloch, *op. cit.*, 1949 and Lucien Febvre, *Combats pour l'histoire*, Paris, Armand Colin, 1953. On the 'Annales school' itself, see François Dosse, *L'histoire en miettes. Des 'Annales' à la 'nouvelle histoire'*, Paris, La Découverte, Pocket, 1987; Guy Bourdé, Hervé Martin, *Les écoles historiques*, Paris, Seuil, 1989, Points Histoire, part. chapter 'L'école des Annales', p. 215-243.

23. Lucien Febvre, *Combats pour l'histoire*, Paris, Armand Colin, 1953. This sentence has been important to me ever since I started work, serving almost as a kind of motto. I explore its implications more fully in: Anne Lehoërff, *L'artisanat du bronze en Italie centrale (1200-725 avant notre ère). Le métal des dépôts volontaires*, Rome, 2007 (Bibliothèque de l'École française de Rome 335).

24. One might remember the stir caused in 2007 by comments made by the President of the French Republic at that time, when he was travelling around Dakar (Senegal), and the stormy debates that followed. Not least an address he gave on the 26th of July 2007 to the University of Cheikh-Anta-Diop de Dakar (Sénégal) – some things he said provoked considerable reaction and controversy, in particular: *"African man has not sufficiently entered History"*. These words referred to the presence of African populations in history, in the European sense of the word, rather than the oral traditions of certain societies, which were not mentioned, and were therefore, it seemed, being excluded from history proper. Viewed from a long-term perspective, this statement is not without irony, the continent of Africa having been one of the first cradles of humanity.

25. Jacques Le Goff, *Histoire et mémoire*, Gallimard [1977], Folio histoire 1988.

26. Jean-Paul Demoule, *Les 10 000 ans oubliés qui ont fait l'histoire. Quand on inventa l'agriculture, la guerre et les chefs*, Paris, Fayard, 2017 stresses this. He notes in particular the beginnings of Protohistory and neolithisation.

27. If one were to indulge in a brutal summing up of these programmes of study in French schools one might say that it is just about the same as it was at the end of the 19th century, only redesigned somewhat to fit in with the trauma of 20th century wars, particular importance being attached to the social aspect: otherwise, we are taught the 'four periods' of history promulgated at the end of the 19th century: Antiquity, with the preamble sketching what came before (but only for very young classes), then the 'Great Mediterranean civilisations', (including the invention of writing and agriculture), then events considered chronologically important, then an increasingly pronounced emphasis on the 20th century with its horrors, its rapid changes and then globalisation. Much space is given to forms of historicised repentance in the explanation of conquests and acts of violence.

28. The questions surrounding periodisation are tackled humorously in Jacques le Goff's last work: *Faut-il couper l'histoire en tranches?*, Paris, 2015.

29. It is worth bearing in mind the recent arguments put forward by Sophie de Beaune, which are representative of this position in *Qu'est-ce que la Préhistoire* ? Paris, Gallimard, Folio histoire, 2016, which asserts on p. 23 that *"prehistory designates both a chronological period and the discipline which studies it"*, whilst highlighting a quotation which states the contrary from Raymond Aron *Paix et guerre entre les nations*, Paris, Calmann-Lévy, [1962], 2004: *"at a given moment in time, an individual may reflect on what has happened to him or her, groups of people may think about their past, or humanity may think about its evolution: this is how autobiography, specific histories and universal histories come into being"*. Prehistorians, on the whole, use the same methods as archaeologists, so it seems intellectually unjustifiable to isolate them. Besides, asserting independence simply perpetuates ancient intellectual territorial disputes and blockages, in a way that is harmful to historical research in the long run.

30. This was originally the subject of my 'Habilitation à Diriger des Recherche' (something a French citizen has to do in order to apply in France for a job as university professor). It was presented to the EHSS on the 31st of October 2009. The title of the thesis was: *By force of arms. The invention of war and metal between the forty-fifth and first centuries DC*. François Hartog was my supervisor and the jury also consisted of: Jean Guilaine, Kristian Kristiansen, Alain Schnapp, Claude Mordant, and Michel Pernot.

31   In 2016 my choice the plural form, "Prehistories" of Europe (Anne Lehoërff *op. cit.* 2016) was a deliberate one, to make a point that Prehistory is not a single entity. The desire to deconstruct myths and fantasies was very much present in my mind and forms the cornerstone of the book. Through writing it I have come to see just how much more needs to be done in order to get prehistory out of its figurative cave (…) so that a more accurate vision of ancient societies might prevail.

Chapter I - WHAT WARS?

32   This narrative concerning a set of weapons belonging to a possible warrior in about 1000 BC, is set out as a preamble over the six chapters; it is based upon real documentation and detailed technical studies in: Anne Lehoërff 2008, 2011, 2012 (ed.), 2017, 2018; Anne Lehoërff, Marc Talon (eds) 2017; Cyril Marcigny *et. al.* 2005; Marianne Mödlinger 2012; Benédicte Quilliec 2007.

33   Anne Lehoërff, Catherine Louboutin (eds), *Archéologie en musée et identiités nationales. Un hértiage en quête de nouveaux défis*, Proceedings of the international conférence, Saint-Germian-en-Laye, 2017, Leiden, Sidestone 2022.

34   *Le Petit Larousse illustré*, Paris, 2005, p. 529. (The most consulted dictionary of the French language).

35   Umberto Ecco, *op. cit.*, Paris, 2006, p. 18 where the author suggests this terminology, periodising war.

36   Machiavelli, *L'arte della Guerra, Tutte il opere storiche e lettere di Niccolò Machiavelli*, 1521.

37   Machiavelli, *Le Prince*, chapter xiv. For studies on Machiavelli: Raymond Aron, *Machiavel et les tyrannies modernes*, Paris, De Fallois, 1993; Patrick Boucheron, *Un été avec Machiavel, Equateurs parallèles*, 2017; Alessandro Fontana (eds), Langues et écritures de la République et de la guerre: études sur Machiavel, Gênes, Name, 2004; Pierre Manent, *Naissances de la politique moderne: Machiavel, Hobbes, Rousseau*, Paris, Gallimard, 2007. For an overview of war and the state in the modern period see: Jean Chagniot, *Guerre et société à l'époque moderne*, Paris, Puf, 2015 ; Laurent Bourquin, Joël Cornette, Hervé Drévillon, *La Monarchie entre Renaissance et Révolution*, Paris, Seuil, 2000, L'univers historique.

38   Machiavelli, *Discorsi sopra la prima deca di Tito Livio*, 1531.

39   Carl von Clausewitz, *Vom Kriege*, 1832.

40   For these two readings of the text see: Raymond Aron, *Penser la guerre, Clausewitz*, 2 volumes, Paris, 1976, this analysis was written during the Cold War and involved a heartfelt rejection of war; also, René Girard: *Achever Clausewitz*, Paris, 2007, which looks at Clausewitz from an anthropological point of view, as a visionary rather than a strategist.

41   This is the thesis of Yuval Noah Harari in: *Sapiens. Une brève histoire de l'humanité*, Albin Michel, 2015, who sees in *sapiens*, the form of *Homo* that was victorious over other subspecies of humans, precisely because of an ability to adapt and evolve, and to think imaginatively and creatively, which made *homo* able to invent, adapt and overcome.

42   The founders of the *Annales* school were amongst the first to criticise the idea of the omnipresence of war in the form of 'histories of battles', which they considered to be too superficial; they stressed the need to open other ways of looking at writing history. For all that, they did not relinquish the subject: Marc Bloch, *Les rois thaumaturges*, 1924 ; *L'étrange défaite*, 1940. This continued to be the case for succeeding generations: Fernand Braudel, *La Méditerranée et le monde méditerranée à l'époque de Philippe II*, Paris, Armand Colin 1949, is also a history of war which takes a long view, constituting a major historiographical event. On Braudel and time, see: Yves Lemoine, *Fernand Braudel, Espaces et temps de l'historien*, Paris, Punctum, 2005. On the 'battle' view of history see : Nicolas Offenstadt, 'Histoire-bataille', in Christian Delacroix, François Dosse, Patrick Garcia, Nicolas Offenstadt (eds) *Historiographies, concepts et débats*, volume 1, Paris, Gallimard, 2010, p. 162-169. On historians and time, there are various views: Michel de Certeau, *L'écriture de l'histoire*, Gallimard, Folio histoire, 1975; Jean Leduc, *Les historiens et le temps. Conceptions, problématiques*, écritures, Seuil, Point histoire, 1999; Krzysztof Pomian, *L'ordre du temps*, Gallimard, Bibliothèque des histoires, 1984.

43   Thomas Hobbes, *Le Léviathan*, [1651], Paris, ed. Sirey, p. 125.

44   See in particular Etienne de la Boétie, *Discours de la servitude volontaire*, written in 1548 when he was not yet 20, no doubt in the context of the violence which took place in the context of the antifiscal revolt in Guyenne which was taking place that very year. In this he distinguishes three types of tyrant who may reach power by election, by violence or by succession. Tyranny ('*voluntary servitude*') comes about not so much through fear (which leads revolt) as through habit, religion and the co-opting of a circle around the tyrant which brings about a cascading, pyramidal effect.

45   Louis Antoine de Bougainville, *Voyages autour du monde*, 2 volumes, Paris, 1771. Here the author relativises the idea of the 'noble savage', but Rousseau does not follow him in this. By contrast, Denis Diderot (1713-1784), in his *Supplément au voyage de Bougainville* (écrit en 1772), Paris, 1796, adopts a position closer to the views of de Bougainville.

| 46 | Jean-Pierre Vernant, *Introduction*, p. 10, in Jean-Pierre Vernant (ed.), *Problèmes de la guerre en Grèce ancienne*, Paris, (1968), 1985.
| 47 | For a selection of works on the subject of war in classical Antiquity see: André Bertrand, *Guerre et violence dans la Grèce antique*, Paris, Fayard, 2014 ; Jean-Nicolas Corvisier, *Guerre et société dans les mondes grecs (490-322 av. J.-C)*, Paris, Armand Colin, collection U, 1999 ; Paul Courbin *La guerre en Grèce à Haute époque d'après les documents archéologiques*, dans Jean-Pierre Vernant (ed) *Problèmes de la guerre en Grèce ancienne*, Paris (1965) 1999, chapter 3, p. 89-120, pl. I-VIII; Montagu Drogo, John, Greek and Roman warfare: battles, tactics and trickery, MBI Pub., 2006; Yvon Garlan, *La guerre dans l'Antiquité*, Paris, 1972; *id. L'homme et la guerre*, dans Jean-Pierre Vernant, *L'homme grec*, Paris, 1993, p. 65-101; Yann Le Bohec, *La guerre romaine. 58 avant J.-C, 235 après J.-C.*, Paris, Tallandier, 2014; Claude Nicolet, *Le métier de citoyen dans la Rome républicaine*, (1988), Paris, Gallimard, 2015; Jean-Pierre Vernant (ed.), *Problèmes de la guerre en Grèce ancienne*, Paris, (1968); John Warry, John Gibson, *Warfare in the classical world: war and the ancient civilisations of Greece and Rome*, Salamander books, 1998. It is interesting that even in the case of modern titles, which take a longer view, divisions between the western and central Mediterranean world and the world of Western and Northern Europe remain the norm: Stefan Chrissanthos, *Warfare in the ancient world: from the Bronze Age to the fall of Rome*, London, Praeger, 2008; Jestice Phyllis *et al.*, *Fighting techniques of the ancient world 3000 BC – AD 500: equipment, combat skills and tactics*, London, Greenhill, 2002.
| 48 | Jack Goody, *The Theft of History*, Cambridge University Press, 2006 (*Le vol de l'Histoire : Comment l'Europe a imposé le récit de son passé au reste du monde*,Paris, Gallimard, coll. « NRF Essais », 2010) ; Serge Gruzinski, *Les Quatre Parties du monde. Histoire d'une mondialisation*, Paris, La Martinière, 2004, *ibid. La Machine à remonter le temps*, Fayard, 2017.
| 49 | This expression is taken from the Jack Goody's title, *Le vol de l'histoire. Comment l'Europe a imposé le récit de son passé au reste du monde*, [2006 for the English edition], Paris, Gallimard, 2010, NRF Essais. By the same author: Jack Goody, *La raison graphique. La domestication de la pensée sauvage*, Paris, Les éditions de minuit, 1977 ; Serge Gruzinski, *La machine à remonter le temps*, Paris, Fayard, 2015; François Hartog, *Anciens, modernes, sauvages*, Paris, Galaade éditions, 2005.
| 50 | Hans Staden, *Nus, féroces et anthropophages*, 1557, Paris, édition Métailié, 2005.
| 51 | Jacques F. Lafitau, *Mœurs des sauvages américains comparées aux mœurs des premiers temps*, 1724. In this he draws parallels between different types of societies and makes links, in a manner original for the time, between what he discovered in Canada and what he knew about antiquity. His work demonstrates powers of observation which sometimes make it possible for us to see him as a founding father of modern ethnology. See: Michèle Duchet, 'De l'histoire morale à la description des mœurs: Lafitau', in Michèle Duchet, *Le partage des savoirs. Discours historique, discours ethnologique*, Paris, La Découverte, 1985, p. 30-52.
| 52 | For the history of archaeology between the 19th and 20th centuries see: Jean-Paul Demoule, Christian Landes (eds), *La fabrique de l'archéologie en France*, Paris, la Découverte, 2009; Alain Schnapp, *La conquête du passé. Aux origines de l'archéologie*, Paris, Carré, 1993; Bruce G. Trigger, *A history of archaeological thought*, Cambridge University Press, [1989], 1994. More specifically, for 'Préhistoire' see: Arnaud Hurel, *La France préhistorienne de 1789 à 1941*, Paris, CNRS, 2007; Annette Laming-Emperaire, *Origines de l'archéologie préhistorique en France. Des superstitions médiévales à la découverte de l'Homme fossile*, Paris, 1964; Nathalie Richard, *Inventer la Préhistoire. Les débuts de l'archéologie préhistorique en France*, Paris, 2008.
| 53 | For the history of archaeology in the 19th and 20th centuries see: Jean-Paul Demoule, Christian Landes (eds), *La fabrique de l'archéologie en France*, Paris, la Découverte, 2009; Alain Schnapp, *La conquête du passé. Aux origines de l'archéologie*, Paris, Carré, 1993; Bruce G. Trigger, *A history of archaeological thought*, Cambridge University Press, [1989], 1994. More specifically with regard to 'prehistory': Arnaud Hurel, *La France préhistorienne de 1789 à 1941*, Paris, CNRS, 2007; Annette Laming-Emperaire, *Origines de l'archéologie préhistorique en France. Des superstitions médiévales à la découverte de l'Homme fossile*, Paris, 1964; Nathalie Richard, *Inventer la Préhistoire. Les débuts de l'archéologie préhistorique en France*, Paris, 2008.

54 This methodology is based upon the laying down of layers as an indicator of successive periods. Thus, unless there has been some disturbance, more ancient periods are further down and more recent levels are higher up. Two contemporary events can be identified if stratigraphic levels can also be identified. This succession of levels is a kind of physical chronology under the ground, but it is 'relative', that is that it shows primarily what came before, after or at the same time. But then, an object present at one level will make it possible to date it (either according to its type, or some other specific means of dating) and this will help to build up an 'absolute' chronology, fixing the events in a time-scale.

55 Alain Schnapp, *Les préadamites : une invention manquée de la préhistoire au XVIIe siècle*, in Anne Lehoërff (ed.), *Construire le temps. Histoire et méthode des chronologies et calendriers des derniers millénaires en Europe occidentale*, actes du colloque international, Lille, 2006, Glux-en-Glenne, 2008 (*Bibracte* 16), p. 33-40.

56 Marc-Antoine Kaeser, *Les Lacustres. Archéologie et mythe national*, Lausanne, Le Savoir suisse, 2004, p. 22-25.

57 Hans-Georg Bandi, *Immagini e riproduzioni di Palafitte nel XIX secolo*, in *Palafitte : mito e realtà*, exhibition catalogue, Verone archaeological museum, 1982, Verona, 1983, p. 15-24.

58 Marc-Antoine Kaeser *op. cit.* 2004 et aussi, Marc-Antoine Kaeser, *Visions d'une civilisation engloutie. La représentation des villages lacustres, de 1854 à nos jours*, Musée national suisse/Latenium, 2004.

59 Anne Lehoërff, Olivier Poncet, 'Un directeur historien. Auguste Geffroy (1820-1895) et l'École française de Rome', dans Michel Gras, Olivier Poncet (éd.), *Construire l'institution. L'École française de Rome, 1873-1895*, Rome, 2015, p. 103-147.

60 Anne Lehoërff, Olivier Poncet *op. cit.* 2015, part. p. 115-120.

61 Anne Lehoërff, *op. cit.*, Paris, Belin 2016, p. 384-386.

62 Carole Fritz (eds), *L'art de la Préhistoire*, Paris, Citadelles & Mazenod, 2017.

63 Anne Lehoërff, *op. cit.*, Paris, Belin 2016, p. 384-386.

64 Hartog François, *Le XIXe siècle et l'histoire. Le cas Fustel de Coulanges*, Paris, Seuil, Points histoire, 2001; Gauchet Marcel, *Philosophie des sciences historiques. Le moment romantique*, Textes de P. Barante, V. Cousin, F. Guizot, J. Michelet, F. Mignet, E. Quinet, A. Thierry, Paris, Seuil, 2002; Ivan Jablonka *L'histoire est une littérature contemporaine. Manifeste pour les sciences sociales*, Paris, Le Seuil, La librairie du XXe siècle, 2014, part.

65 Claude Blanckaert (ed.), *Les politiques de l'anthropologie. Discours et pratiques en France (1860-1940)*, Paris, 2001; Claude Blanckaert (ed.), *Le musée. Histoire d'un musée laboratoire*, Paris, Musée de l'Homme, 2015; Christine Laurière, *Paul Rivet. Le savant et le politique*, Paris, Publications scientifiques du Muséum national d'histoire naturelle, 2008.

66 Claude Lévi-Strauss, *Tristes tropiques*, Paris, Plon, 1955.

67 Quoted by Lawrence Keeley, *Les guerres préhistoriques* [translation of *War before civilization*, 1996], Paris, édition du Rocher, 2002, p. 30. One of ethnology's pioneering works by Malinowski is: *Les Argonautes du Pacifique Occidental*, published in 1922, translated into many languages (Gallimard) for the French edition which is frequently reprinted.

68 Pierre Clastres, *Archéologie de la violence. La guerre dans les sociétés primitives. Essai*, Revue Libre, [1977], Éditions de l'Aube, édition 2010, p. 7-8.

69 This is also the notion that forms the basis of the principles elaborated by the sociologist Spencer in his *Principes de sociologie*, used and quoted by Clastres, *op. cit.* 2010, p. 12.

70 Christophe Darmangeat 2021

71 Ivan Jablonka *op. cit.* 2014.

72 It is indeed high time to break down such barriers and old paradigms, which are cumbersome and fail to correspond to present day needs or scientific realities. In order to escape them, to free ourselves from them, no doubt such questions will have to be considered in depth, and we should not hesitate to overturn the present state of affairs, including our habits as researchers, at an academic level and in the education system. It would not be right to share Sophie de Beaune's reticence with regard to the isolation of the Neolithic and Prehistory, using the pretext that *"the inclusion of the Neolithic in prehistory is ratified in academic institutions and it would be very difficult nowadays to undo this separation"*. *op. cit.* 2016, p. 26. It is academic researchers who create the various frameworks. If such frameworks fail to correspond to scientific results, it is the duty and the responsibility of intellectuals to change the present state of affairs.

73 Paul Jamin, '*La fuite devant le mammouth*', 1885, Musée de l'Homme, Paris.

74 Paul Jamin, '*Le rapt à l'Âge de pierre*', 1888, musée Saint Rémi Reims.

75 Jean Guilaine *op. cit.* 2017 ; Marc-Antoine Kaeser *op. cit.* 2004; Anne Lehoërff *op. cit* 2016, p. 299-335 and Anne Lehoërff, 'Guerres et inégalités sociales à l'Âge du bronze', dans Jean Guilaine, Dominique Garcia (eds) *La Protohistoire*, published on the occasion of the international Union of Sciences of Pre-and Proto-history, Paris, juin 2018, Paris, Hermann, 2018, p. 283-295.

76 Jean-Paul Demoule, *On a retrouvé l'histoire de France. Comment l'archéologie raconte notre passé*, Robert Laffont, 2012.

77 Alain Deyber, *Vercingétorix chef de guerre*, Lemme, 2017; Christian Goudineau, *Le dossier Vercingétorix*, Paris, Babel, 2001 ; Anne Lehoërff, 'Vercingétorix, l'homme d'une conclusion ?', *op. cit.* 2016, p. 511-518; Serge Lewuillon, *Vercingétorix ou le mirage d'Alesia*, Paris, Complexe, 1999.

78 People were even aware of a few famous times when the Celts inspired fear throughout the Mediterranean world: in Rome on the Capitol when the cries of geese avoided a disaster for the Romans, on 18 July 390 BC, according to Livy (or 386 according to Polybius), at Delphi in 279/278 BC where Pythia saved the sanctuary (Diodorus of Sicily, XXII, 13: Pausanius, X, 21-22), when the armies of Alexander and Galatea did not cease from combat.

79 The site has now become a European research centre with its own museum of Celtic civilisation. Archaeological excavations continue each year, alongside international scientific conferences for students.

80 For the construction of the narrative by historians see: Sylvain Venayre, *Les origines de la France. Quand les historiens racontaient la France*, Paris, Seuil, 2013; see too, by the same author, for a deconstruction of the myths in cartoon form: Sylvain Venayre, Étienne Davodeau, *La Balade nationale. Les origines*, Paris, La Revue dessinée-La Découverte, Histoire dessinée de la France, volume 1, 2017.

81 Here, the role of Ernest Lavisse in the education of numerous generations was very important, not least with regard to his '*L'histoire de France illustrée depuis les origines jusqu'à la Révolution*', reedited and reprinted on several occasions, and which formatted the minds of generations of pupils. A veritable figurehead in the national story, he held a key position at the head of the academic system, as an iconic historian whose thinking dominated and gave legitimacy from the III Republic on. Julius Caesar was the heroic civiliser of the valiant but inferior Gauls. From this perspective, the 'pre-Celtic savages' were not likely to get much of a look in...

82 Ludivine Pechoux (ed.), *Les Gaulois et leurs représentations*, Paris, Errance, 2011.

83 A picture painted in 1893 and kept in the musée des Beaux-Arts de La Rochelle. For a study, see: François Malrain, Matthieux Poux (eds), *Qui étaient les Gaulois*, Paris, Lamartinière, 2011, p. 77.

84 The illustration can be seen in Ludivine Péchoux (ed.) *op. cit.* 2011, p. 20.

85 John Powell, *Weapons and warfare*, Pasadena, Salem press, 2010; Antony Snodgrass, *Early Greek armour and Weapons from the end of Bronze Age to 600 B.C*, Édimbourg, 1964; in addition, the topic of war was on the programme for the aggregation in France in 1999 leading to the publication of a number of theses from 1999 to 2001.

86 John Keegan, *Histoire de la guerre. Du Néolithique à la guerre du Golfe*, Paris, Dagorno, 1996 for the French translation.

87 Lawrence Keeley, *op. cit.* [1996], 2002, chapter I, 'L'idéalisation du passé'.

88 Lawrence Keeley *op. cit.* 1996, p. 14.

89 See, for example, Pierre Vidal-Naquet's: 'Pourquoi et comment je suis devenu historien', in *Le choix de l'histoire*, Arléa, 2004, p. 13-50. From the first lines of this piece, he stressed the importance of one of the earliest of these written texts in 1948 in *Imprudence*, 'We did not make war', reminding us of his Jewish origins, the tragic disappearance of his parents in 1944 and his denunciations of the atrocities committed in the Algerian war, then largely hushed up in the wake of the Aubin affair. For the present generation of grandchildren, see Ivan Jablonka, *L'histoire des grands-parents que je n'ai pas eus*, Paris, le Seuil, 2012, Librairie du XXIe siècle.

90 I am thinking of Jean-Pierre Vernant (1914-2007) for example on antiquity, which sometimes came from the seminaries of Alain Schnapp (born after the Second World War), and Pierre Vidal-Naquet (1930-2006), who represent the three generations.

91 Jean-Pierre Vernant, *La traversée des frontières*, Paris, Seuil, 2004, p. 19.

92 Lawrence Keeley, *op. cit.* 1996, p. 14.

93 In the French system, the *agrégation* is a competitive examination which one must pass in order to become a history (or geography) teacher in a *lycée* (higher level secondary school).

94 Pierre Vidal-Naquet on the Aubin affair.

95	Our approach to history and the way we write it was affected. This worry is at the heart of: Roger Chartier, *Au bord de la falaise. L'histoire entre certitudes et inquiétude*, Paris, Albin Michel, 2009; François Hartog, *Croire en l'histoire*, paris, Flammarion, 2013; Gérard Noiriel, *Sur la crise de l'histoire*, Paris, Belin, 1996.
96	Pierre Nora (ed.), *Les lieux de mémoires*, Paris, Gallimard, Bibliothèque illustrée des histoires (3 volumes: 'La République', 'La Nation', 'La France'), 1984-1997.
97	This introspection even took on an intellectual form, becoming the norm in France in the context of universities' pursuit of human sciences: in 1987 Pierre Nora published texts by seven historians entitled: *Essais d'ego-histoire*; on 23 November 1988 in France, an announcement was made that the HDR (*l'Habilitation à diriger des recherches*) had to include a memoir written by applicants about themselves. This was soon baptised in academic jargon an 'ego-history'. Amongst the most successful examples, which combines humour, self-mockery and mockery of the exercise required was: Sylvain Venayre, *Disparu. Enquête sur Sylvain Venayre*, Paris, Les Belles Lettres, 2012.

Chapter II - RESEARCH 'EVIDENCE'

98	This notion is taken from: Ivan Jablonka, *L'histoire est une littérature contemporaine*, op. cit., p. 7.
99	Alain Corbin, *Le monde retrouvé de Louis-François Pinagot*, Paris, Flammarion, 1998, who set himself the task of writing the story of an anonymous person from the 19th century (20 June 1798 – 31 January 1876, according to state records), who lived in le Perche, and was chosen 'randomly' from the archives. The historian thus taking it upon himself to write about 'people submerged by time'.
100	Ivan Jablonka, *L'histoire est une littérature contemporaine*, op. cit., p. 164.
101	Successive hypotheses have been anchored in the times that have produced them, from medieval legends to quite wild theories in the 1960s and 1970s when the thought was even entertained that megaliths were created by men coming from other planets, in the context of the conquest space and fascination in 'extra-terrestrial' worlds. See: Anne Lehoërff, *Préhistoires d'Europe*, op. cit., chapter V.
102	For a good guide to Palaeolithic art see: Carole Fritz (ed.), *L'art de la Préhistoire*, op. cit.
103	Elena Man-Estier, Patrick Paillet, 'La "scène du puits" de Lascaux ou les multiples récits issus des profondeurs du temps', *in* Anne Lehoërff (ed.), 'Dossier: La Préhistoire', *La Nouvelle Revue française*, op. cit., p. 130-135.
104	Jean Guilaine, Jean Zammit, *Le sentier de la guerre. Visages de la violence préhistorique*, Paris, Seuil, 2001, p. 90.
105	*Ibid.*, p. 150.
106	*Ibid.*, the chapter 'L'agriculture : le calme ou la tempête ?' gives several examples.
107	On the iconography of the Palaeolithic period see: Carole Fritz (ed.), *L'art de la Préhistoire, op. cit.*; of Protohistory (Neolithic-Metal Age): Venceslas Kruta, *L'Europe des origines. La Protohistoire, 6000-500 avant J.-C*, Paris, Gallimard, 'L'univers des formes', 1992 ; of the Bronze Age: *L'Europe au temps d'Ulysse. Dieux et héros de l'âge du bronze*, catalogue de l'exposition, Paris, 1999; of the Iron Age: Christiane Éluère, *L'art des Celtes*, Paris, Citadelles & Mazenod, 2004. For a study of the most ancient figurative representations in Europe see: Jean-Paul Demoule, *Naissance de la figure. L'art du Paléolithique à l'Âge du fer*, Paris, Gallimard, 'Folio histoire', 2017 (first edition: 2007). On depictions specifically related to warriors see: Franco Marzatico, Paul Gleirscher (eds), *Guerrieri, Principi ed Eroi fra Danubio e il Po dalla Preistoria all'Alto Medioevo*, catalogue de l'exposition, Trente, Castello Del Buonconsiglio, 2004.
108	Richard Harrison, *Symbols and Warriors. Images of the European Bronze Age*, Bristol, Western Academic and Specialist Press Limited, 2004.
109	Christiane Éluère, *L'art des Celtes*, op. cit., Anne Lehoërff, *Préhistoires d'Europe*, op. cit., p. 401.
110	Christiane Éluère, *L'art des Celtes*, op. cit.
111	For a detailed study of each decorated panel see: Christian Goudineau (eds), *Religion et société en Gaule*, Paris, Errance, 2006, part. p. 53-77. For details of each panel see also: Anne Lehoërff, *Préhistoires d'Europe*, op. cit., p. 50-52.
112	Yves Desfossés, Gilles Prilaux, Alain Jacques, *L'archéologie de la Grande Guerre*, Rennes-Paris, Éditions Ouest-France/Inrap, 2008.
113	Jean Guilaine, Jacques Sémelin (eds), *Violences de guerre, violences de masse. Une approche archéologique*, Paris, La Découverte, 2016.

114 Which does not mean that results are always forthcoming. As Georges Duby reminds us, the study of physical data is not always easy: *"Remnants of military equipment dating from this time [1214] are very rare indeed. For a long time it had not been the custom for the dead to bear their weaponry with them into the tomb, the privileged place for archaeological finds. And aging weapons were hardly ever kept or put to one side in the dwelling places of nobles. They were used straight away to make new ones since iron was still scarce at the time."* Georges Duby, *Le dimanche de Bouvines*, Paris, Gallimard, 'Folio histoire', 1985, p. 35 (first edition: 1973).

115 *Ibid.*

116 Olivier Buchsenschutz and Alain Schnapp, 'Alesia', *in* Pierre Nora (eds), *Les lieux de mémoire, op. cit*, tome III, p. 4103-4140 ; Jean-Louis Voisin, *Alesia*, Paris, Perrin, 2014. For a recent survey of the subject: Michel Reddé, Siegmar von Schnurbein (eds), *Alesia et la bataille du Teutoburg. Un parallèle critique des sources*, Actes du colloque organisé à l'Institut historique allemand de Paris, Supplément à *Francia*, 2008 ; and also: Christian Goudineau, 'Le mythe Gaulois', *in* Jean-Paul Demoule, Bernard Stiegler (eds), *L'avenir du passé. Modernité de l'archéologie*, Paris, La Découverte, 2008, p. 212-222 ; Anne-Marie Thiesse, *La création des identités nationales. Europe*, XVIIIe -XXe siècle, Paris, Seuil, 1999. For the most recent survey of the Gauls: Jean-Louis Brunaux, *Nos ancêtres les Gaulois*, Paris, Seuil, 2008 et *Les Celtes. Histoire d'un mythe, op. cit.* ; John Collis, *The Celts, Origins, Myths, Inventions*, London, The History Press, 2003. In a similar vein, on debates about the renewal of 'national identity' see: Armelle Bonis, Joëlle Burnouf, Jean-Paul Demoule (eds), 'Archéologie et passions identitaires', *Les Nouvelles de l'archéologie*, n° 67, printemps 1997 ; Jean-Paul Demoule, 'L'archéologie de la France : un refoulement national ?', *in* Jean-Paul Demoule, Bernard Stiegler (eds), *L'avenir du passé, op. cit.*, p. 223-245.

117 There are various views on this topic, including: Pierre Nora (ed.), *Les lieux de mémoire, op. cit.*

118 In the spring of 2017, the discovery of the remains of *homo sapiens* at Djebel Irhoud (Morocco) made it clear that our direct biological ancestors were around about 100,000 years earlier than hitherto believed, which then dated to 200,000 BC on the basis of remains found in Ethiopia.

119 Jean Guilaine, Jean Zammit, *Le sentier de la guerre, op. cit.* ; Jean-Paul Demoule, 'La violence', Dossier : *Le Néolithique à l'origine du monde contemporain, Documentation photographique*, n° 8117, mai-juin 2017, p. 50-51. Philippe Lefranc, Anthony Denaire, Christian Jeunesse (eds), *Données récentes sur les pratiques funéraires néolithiques de la plaine du Rhin supérieur*, Oxford, Archaeopress, 2014. For an overview of the European Neolithic period: Chris Fowler, Jan Harding, Daniela Hofmann (eds), *The Oxford Handbook of Neolithic Europe*, Oxford, Oxford University Press, 2015.

120 Jiri Hrala, Radka Sumberova, Milos Vavra (eds), *Velim: a Bronze Age fortified site in Bohemia*, Prague, Institut d'archéologie, 2000.

121 Niels Andersen, 'Causewayed Enclosures in Northern and Western Europe', Chris Fowler, Jan Harding, Daniela Hofmann (eds), *The Oxford Handbook of Neolithic Europe, op. cit.*, p. 795-812.

122 Some authors involved in the study are still uncertain as to the precise location of the battle. Some see in it the site of a large scale battle with 4000 combatants and a death toll of 25%; others think it was a smaller scale sacrificial site: Gundula Lidke, Ute Brinker, Detlef Jantzen, Anne Dombrowsky, Jana Dräger, Joachim Krüger, Thomas Terberger, 'Warfare or sacrifice? Archaeological research on the Bronze Age Site in the Tollense Valley, Northeast Germany', Christian Horn, Kristian Kristiansen (eds), *Warfare in Bronze Age Society*, Cambridge, Cambridge University Press, 2017, p. 175-192; Detlef Jantzen, Thomas Terberger, 'Gewaltsamer Tod im Tollensetal vor 3200 Jahren', *Mitteilungen zur christlichen Archäologie*, July 2011; Krüher Joachim, Lidke Gundula, Lorenz Sebastian, Terberger Thomas (ed), Tolensetal 1300 v. Chr. Das älteste Schlachtfeld Europas, Darmstadt, WBG Theiss, 2020.

123 François de Polignac, *La naissance de la cité grecque : cultes, espace et sociétés*, VIIIe-VIIe siècle avant J.-C., (1984), Paris, La Découverte, 1995; Madeleine Jost, *Aspects de la vie religieuse en Grèce*, Paris, Sedes, 1992; Krzysztof Ulanowski (ed.), *The Religious Aspects of War in the Ancient Near East, Greece, and Rome*, Leyde-Boston, Brill, 2016.

124 Bruno Maureille, *Les origines de la culture. Les premières sépultures*, Paris, Le Pommier-Cité des sciences et de l'industrie, 2004. Alain Froment, Hervé Guy (eds), *Archéologie de la santé*, Paris, La Découverte, 2019.

125 Carole Fritz (ed.), *L'art de la Préhistoire, op. cit.*

126 Philippe Barral, 'Des dieux sans domicile ?', François Malrain, Matthieu Poux (eds), *Qui étaient les Gaulois ?, op. cit.*, p. 131-143.

127 Jean-Louis Brunaux, Bernard Lambot, *Guerre et armement chez les Gaulois (450-52 avant J.-C.)*, Paris, Errance, 1987. For an overview see: Patrice Arcelin, Jean-Louis Brunaux (eds), *Cultes et sanctuaires en France à l'âge du fer*, Paris, CNRS éditions, 2003.

128   For a recent survey see: Thierry Lejars, with contributions by Kurt W. Alt et Peter Jud, Nadine Dieudonné-Glad *et al.*, *La Tène, un site, un mythe 3*, Lausanne, *Cahiers d'archéologie romande*, 2013.

129   François Malrain, Matthieu Poux (eds), *Qui étaient les Gaulois ?*, *op. cit.*, p. 102-103; Anne Lehoërff, *Préhistoires d'Europe*, *op. cit.*, p. 448.

130   Christophe Maniquet, 'Le dépôt cultuel du sanctuaire gaulois de Tintignac à Naves (Corrèze)', *Gallia*, volume 65, 2008, p. 273-326.

131   For the methodology of radiocarbon dating see: Jacques Évin, Georges-Noël Lambert, Loïc Langouet, Philippe Lanos, Christine Oberlin, *La datation en laboratoire*, Paris, Errance, 1998.

132   See for example certain texts which are troubling from this point of view, including the discovery of the body of the victim in two different places, in Ivan Jablonka, *Laëtitia ou la fin des hommes*, Paris, Seuil, 2016. Also troubling is the homonymy between the two places where the body was discovered, that of a young woman called Laëtitia Perrais, and that of a Celtic prince: Lavau in Loire-Atlantique for the first and Lavau in Aube for the second.

133   Jean Guilaine, Jacques Sémelin (eds), *Violences de guerre, violences de masse, op. cit.* Though the question of Palaeolithic war is posed at the beginning, most of the work concerns more recent periods and contemporary conflicts in particular, and this is in a representative manner, in a present-day context. This work is an extension of a previous work: Jean Guilaine, Jean Zammit, *Le sentier de la guerre, op. cit.* This work is a journey through time, from the Neanderthal to the end of the Bronze Age (the beginning of the 1st millennium BC). Taking each epoch in turn, the authors look at evidence of violence in an approach based on physical clues, in an anthropological manner (in the sense of physical anthropology and the study of marks on bones) and in the context of more classical form of archaeology based upon objects and sites.

134   For details about the examples and illustrations see: Jean Guilaine, Jean Zammit, *Le sentier de la guerre, op. cit.*; Marylène Patou-Mathis, *Préhistoire de la violence et de la guerre*, Paris, Odile Jacob, 2013; Jean Guilaine, Jacques Sémelin (eds), *Violences de guerre, violences de masse, op. cit.*

135   The most ancient periods, approached from the perspective of violence, have logically been included in studies of war ever since the appearance of Lawrence Keeley's work: *Les guerres préhistoriques, op. cit.*, and even more recently and specifically in the Palaeolithic period: Paléolithique, Marylène Patou-Mathis, *Préhistoire de la violence et de la guerre, op. cit.*

136   Bruno Boulestin (*Approche taphonomique des restes humains. Le cas des mésolithiques de la grotte des Perrats et le problème du cannibalisme en préhistoire récente européenne*, British Archaelogical Reports International Series 776, Oxford, Archaeopress, 1999) who studied these bones clearly sees in them a practice of butchery leaving marks exactly the same on the bones of animals that had been cut up for food.

137   Moreover there is no place for the Bronze Age in: Jean Guilaine, Jacques Sémelin (eds), *Violences de guerre, violences de masse, op. cit.*

138   Gundula Lidke *et al.*, 'Warfare or sacrifice?', Christian Horn, Kristian Kristiansen (eds), *Warfare in Bronze Age Society, op. cit.*; Nick Thorpe, 'Warfare in the European Bronze Age', Harry Fokkens, Anthony Harding (eds), *The Oxford Handbook of the European Bronze Age*, Oxford, Oxford University Press, 2013, p. 234-247.

139   Dominique Garcia, 'Religion et société. La Gaule méridionale', Christian Goudineau (eds), *Religion et société en Gaule, op. cit.*, p. 135-155.

Chapter III - WHEN METAL SPEAKS

140   The procedure used by Thomsen follows a logic that was widespread in Europe for classification of collections materials and collections of all sorts in the modern period and which largely determined the creation of archives and museums: Michel Foucault, *Les mots et les choses. Une archéologie des sciences humaines*, Paris, Gallimard, 1966; Alain Schnapp, *La conquête du passé. Aux origines de l'archéologie, op. cit.* Pour les premières, Bruno Galland, *Les archives*, Paris, PUF, 'Que-sais-je ?', 2016; Krzysztof Pomian, 'Les archives. Du trésor des chartes au Caran', Pierre Nora (ed.), *Les lieux de mémoire, op. cit.*, volume III, p. 3999-4066; for the latter, Dominique Poulot, *Musée, nation, patrimoine, 1789-1815*, Paris, Gallimard, 1997; Dominique Poulot, *Patrimoine et musées. L'institution de la culture*, Paris, Hachette Éducation, 2001; Dominique Poulot, *Musée et muséologie*, Paris, La Découverte, 2005; Hedley Swain, *An introduction to Museum Archaeology*, Cambridge, Cambridge University Press, 2007. These classifications fit in more broadly with the establishment of academic disciplines and 19th century discourse: Christian Delacroix, François Dosse, Patrick Garcia, *Les courants historiques en France*, Paris,

	Armand Colin, 1999; Marcel Gauchet, *Philosophie des sciences historiques. Le moment romantique, op. cit.*; François Hartog, *Le XIXe siècle et l'histoire. Le cas Fustel de Coulanges, op. cit.* For the specifically French aspect of this approach see: Sylvain Venayre, *Les origines de la France. Quand les historiens racontaient la nation, op. cit.*
141	Arentzen, W., 2009: L.J.F Janssen en de Oudheden uit Hilversum, in: L.J.F. Jansen (1856 facsilime), *Hilversumse Oudheden. Eene bijdrage tot de ontwikkelingsgeschiedenis der vroegste Europesche volken*, Leiden (Sidestone Press), ix-xiii. Meyer, E., 1953: *Heinrich Schliemann. Briefwechsel I*, Berlijn.
142	He was not alone. Other contemporaries of his were working along the same lines, and he was able to draw their ideas together see: Christophe Delage, 'Once upon a time... the (hi)story of the concept of the 'chaîne opératoire', in French prehistory', art. cit.
143	Alain Testart, *Avant l'histoire. L'évolution des sociétés de Lascaux à Carnac*, Paris, Gallimard, 2012. p. 190.
144	See the contribution of Caroline Robion-Brunner *in* François-Xavier Fauvelle (ed.), *Civilisations de l'Afrique ancienne*, Paris, Belin, 2018.
145	The formulation comes from the evocative title of: Christopher Pare (ed.), *Metals Make the World Go Round. The Supply and Circulation of Metals in Bronze Age Europe*, Actes du colloque de l'université de Birmingham, juin 1997, Oxford, Oxbow Books, 2000.
146	The evolutionist and linear vision of societies began to be criticised from the beginning of the 20th century, within the context of certain trends in anthropology which favoured the diversity of societies; yet the earlier view re-emerges here and there showing that the idea of 'primitive societies' had not entirely disappeared, even if it was masked by the more acceptable term of 'traditional society'. One finds traces of this in contemporary writings for example: Barthélémy Courmont, *La guerre*, Paris, Armand Colin, 2007, introduction, p. 5: "*Trying to get an overview of war in history means investigating its evolution, over the differences between cultures, the levels of advancement and technological capacities of some civilisations compared to others.*" This work was essentially about contemporary conflicts and sees war as starting with the Greeks.
147	Paul Craddock, *Early Metal Mining and Production*, London, Archetype, 2010 (first edition: 1995); *Le premier or de l'humanité en Bulgarie. 5e millénaire*, catalogue de l'exposition au musée des Antiquités nationales de Saint-Germain-en-Laye, Paris, Réunion des musées nationaux, 1989; William O'Brien *Prehistoric Copper Mining in Europe, -5500/-500 BC*, Oxford, Oxford University Press, 2014; Christian Strahm, 'L'introduction et la diffusion de la métallurgie en France', Paul Ambert, Jean Vaquer (eds), *La première métallurgie en France et dans les pays limitrophes*, actes du colloque de Carcassonne, 28-30 septembre 2002, Paris, Société préhistorique française, 2005 (Mémoire de la Société préhistorique française, XXXVII), p. 27-35.
148	Peter Clark (ed.), *The Dover Bronze Age Boat in context: Society and Water transport in Prehistoric Europe*, Oxford, Oxbow Books, 2004; Anne Lehoërff (ed.), *Par-delà l'horizon. Sociétés en Manche et mer du Nord il y a 3 500 ans/ Beyond Horizon. Societies of the Channel and North Sea 3500 years ago/ Voorbij de Horizon. Samenlevingen in Kanaal en Noordzee 3500 jaren geleden*, Paris, Somogy, 2012.
149	Joakim Goldhahn, Johan Ling, 'Bronze Age rock art in northern Europe: contexts and interpretations', Harry Fokkens, Anthony Harding (eds), *The Oxford Handbook of the European Bronze Age, op. cit.*, p. 270-290.
150	A paper on this topic was presented at a conference organised by Jean Guilaine and Jacques Sémelin, as yet unpublished: Anne Lehoërff, *Préhistoires d'Europe, op. cit.*, p. 248 ; Klavs Randsborg, *Hjortspring: warfare and sacrifice in Early Europe*, Aarhus, Aarhus University Press, 1996.
151	Anne Lehoërff, *Préhistoires d'Europe, op. cit.*, p. 48-50; Harald Meller (eds), *Der geschmiedete Himmel. Die weite Welt im Herzen Europas vor 3600 Jahren*, Stuttgart, Konrad Theiss, 2004 ; Harald Meller, 'The sky disc of Nebra', Harry Fokkens, Anthony Harding (eds), *The Oxford Handbook of the European Bronze Age, op. cit.*, p. 266-269.
152	On exchanges in general see: Peter Clark (ed.), *The Dover Bronze Age Boat in context: Society and Water transport in Prehistoric Europe*, Oxford, Oxbow Books, 2004 ; Barry Cunliffe, *Facing the Ocean: The Atlantic and its peoples*, Oxford, Oxford University Press, 2001; Barry Cunliffe, *By Steppe, Desert and Ocean: the Birth of Eurasia*, Oxford, Oxford University Press, 2015; Jean Guilaine (eds), *Matériaux, productions, circulations du Néolithique à l'Âge du Bronze*, Séminaire du Collège de France, Paris, Errance, 2002; Kristian Kristiansen, Thomas Larsson, *The Rise of Bronze Age Society. Travels, Transmissions and Transformations*, Cambridge, Cambridge University Press, 2005; Anne Lehoërff, Marc Talon (eds), *Movement, Exchange and Identity in Europe in the 2nd and 1st Millennia BC: Beyond Frontiers, op. cit.*
153	André Leroi-Gourhan, *Les religions de la Préhistoire*, Paris, PUF, 1964, p. 4, referring to methods of approach to the study of Prehistory.

154   Alain Schnapp, *La conquête du passé. Aux origines de l'archéologie, op. cit.*

155   Jean-Pierre Mohen, Gérard Bailloud, *La vie quotidienne. Les fouilles du Fort-Harrouard*, Paris, Picard, 1987. (L'Âge du bronze en France 4).

156   My first study was about these remains in the Padan plain (Italy) at the end of the 2nd millennium. At the start of the 1990s I had no difficulties gaining access to this data, but sometimes I was asked what I intended to do with it, the interest in this kind of study did not then seem obvious. An article was based on this master's thesis: Anne Lehoërff, 'Les moules de l'Âge du bronze dans la plaine orientale du Pô. Vestiges de mise en forme des alliages base cuivre', *Padusa*, XVIII, 1992, p. 131-243.

157   Hoards exist during Neolithic (and probably Paleolithic), but their number was increasing a lot during Bronze Age. See for example : Karsten Wentink, *Ceci n'est pas une hache. Neolithic Depositions in the Northern Netherlands*, Leiden, Sidestone Press, 2006.

158   It is worth bearing in mind that the use of metal detectors is forbidden in France and removing metal goods from the soil is illegal, liable to prosecution, as per the law of *7 juillet 2016, Code du patrimoine, livre V*. This practice is legal in some European countries, which can give rise to debate. Some metal hoards have been discovered in this way, but they are deprived of their archaeological context and lay-out (which only a professional archaeologist can identify). Such discoveries therefore are only of limited interest, to the extent that collections of items made formerly in antiquarian days are no longer admissible in 21st century archaeology. Professional excavations encouraged in France, for example, stress the importance of accounting for the actual groupings that demonstrate the complexity of such practices as hoard-burials and the arrangement of the objects.

159   Michel Pernot (ed.), *Quatre mille ans d'histoire du cuivre. Fragments d'une suite de rebonds*, Bordeaux, Presses universitaires, 2017; Michel Pernot, Frank Montheillet, 'Archéométallurgie du formage : le martelage des alliages à base de cuivre à l'époque protohistorique. Premiers résultats', *Revue de métallurgie*, vol. 91, n° 5, mai 1994, p. 849-861. On technical vocabulary and a recent survey: Jean-François Piningre, Michel Pernot, Véronique Ganard, *Le dépôt d'Evans (Jura) et les dépôts de vaisselles métalliques de bronze en France au Bronze final*, 37e supplément de la *Revue archéologique de l'Est*, 2015.

160   Such hierarchies of objects are also found for some categories of non-metallic materials: ceramics, present everywhere in Europe from the start of protohistory (6th millennium for a large part of Europe), have a similarly very unequal status: ordinary ceramics (common or everyday) are just that, but fine ceramics, particularly if decorated, are treated in a privileged way, particularly if imported. Exogenous ceramics, imported from Attica (with black and red pictures) discovered in Iron Age protohistoric contexts (particularly in very rich tombs referred to as 'princely'), capture our interest most of all. Lithic materials (the technical term for rocks) have a limited aura amongst experts, other than some very beautiful objects, like the large polished axes of the final Neolithic or arrowheads with very long central stems from the upper Bronze Age from the west of Armorica. The status of human remains has changed over the course time, also sometimes commercially trafficked, even though this is now illegal.

161   As the head of the European project from 2011 to 2015 ('BOAT 1550 BC') I commissioned the project's exhibition and I had to deal with such phenomena: specific showcases, security measures, adapting to museum display policies in order to respect public expectations in writing the brochure and setting out a visitors' route. See: Anne Lehoërff, *Par-delà l'horizon, op. cit.* for the exhibition publication.

162   Anne Lehoërff, 'La métallurgie du bronze : techniques, usages et sociétés/Bronze Age metalcraft : technics, uses and societies', Jean Guilaine, Dominique Garcia (eds), *Protohistoire de la France : quarante ans de découvertes. Néolithique, Âge du bronze, Âge du fer, op. cit.*

163   Sylvain Venayre, *Disparu !, op. cit.*, chapter IV, 'Le message'.

164   Oscar Montelius, *Les temps préhistoriques en Suède et dans les autres pays scandinaves*, traduction de Salomon Reinach, Paris, Ernest Leroux éditeur, 1895.

165   Though metallurgy (as a technical component) is as good as absent from university archaeological teaching whilst stone and ceramics teaching is omnipresent.

166   The metallurgist is still the specialist who is least often consulted on site, which is a shame. People are more likely to call upon the services of a restorer, though such work should go on alongside that of the technologist. The paucity of training opportunities in metal archaeology, alongside this notion of the 'work of art', applied to metal, goes some way to explain this situation and the delay in setting up of *ad hoc* procedures which would be helpful to all aspects of research and conservation.

167   Anne Lehoërff, 'Le travail en laboratoire au service de l'histoire de l'artisanat métallurgique du début du premier millénaire avant notre ère en Italie', *Mélanges de l'École française de Rome*, tome 111, n 2, 1999, p. 787-846 ; Anne Lehoërff, 'Le métal archéologique du côté du laboratoire : mythes et réalités d'un matériau', Sylvie Boulud-Gazo, Théophane Nicolas (eds), *Artisanats et productions à l'Âge du bronze*, Séances de la Société préhistorique française, 4, Paris, Association pour la promotion des recherches sur l'Âge de bronze- Société préhistorique française, 2015, p. 97-108.

168   Authors, like Diodorus, give information about where mines were situated: *"It [the Island of Elba] possesses much ferrous rock which is cut up with a view to casting and the preparation of the iron, because there is an abundance of such ore."* (Diodorus, V, 13, 1 pour l'île d'Elbe - Aithaleia); Pliny the Elder, books XXXIII and XXXV in which real technical processes are adumbrated, regarding options of various mines for various ores and manufacturing in the true sense of the word.

169   Studies on how mines worked in the context of ancient populations were also tackled in a richly illustrated 16th century work *De re metallica* (Basle 1556) by Georgius Agricola (1494-1555) which was very successful and went into many editions in German, English and finally French. Agricola was a great traveller, humanist and is considered one of the founders of mineralogy related to metalcraft. For his contributions concerning mines see: Michel Angel, *Mines et fonderies au* XVIe *siècle d'après De re metallica*, Paris, Les Belles Lettres-Total Édition Presse, 1989 ; Marco Antonio Della Fratta et Montalbano, *Pratica minerale. Trattato*, Bologne, per li Manolessi, 1678.

170   For a large-scale survey see: R. J. Forbes, *Studies in Ancient Technology*, 9 vol., Leiden, E. J. Brill, 1955-1957; R. F. Tylecote, *A History of Metallurgy*, Boca Raton (Florida), CRC Press, 1992 (first edition: *A Early History of Metallurgy in Europe*, London, Longman, 1987).

171   For these years in particular see: Jean-Pierre Mohen, Christiane Éluère (eds), *Découverte du métal*, Paris, Picard, 1991, and *Le premier or de l'humanité en Bulgarie, 5e* millénaire, *op. cit.*

172   Flint deposits are exploited for local use in different places in Europe, but others are also sought for high quality manufacture which is exported over long distances, like the flint from Grand-Pressigny. Jacques Pelegrin, 'La production des grandes lames de silex du Grand-Pressigny', Jean Guilaine (eds), *Matériaux, productions, circulations du Néolithique à l'Âge du Bronze, op. cit.*, p. 131-148.

173   For a bibliography specific to iron see: Radomir Pleiner, *Archaeometallurgy of Iron*, Prague, Archaeological Institute CSAV, 1989, for a more general view: Jean-Paul Guillaumet, *Paléomanufacture métallique. Méthode d'étude*, Paris, Infolio, 2003 most of which deals with iron metallurgy; Jean-Pierre Mohen, Métallurgie préhistorique. Introduction à la paléométallurgie, Paris, Masson, 1990, chapter VI; également Forbes, Studies in Ancient Technology, *op. cit.*, and Tylecote, A History of Metallurgy, *op. cit.*

174   The terminology: Michel Mangin (ed.), *Le fer*, Paris, Errance, 2004, quoted by Jean-Paul Guillaumet, *Paléomanufacture métallique, op. cit.*

175   This is all too common in publications, even in 2017: Jean-Paul Demoule, *Les dix millénaires oubliés qui ont fait l'histoire, op. cit.*, article 'Bronze' dans le glossaire, p. 254: 'Le bronze est un alliage de cuivre, avec environ 10 % d'étain.' ('Bronze is copper alloy with about 10% tin').

Chapter IV - A LIST OF WEAPONS

176   The sum of objects comes potentially to several thousand, though this is not the place for a detailed inventory. Rather than an illusion of exhaustiveness and a boring list of objects studied more or less closely, the choice has been made here to select representative types and some individually representative, even emblematic, examples. The scientific literature and bibliographical references include illustrations from which they can be recognised.

177   Anthony Harding, *Warriors and Weapons in Bronze Age Europe, op. cit.*, p. 99 for estimates in England which estimate that there is a known Bronze Age sword for every 240 square kilometre; Christian Horn, Kristian Kristiansen, 'Contextualizing Bronze Age Warfare: the emergence of Martial arts', Christian Horn, Kristian Kristiansen (eds), *Warfare in Bronze Age Society, op. cit.*, 2017, p. 1-17, part. p. 3; other contributions also in: Marion Uckelmann, Marianne Mödlinger (eds), *Bronze Age Warfare*, Oxford, Archaeopress (British Archaeological Reports International Series 2255), 2011.

178   Gordon Childe, *The Dawn of European Civilization*, London-New York, Trubner-Knopf, 1925.

179   In the Near East, the first hafted axes are more ancient but they remain shorter for a long while and analyses of their composition show that a percentage of arsenic was used rather than tin. They evolve only later and do not figure in Mesopotamian iconography, as noted in: Guillaume Gernez, *Les armes du Proche-Orient ancien. Des origines à 2000 av. J.-C*, Paris, Errance, 2017, p. 43. The combat axe and the spear seem to have been favoured in the Mediterranean where metalcraft nevertheless developed early.

180   Archaeological publications and the museum catalogues illustrate these kinds of objects. For a study of these typical objects see: Anne Lehoërff, *Préhistoires d'Europe, op. cit.*, p. 324-325 ; also: Franco Marzatico, Paul Gleirscher (eds), *Guerrieri, Principi ed Eroi fra Danubio e il Po dalla Preistoria all'Alto Medioevo, op. cit.*

181   Anne Lehoërff, *Préhistoires d'Europe, op. cit.*, p. 290-297.

182   Studies made by various researchers show that swords were indeed used in fighting. I carried out a certain number. See also on this specific point: Bénédicte Quilliec, *L'épée atlantique : échanges et prestige au Bronze final*, Paris, Société préhistorique française, 2007 (Mémoire de la SPF XLII).

183   Anne Lehoërff, 'Le métal au service de la guerre dans l'Europe de la Protohistoire', Michel Pernot (ed.), *Quatre mille ans d'histoire du cuivre, op. cit.*, p. 103-115 ; Anne Lehoërff, 'The imaginary Crested helmet of Vercingetorix: what is creativity in Bronze Age metal production', Joanna Sofaer (ed.), *Considering Creativity: Creativity Knowledge and Practice in Bronze Age Europe*, Oxford, Archaeopress, 2018, chapter v.

184   Reflections on the role of the sword are found in the pioneering work on this weapon and its place in the Bronze and indeed the Iron Age: Anthony Harding, *Warriors and Weapons in Bronze Age Europe, op. cit.* ; Kristian Kristiansen, 'The Tale of the Sword. Swords and Swordfighters in the Bronze Age Europe', *Oxford Journal of Archaeology*, vol. 21, n° 4, November 2002, p. 319-332; Richard Osgood, *Warfare in the Late Bronze Age of North Europe*, Oxford, Archaeopress, 1998 (British Archaeological Reports International Series 694); Christopher Pare, *Swords, Wagon-Graves and the Beginning of the Early Iron Age in Central Europe*, Séminaire de l'université de Marburg 37, 1991; Radomir Pleiner, *The Celtic Sword*, Oxford, Oxford University Press, 1993; Marion Uckelmann, Marianne Mödlinger (eds), *Bronze Age Warfare, op. cit.*

185   For specific information about these swords see: Peter Schauer, *Die Schwerter in Süddeutschland, Österreich und der Schweiz*, Munich, Beck, 1971 (*PBF* IV.2), p. 193-195. For a broader context: Pierre-Yves Milcent, *Le temps des élites en Gaule atlantique. Chronologie des mobiliers et rythmes de reconstitution des dépôts métalliques dans le contexte européen (XIIIe-VIIe s. av. J.-C.)*, Rennes, Presses universitaires de Rennes, 2012.

186   Anne Lehoërff, 'L'Âge du bronze est-il une période historique ?', Dominique Garcia (ed.), *L'Âge du bronze en Méditerranée. Recherches récentes, op. cit.*

187   No example of sand-casting has been found from protohistorical times, but this process leaves practically no physical traces.

188   The Trundholm sun chariot (Denmark) dating from this period could not have been produced other than by a process of lost wax using a non-permanent mould. For an illustration of this point see: Anne Lehoërff, *Préhistoires d'Europe, op. cit.*, p. 240.

189   Anthony Harding, *Warriors and Weapons in Bronze Age Europe, op. cit*, p. 107 for examples of swords made of organic materials.

190   For the method and the results see: Anne Lehoërff, *L'artisanat du bronze en Italie centrale (1200-725 avant notre ère). Le métal des dépôts volontaires, op. cit.*, part. p. 241-242.

191   See: Jean-Louis Brunaux, Bernard Lambot, *Guerre et armement chez les Gaulois (450-52 avant J.-C.), op. cit.*; Franck Mathieu, *Le guerrier gaulois. Du Hallstatt à la conquête romaine*, Paris, Errance, 2007.

192   Thus, Jean-Noël Corvisier, *Guerre et société dans les mondes grecs (490-322 av. J.-C.)*, Paris, Armand Colin, 1999 uses the three words in the same sentence, in French, p. 13: "Pour l'essentiel, il [l'armement offensif] s'agit d'une lance ou d'un long javelot à pointe large, tenu à deux mains comme une pique pour frapper d'estoc. [...] Essentially, this is a spear with a broad point, held in two hands like a lance for stabbing."

193   François Bon, *Préhistoire. La fabrique de l'homme*, Paris, Seuil, 2009, p. 210.

194   *Ibid.*, note 2. Voir aussi Jacques Jaubert, *Chasseurs et artisans du Moustérien*, Paris, La Maison des Roches, 1999.

195   Jean-Luc Piel-Desruisseaux *Outils préhistoriques. Du galet taillé au bistouri d'obsidienne*, Paris, Dunod 2007, p. 162-167.

196   This is the vocabulary to designate the point. See: André Leroi-Gourhan (eds), *Dictionnaire de la préhistoire*, Paris, PUF, 1988, p. 68.

197   Yves Lanchon, Philippe Marquis, *Le premier village de Paris, il y a 6 000 ans. Les découvertes archéologiques de Bercy*, Paris, Paris Musées, 2000.

198   François Bon, *Préhistoire. La fabrique de l'homme, op. cit.*, p. 214.

199   Some fine examples and interesting reflections in: Pierre Pétrequin, Jean Vaquer, 'Masses, sphéroïdes et haches de pierre à perforation transversale', in *Signes de richesse. Inégalités au Néolithique*, Paris, Réunion des Musées nationaux, 2015, p. 29-34.

200 The first key reference is John Coles, 'European Bronze Age shields', *Proceedings of the Prehistoric Society*, vol. 28, 1962, p. 156-170. For a recent contribution, Marion Uckelmann, 'Protection, apparat et culte. De la fonction du bouclier à l'Âge du bronze', Luc Baray, Matthieu Honegger, Marie-Hélène Dias-Meirinho (eds), *L'armement et l'image du guerrier dans les sociétés anciennes. De l'objet à la tombe*, Dijon, Presses universitaire de Dijon, 2011, p. 270-278.

201 Harrison, Richard, *Symbols and Warriors. Images of the European Bronze Age*, Western Academic, Bristol, 2004.

202 Kristian Kristiansen, 'The emergence of warrior aristocracies in later European prehistory and their long-term history', John Carman, Anthony Harding (eds), *Ancient Warfare*, Gloucestershire, Sutton Publishing, 1999, p. 175-189, part. p. 178.

203 This figure of 13% is given by Marion Uckelmann, 'Protection, apparat et culte. De la fonction du bouclier à l'Âge du bronze', art. cit., p. 273. It would be worth checking the method of analysis to make sure this included no corroded parts which would have increased the tin levels. Only a sample (and not a surface analysis or powder micro-fragments), with a diagram of the section analysed would guarantee the reliability of the result.

204 One of the very first precise studies is: Léon Coutil, *Casques antiques proto-étrusques, mycéniens, grecs, gaulois et romains*, Mémoires de la Société préhistorique française, tome III, 1913-1914 ; Le Mans, Imprimerie Monnoyer, 1915, p. 163-225. This category is included in Anthony Harding, *Warriors and Weapons in Bronze Age Europe*, op. cit., which uses different categories without however tackling the technological aspect.

205 This is the Chalcidian type III helmet from the Odescalchi collection (inventory number 1720), Anne Lehoërff, 'L'Âge du bronze est-il une période historique ?', Dominique Garcia (ed.), *L'Âge du bronze en Méditerranée. Recherches récentes*, op. cit.

206 For the principles derived from physical sciences see, from amongst very many works: Jean Philibert, Alain Vignes, Yves Bréchet, Pierre Combrade, *Métallurgie du minerai au matériau*, Paris, Masson, 1998; Claude Volfovsky (ed.), *La conservation des métaux*, Paris, CNRS Éditions, 2001.

207 It is for this reason that one of the Norman helmets was bought by Ladislao Odescalchi. Anne Lehoërff, 'L'Âge du bronze est-il une période historique ?', Dominique Garcia (ed.), *L'Âge du bronze en Méditerranée. Recherches récentes*, op. cit. See also Cyril Marcigny et al., La Normandie à l'aube de l'histoire, op. cit.

208 These analyses were made on the basis of micro-sampling which made it possible a visualisation of the section analysed, according to a procedure defended in Anne Lehoërff, 'Le métal archéologique du côté du laboratoire : mythes et réalités d'un matériau', Sylvie Boulud-Gazo, Théophane Nicolas (eds), *Artisanats et productions à l'Âge du bronze*, op. cit.

209 It is kept in the museum of Musée d'archéologie nationale (Saint-Germain-en-Laye) inv. number 358.

210 See: Pierre Sauzeau, Thierry Van Compernolle (eds), *Les armes dans l'Antiquité. De la technique à l'imaginaire*, Actes du colloque international du SEMA (Montpellier, 2003), Montpellier, Presses universitaires de la Méditerrannée, 2007, p. 13-33, part. p. 28-31.

211 Christiane Éluère, *L'art des Celtes*, op. cit., p. 191.

212 Christophe Maniquet, 'Le dépôt cultuel du sanctuaire gaulois de Tintignac à Naves (Corrèze)', art. cit.

213 In 1910 in volume II of his *Manuel*, Joseph Déchelette made an allusion to the front part of a leather breast-plate found in 1834 near Picquigny in the Somme, of which there is no drawing and no remnants.

214 Marianne Mödlinger, 'European Bronze Age cuirasses. Aspects of chronology, Typology, Manufacture', art. cit.

215 For example: Alain Bulard, 'Un dépôt de neuf cuirasses découvert à Paris au XVIIe siècle', *Revue archéologique d'Île de France*, n° 1, 2008, p. 125-132.

216 Musée d'Archéologie nationale, Saint-Germain-en-Laye. Anne Lehoërff, 'Les cuirasses de Marmesse (Haute-Marne), un artisanat d'exception', art. cit., p. 95-106.

217 Musée d'Archéologie nationale, Saint-Germain-en-Laye, et musée de l'Armée, Invalides, Paris ; Jean-Pierre Mohen, 'Étude comparée de deux cuirasses hallstattiennes, la cuirasse "de Grenoble" et la cuirasse "de Naples"', *Annales du Laboratoire de recherche des musées de France*, 1970, p. 65-80.

218 Waldemar Deonna, *Les cuirasses hallstattiennes de Fillinges au musée d'Art et d'Histoire de Genève*, in *Préhistoire*, tome III, Paris, E. Leroux, 1934, p. 93-143, part. p. 96. This version is questioned by Peter Schlauser, *Die Urnenfelderzeitlichen Bronzepanzer von Fillinges*, Jahrbuch des Römisch-Germanischen Zentralmuseums Mainz, n° 25, 1978, p. 92-130, who thinks they were spread over and area of 1 à 2 m^2.

219 In the systems of present-day chronological correspondences, this fork corresponds to Ha A2/Ha B1 in the German system, or BF IIb-IIIa in the French system, that is 1100-950 BC.

220 Musée d'Archéologie nationale (MAN), inventory number 2757, collection Verchère de Reffye.

221   This calculation was carried out through sampling, using the following formula, based on measurements made of microstructures observed during metallography: final thickness of the sheet metal (between 0.4 and 0.5 millimetres), of sulphur (FF inclusion, on average 40 to 50 mm in the context of a biaxial type reshaping For the reference see: Anne Lehoërff, *L'artisanat du bronze en Italie centrale (1200-725 avant notre ère). Le métal des dépôts volontaires, op. cit.*

222   Anne Lehoërff, 'Les cuirasses de Marmesse (Haute-Marne), un artisanat d'exception', *art. cit.*

223   Knowing that the density of material is 9, that the average weight of a front or rear part of the breastplate is 1.5 kilogram, that the reshaping is in the order of about 90%, the volume of metal for a main piece will be about 100 cubic centimetres for a final surface of approximately a quarter of square metre, and therefore a blank of about 12 square centimetres for a thickness of about 10 millimetres (maximum). If one weighs the figure with the loss of thickness due to polishing (a measurable loss for in terms of the shaped indentations still visible on the rear side), we arrive at about 0.8 centimetres, which would still be thick for a bronzemaker nowadays.

224   The material analysed at Marmesse is also an alloy of 9% tin about which includes, as in Saint-Germain-du-Plain, traces of sulphurs in non-negligible proportions for such levels of plastic reshaping. These analyses were made on the basis of samples on the front breastplate of 86197, the metal-sheeting from the edge of 83754 and the back plate of 83758.

225   The value is then a weight of approximately 3 kilograms for the breastplates in their present state. Taking into about the loss due to the gaps, to the effects of corrosion and adding the weight of the internal padding, the total must have been in the order of 5 kilograms, of which 4 kilograms was metal.

226   The presence of a second phase rich in tin at the edges is common in metal sheets made of copper alloys from these periods, but not to such an extent.

227   Christiane Éluère, *L'art des Celtes, op. cit.*, fig. 111.

228   Anne Lehoërff, 'Les dépôts métalliques de Cannes-Écluse (Seine-et-Marne). Étude technique des jambières du dépôt 1', *Revue archéologique de l'Est*, volume 58, 2009, p. 439-451.

229   André Leroi-Gourhan, *Le geste et la parole*, volume I : *Technique et langage*, Paris, Albin Michel, 1964, p. 242.

Chapter V - OFF TO WAR

230   In 2016, Inrap (*Institut national de recherches archéologiques preventives*) held a conference on the subject, the papers to appear in 2018.

231   Marylène Patou-Mathis, *Préhistoire de la violence et de la guerre, op. cit.*

232   Pierre Clastres, *Archéologie de la violence. La guerre dans les sociétés primitives, op. cit.*

233   Jean Guilaine, Jean Zammit, *Le sentier de la guerre, op. cit.*, p. 152-168 for the main engravings.

234   *Ibid.*, p. 179ff and the map showing sites in France, p. 180.

235   Anne Lehoërff, *Préhistoires d'Europe, op. cit.*, p. 238.

236   For general works on the Neolithic period and an analysis of social inequality see: Jean-Paul Demoule, *Les dix millénaires oubliés qui ont fait l'histoire, op. cit.*; Jean Guilaine, *Les chemins de la Protohistoire, op. cit.*; Chris Fowler *et al.*, *The Oxford Handbook of Neolithic Europe, op. cit.* For archaeological and anthropological works dealing more specifically with this question see: Jared Diamond, *De l'inégalité parmi les sociétés. Essai sur l'homme et l'environnement dans l'histoire*, traduction de Pierre-Emmanuel Dauzat, Paris, Gallimard, 'NRF Essais', 2000; Brian Hayden, *L'homme et l'inégalité. L'invention de la hiérarchie durant la Préhistoire*, Paris, CNRS Éditions, 2008.

237   Maurice Godelier, 'Chefferies et États, une approche anthropologique', Pascal Ruby (ed.), *Les princes de la Protohistoire et l'émergence de l'État*, Naples-Rome, Publications de l'École française de Rome, 1999, p. 20.

238   Marshall Sahlins, *Stone Age Economics*, Chicago, Aldine-Atherton, 1972.

239   It is for this reason that locating the conventional end of 'prehistory' at this point, as far as terminology is concerned, and using that of 'protohistory' from the development of agricultural societies is clearly justified. It is a way out of the evolutionist vision of the 19th century associated with the 'Stone Age' and including the multiple aspects of the new world. See: Jean Guilaine, *Les chemins de la Protohistoire, op. cit.*, chapter I, 'Protohistoire et histoire globale' ; Jean Guilaine, Dominique Garcia (eds), *Protohistoire de la France : quarante ans de découvertes. Néolithique, Âge du bronze, Âge du fer, op. cit.*; Anne Lehoërff, 'Les paradoxes de la Protohistoire française', *art. cit.*, and 'L'Âge du bronze est-il une période historique ?', Dominique Garcia (ed.), *L'Âge du bronze en Méditerranée. Recherches récentes, op. cit.*

240   Anne Lehoërff, *Préhistoires d'Europe, op. cit.*, p. 85.

241 Anne-Marie Pétrequin, Pierre Pétrequin, *Objets de pouvoirs en Nouvelle-Guinée. Approche ethnoarchéologique d'un système de signes sociaux*, avec la collaboration d'Olivier Weller, Paris, Réunion des musées nationaux, 2006.

242 Maurice Godelier, 'Chefferies et États, une approche anthropologique', *in* Pascal Ruby (eds), *Les princes de la Protohistoire et l'émergence de l'État, op. cit.*, p. 19, distinguishes only six types of kinship in the world.

243 Maurice Godelier, 'Chefferies et États, une approche anthropologique', Pascal Ruby (ed.), *Les princes de la Protohistoire et l'émergence de l'État, op. cit.*, p. 20.

244 Anne Lehoërff, 'Le métal au service de la guerre dans l'Europe de la Protohistoire', Michel Pernot (eds), *Quatre mille ans d'histoire du cuivre, op. cit.*, p. 103-115 ; Anne Lehoërff, 'Guerres et inégalités sociales à l'Âge du bronze/Warfare and social inegalities during Bronze Age Europe', Jean Guilaine, Dominique Garcia (eds), *Protohistoire de la France : quarante ans de découvertes. Néolithique, Âge du bronze, Âge du fer, op. cit.*

245 Marcel Mauss, 'Essai sur le don. Forme et raison de l'échange dans les sociétés archaïques (1902-1903)', *L'Année sociologique*, seconde série, 1923-1924.

246 Maurice Godelier, 'Chefferies et États, une approche anthropologique', Pascal Ruby (ed.), *Les princes de la Protohistoire et l'émergence de l'État, op. cit.*, p. 19-30. For a broader overview by the same author: Maurice Godelier, *Aux fondements des sociétés humaines. Ce que nous apprend l'anthropologie*, Paris, Albin Michel, 2007.

247 Christian Horn, Kristian Kristiansen (eds), *Warfare in Bronze Age Society, op. cit.*, p. 3.

248 On the notion of combat: Wolfgang Sofsky, *Traité de la violence*, Paris, Gallimard, 'Nrf Essais', 1998, chapter VIII, 'Le combat'. Here the author sets out in particular links between combat, the regulated duel, the agon and the way events follow on from one another, phases of combat eventually leading to peace.

249 Authors writing in English do not hesitated to use the words 'swordsmen' or 'sword-fighters' to designate these warriors: 'The Tale of the Sword. Swords and Swordfighters in the Bronze Age Europe', *art. cit.*; Barry Molloy, 'Swords and Swordsmanship in the Aegean Bronze Age', *American Journal of Archaeology*, vol. 114, n° 3, July 2010, p. 403-428.

250 The hoplite could have a short sword, the *xiplos*, but this does not play a determining role in combat strategy involving hoplites.

251 With respect to more ancient periods, combats of the Mycenaean periods do however include swords and individual confrontations. The 12th century BC marks precisely a break in history and modes of combat in the Mediterranean region: Robert Drews, *The End of the Bronze Age: Changes in Warfare and the Catastrophe ca. 1200 BC*, Princeton, Princeton University Press, 1993. For a more catastrophist view: Eric Cline, *1177 BC. The Year Civilization Collapsed*, Princeton, Princeton University Press, 2014 (for the French edition: *1177 avant J.-C. Le jour où la civilisation s'est effondrée*, Paris, La Découverte, 2015). The author offers a *tour-d'horizon* of the central and eastern Mediterranean world without, however, considering more northern areas in order to make possible comparisons. He deals only with the 'civilisations' (there is a map at the start of the book) of Greece to Egypt (the western part) to the eastern banks as far as the Persian Gulf (the south and eastern extended areas). This is supposed to be seen as a global historical perspective, but as is so often the case, the non-Mediterranean, regions of Europe, which were also involved in the Bronze Age, are not mentioned.

252 Guillaume Gernez, *Les armes du Proche-Orient ancien. Des origines à 2000 av. J.-C, op. cit.*

253 Kristian Kristiansen, 'The emergence of Warrior Aristocraties in Later European prehistory and their Long-Term History', John Carman, Anthony Harding (eds), *Ancient Warfare, op. cit.*, p. 175-189, part. p. 178-180; Skogstrand, Lisbeth, Warriors and the Other Men. *Notions of Masculinity from the Late Bronze Age to the Early Iron Age in Scandinavia*, Oxford, Archeopress Archaeology, 2016.

254 Richard Harrison, *Symbols and Warriors. Images of the European Bronze Age, op. cit.*

255 The question has been asked above all regarding the ancient world and, for protohistory, essentially with regard to the Iron Age and the burials with chariots from the Iron Age: Peter Greenhalgh, *Early Greek Warfare: horsemen and chariots in the Homeric and Archaic Ages*, Cambridge, Cambridge University Press, 1973; *Le cheval symbole de pouvoir dans l'Europe préhistorique*, Catalogue de l'exposition, musée de Préhistoire d'Île-de-France, Nemours, 2001; Patrice Méniel, *Chasse et élevage chez les Gaulois (450-52 av. J.-C.)*, Paris, Errance, 1987 ; Christopher Pare, *op. cit.* 1998; Stuart Piggott, *The Earliest Wheeled Transport, from the Atlantic Coast to the Carpatian Sea*, London, Thames and Hudson, 1983; Philip Sidnell, *Warhorse. Cavalry in Ancient Warfare*, London, Hambledon Continuum, 2006.

256 The site of Illerup Adal near Alken (Denmark) yielded the remains of almost 200 humans all of which had suffered various violent traumas. Buried in bogland, they are considered to be a sacrificial deposition of men after a battle that was lost (elsewhere) and that this was not the place where the battle took place.
257 Radomi Pleiner *The Celtic Sword*, Oxford, Clarendon Press, 1993.
258 Anne Lehoërff, *Préhistoires d'Europe*, op. cit., chapter x.
259 François Malrain, Matthieux Poux (eds), *Qui étaient les Gaulois ?*, op. cit., p. 110.
260 Jean-Louis Arcelin, Jean-Louis Brunaux, *Cultes et sanctuaires en France à l'âge du fer*, op. cit.; Jean-Louis Brunaux, Bernard Lambot, *Guerre et armemement chez les Gaulois (450-52 avant J.-C.)*, op. cit.
261 Dominique Garcia, 'Religion et société. La Gaule méridionale', Christian Goudineau (ed.), *Religion et société en Gaule*, op. cit., chapter v.
262 For a consideration of the modern period, in particular debates between Protestants and Catholics against the backdrop of discoveries outside Europe, see: *Une sainte horreur ou le voyage en Eucharistie xvie-xviiie siècle*, Paris, PUF, 1996.
263 Alain Testart (ed), *Les armes dans les eaux. Questions d'interprétation en archéologie*, Paris, Errance, 2013. This work has the impressive ambition of imposing an interpretive method upon the subject. The result is stimulating even though the arguments used to refute theses involving religion are debatable (no ethnological examples, therefore a very improbable thesis). Also, most importantly, the positioning of ethnology with respect to archaeological data creates problems since the author questions archaeology's analytical and interpretive capacity when the latter is not based on ethnology or 'history' (p. 9). A position which is at the least debatable and which condemns archaeology as being fundamentally ineffective.
264 Caroline von Nicolai, 'Historique des interprétations du xixe siècle à nos jours', Alain Testart (ed.), *Les armes dans les eaux. Questions d'interprétation en archéologie*, op. cit, p. 17-51.
265 One might mention Alain Testart's only argument, *Les armes dans les eaux. Questions d'interprétation en archéologie*, op. cit., p. 9: "I have always been astonished at what archaeologists have supposed in order to interpret their finds, a ritual of offerings or sacrifices of weapons in waters whilst there is no example in societies textually documented or oral investigations, that is to say, neither in history, nor in ethnology." The fact that there are no examples in anthropology from recent societies outside Europe is not enough to exclude such hypotheses. From this author's point of view, only a rational understanding would be acceptable to explain hoards in wet places. This is to forget that the practice also concerns burials in earth and that this behaviour comes from an original practice which has to be considered as such during Europe's Metal Ages.
266 Conan Doyle, *The Sign of the Four* (French edition from 1896 with Hachette under the title *La marque des quatre*), second adventure of Sherlock Holmes.
267 Specifically linked to war: Anne Jacquemin, 'Guerres et offrandes dans les sanctuaires', *Pallas*, n° 51, 1999, p. 141-157; Raoul Lonis, *Guerre et religion en Grèce à l'époque classique. Recherches sur les rites, les dieux, l'idéologie de la victoire*, Besançon, Université de Franche-Comté, 1979.
268 Richard Bradley, *The Passage of Arms. An archaeological analysis of prehistoric hoards and votive deposits*, Cambridge, Cambridge University Press, 1990, and Richard Bradley, 'Hoards and the deposition of Metalwork', Harry Fokkens, Anthony Harding (ed.), *The Oxford Handbook of the European Bronze Age*, op. cit., p. 121-139; John Chapman, *Fragmentation in Archaeology. People, Places and Broken Objects in the prehistory of South Eastern Europe*, London, Routledge, 2000.
269 Christian Goudineau (ed.), *Religion et société en Gaule*, op. cit.
270 François Malrain, Matthieux Poux (eds), *Qui étaient les Gaulois ?*, op. cit., p. 110.

Chapter VI - WAR IN ALL ITS STATES

271 Jean-Pierre Vernant, *L'individu, la mort, l'amour. Soi-même et l'autre en Grèce ancienne*, Paris, Gallimard, 1989, p. 41-79
272 Patrice Brun, *Princes et princesses de la Celtique. Le premier Âge du fer (850-450 av. J.-C)*, Paris, Errance, 1987; Kristian Kristiansen, *Europe Before History*, Cambridge, Cambridge University Press, 1998.
273 Carole Fritz (ed.), *L'art de la Préhistoire*, op. cit.; Patrick Paillet, *Les arts préhistoriques*, Rennes, Ouest-France, 2006; Stéphane Petrognani (ed.), *De Chauvet à Lascaux. L'art des cavernes, reflet de sociétés préhistoriques en mutation*, Paris, Errance, 2013.
274 Marija Gimbutas, *The Gods and Goddesses of old Europe 7000 to 3500 BC: Myths, Legends and Cult Images*, Berkeley-Los Angeles, University of California Press, 1974 (for the French edition: *Le langage de la déesse*, Paris, éditions des Femmes, 2006).
275 Jacques Cauvin, *Naissance des divinités, naissance de l'agriculture : la révolution des symboles au Néolithique*, Paris, CNRS éditions, 1994.

276 Jean-Paul Demoule, dans *Les dix millénaires oubliés qui ont fait l'histoire, op. cit.*, chapter IX, 'Qui a inventé la domination masculine ?'; Alain Testart, *La déesse et le grain. Trois essais sur les religions néolithiques*, Paris, Errance, 2010.

277 Jean-Paul Demoule, Dossier : *Le Néolithique à l'origine du monde contemporain, op. cit.*, p. 54.

278 Claudine Cohen, *Femmes de la préhistoire*, Paris, Belin, 2016 p. 96-97, writes in a similar vein: "*The loss of visible manifestations of the woman's oestrus ascribes to sexuality a symbolic register at the very start of humankind, with its rules and social dimension, that is a wholly different status than just the performance of a physiological function.*"

279 See in particular: Maurice Godelier, *L'énigme du don*, Paris, Fayard, 1996; Françoise Héritier-Augé, Élisabeth Copet-Rougier, *Les complexités de l'alliance*, volume 1 : *Les systèmes semi-complexes*, Paris, Éditions des Archives contemporaines, 1990; Claude Lévi-Strauss, *Tristes Tropiques, op. cit., Le totémisme aujourd'hui*, Paris, PUF, 1962, and *La pensée sauvage*, Paris, Plon, 1962.

280 Adrienne Mayor, *Les Amazones. Quand les femmes étaient les égales des hommes (VIIIe av. J.-C.-Ier apr. J.-C.)*, translated from the English by Philippe Pignarre, Paris, La Découverte, 2017. The area studied in this book stretches from the Ukraine to modern day China including the areas round the Black Sea. The author uses texts from antiquity, Greek iconography and archaeology from the Scythian plains and the kurgans too as well as the north of China. The inclusion of this archaeological data opens interesting perspectives from this point of view, in a committed work, aiming essentially to provide a forceful demonstration of the reality of the concept of the Amazon, divided into three types (p. 53), including non-Greek female warriors. For the archaeology of these regions see: Iaroslav Lebedynsky, *Les Scythes. La civilisation nomade des steppes VIIe-IIIe siècles av. J.-C.*, Paris, Errance, 2001; Chriss Webber, *The Gods of Battles. The Thracians at War, 1500 BC-AD 150*, Barnsley, Pen & Sword Books, 2011.

281 Adrienne Mayor, *Les Amazones. Quand les femmes étaient les égales des hommes (VIIIe av. J.-C.-Ier apr. J.-C.), op. cit.*, p. 88-89 and chapter XIII for a list of weapons by category. The metalcraft is iron.

282 *Ibid.*, chap. IV and XIII.

283 Claude Rolley (ed.), *La tombe princière de Vix*, Paris, Picard, 2003.

284 Maurice Godelier, 'Chefferies et États, une approche anthropologique', Pascal Ruby (ed.), *Les princes de la Protohistoire et l'émergence de l'État, op. cit.*

285 Mythical 'Amazons' do not work a model because they are present in a place where they are not supposed to be. The rich tombs of central Asia Minor cannot be considered as the last resting places of 'Amazons' (Adrienne Mayor, *Les Amazones. Quand les femmes étaient les égales des hommes (VIIIe av. J.-C.-Ier apr. J.-C.), op. cit.*, but simply a feminine component in a normed system (funerary rituals being the fullest expression) which involves the presence of men and women. It is unknown in the west of Europe for anything like this to have taken place.

286 Pascal Brioist, Hervé Drévillon, Pierre Serna, *Croiser le fer. Violence et culture de l'épée dans la France moderne (XVIe-XVIIIe siècle)*, Ceyzérieu, Champ Vallon, 2002 ; François Guillet, *La mort en face. Histoire du duel de la Révolution à nos jours*, Paris, Aubier, 2008; Victor Kiernan, *The Duel in European History*, London, Zeed Books, 2016 (first edition: 1988).

287 This episode is related in Denis Bertholet, *Claude Lévi-Strauss*, Paris, Plon, 2003, p. 378-379. For a more recent biography, see also Emmanuelle Loyer, *Lévi-Strauss*, Paris, Flammarion, 'Grandes Biographies', 2015.

288 Nicolas Mariot, 'Faut-il être motivé pour tuer ? Sur quelques explications aux violences de guerre', *Genèses*, n° 53, 2003/4, p. 154-177.

289 Thomas Hobbes, *Léviathan*, 1651, éd. Paris, 2007, p. 224.

290 These enclosures were, and sometimes still are, seen as territorial markers associated with displaying power rather than being a real protection in the context of conflicts. See: Chris Fowler, Jan Harding, Daniela Hofmann (eds), *The Oxford Handbook of Neolithic Europe, op. cit.*

291 Christian Horn, Kristian Kristiansen (eds), *Warfare in Bronze Age Society, op. cit.*, p. 1.

292 These results are from studies by Johannes Müller: 'Demographic traces of technological innovation, social change and mobility: from 1 to 8 million Europeans (6000-2000 BC)' mentioned in Christian Horn, Kristian Kristiansen (eds), *Warfare in Bronze Age Society, op. cit.*, p. 15.

293 Étienne de La Boétie, *De la servitude volontaire*, 1576, Paris Gallimard 2008.

294 For an analysis which arises increasing from these questions see: Nathan Schlanger, Anne-Christine Taylor (eds), *La Préhistoire des autres. Perspectives archéologiques et anthropologiques*, Paris, La Découverte- Inrap 2012; André Delpuech, 'Il est des situations dont il faut s'accommoder', *Les Nouvelles de l'archéologie*, n° 147, March 2017, p. 61-72. See also, for a broader survey of the question of the 'savage' and the 'other' in mental and intellectual constructions: François-Xavier Fauvelle, À la recherche du sauvage idéal, Paris, Seuil, 2017; François Hartog, *Anciens, modernes, sauvages, op. cit.*; Marshall Sahlins, *La découverte du vrai sauvage*, English version by Claudie Voisenat, Paris, Gallimard, 'Bibliothèque des sciences humaines', 2007.

295 "*A State is a human community which claims the monopoly of the legitimate use of violence over a given territory.*" Max Weber, *Le savant et le politique*, 1919, Paris, 10/18, 2002). This definition should not to be confused with the idea of 'nation'. See extensions of Max Weber's thinking in Max Weber, Économie et société, 1921, Paris, Pocket, 2003.

296 A general overview of the concept: Pierre Bourdieu, *Sur l'État. Cours au Collège de France (1989-1992)*, Paris, Seuil, 2012 ; Alain Cambier, *Qu'est-ce que l'État ?*, Paris, Vrin, 'Chemins philosophiques', 2004.

297 Pierre Clastres, *La société contre l'État. Recherches d'anthropologie politique*, Paris, Les Éditions de Minuit, 1974.

298 Pierre Clastres, *Archéologie de la violence. La guerre dans les sociétés primitives, op. cit.*

299 For example, Philippe Contamine, *La guerre au Moyen Âge*, Paris, PUF, 1980. Hervé Drévillon et Paul Vo-Ha, séminaire 'Guerre et société à l'époque moderne', septembre-décembre 2017-janvier-avril 2018, université Paris-I Panthéon-Sorbonne. See also Hervé Drévillon (eds), *les Rois absolus (1629-1715)*, Paris, Berlin, coll. 'Histoire de France, 2011 et *L'individu et la guerre,* Paris, Belin, 2013.

300 Jack Goody, *La raison graphique. La domestication de la pensée sauvage, op. cit.*

301 Robin Osborne, Barry Cunliffe (eds), *Mediterranean Urbanization 800-600 BC*, Oxford, Oxford University Press, 2005.

302 Present day digital language is a new form of response to this same question of figures, thresholds and distances. It can cope with gigantic masses of data. It is also a language that is articulated and normed in a way that has gone far beyond its initial frame of reference, and has legitimised its own developments in the Internet, the 'Web'. This arises out of a double definition that is paradoxical almost to the extent of being contradictory, for it is at the same time physical and non-physical. This contradiction is so powerful that most people are not aware nowadays of what does and what does not leave traces regarding their online activity. The idea of an 'archive' for a future historian is not always clear in terms of what has been stored and what has not.

303 For overviews of the European Bronze Age and it diversity: Jacques Briard, *L'Âge du bronze en Europe, Économie et société, 2000-800 avant J.-C*, Paris, Errance, 1997; Harry Fokkens, Anthony Harding (eds), *The Oxford Handbook of the European Bronze Age, op. cit.*, p. 270-290 ; Anthony Harding, *European Societies in the Bronze Age*, Cambridge, Cambridge University Press, 2000; Kristian Kristiansen, *Europe Before History, op. cit.*; Klavs Randsborg (ed.), *Absolute Chronology. Archaeological Europe 2500-500 BC*, actes du colloque de Vérone, 1995, *Acta Archaeologica*, n° 67, p. 99-120.

304 Christian Horn, Kristian Kritiansen (eds), *Warfare in Bronze Age Society, op. cit.*, p. 237.

305 Fernand Braudel, *Civilisation matérielle et capitalisme*, xve-xviiie siècle, tome III: *Le temps du monde*, Paris, Armand Colin, 1979; Francois-Xavier Fauvelle (ed.), *Civilisations de l'Afrique ancienne, op. cit.* ; William Graham Lister Randles, *L'Empire du Monomotapa du xve au xixe siècle*, Paris-La Haye, École des hautes études en sciences sociales-Mouton, 1975.

306 Maurice Godelier, 'Chefferies et États, une approche anthropologique', Pascal Ruby (ed.), *Les princes de la Protohistoire et l'émergence de l'État, op. cit.*, p. 26.

307 This major break was for a long while under-estimated and poorly integrated into history, as certain archaeologists have lamented: Jean-Paul Demoule, *Les dix millénaires oubliés qui ont fait l'histoire, op. cit.*

308 Jean Guilaine, *La seconde naissance de l'homme. Le Néolithique*, Paris, Odile Jacob, 2015, and *Les chemins de la Protohistoire, op. cit.*

309 Maurice Godelier, 'Chefferies et États, une approche anthropologique', Pascal Ruby (ed.), *Les princes de la Protohistoire et l'émergence de l'État, op. cit.*

310 Georges Dumézil, *Aspects de la fonction guerrière chez les Indo-Européens*, Paris, PUF, 1956.

311 Amongst the last overviews questioning the myth of Indo-Europeans, *Mais où sont passés les Indo-Européens. Le mythe d'origine de l'Occident*, Paris, Seuil, 2014, 'La librairie du XXIe siècle'.

312 Georges Dumézil, *Mythes et épopée. L'idéologie des trois fonctions dans les épopées des peuples indo-européens*, Paris, Gallimard, 1968.

313 Gordon Childe, *The Dawn of European Civilization, op. cit.*

314 Joëlle Cornette (ed.), Damien Agut, Juan Carlos Moreno-Garcia, *L'Égypte des pharaons*, Paris, Belin, coll. 'Mondes Anciens', 2016; Joëlle Cornette (eds), Francis Joannès, Bertrand Lafont, Philippe Clancier, Aline Tenu, *La Mésopotamie*, Paris, Belin, coll. 'Mondes Anciens', 2017.

315 Guillaume Gernez, *Les armes du Proche-Orient ancien. Des origines à 2000 av. J.-C., op. cit.*, part. p. 42-43 for the sword.

316 On this precise point see: Jean Guilaine, Jean Zammit, *Le sentier de la guerre, op. cit.*, p. 269.

317 Jean Guilaine, Jean Zammit, *Le sentier de la guerre, op. cit.*, p. 265 ; Jean-Paul Demoule, *Les dix millénaires oubliés qui ont fait l'histoire, op. cit.*

318 Dan Howard, *Bronze Age Military Equipment*, Barnsley, Pen & Sword Books, 2012. On the link between high technology skills and the long sword (not the short dagger) in the Mediterranean era see: Barry Molloy, 'Swords and Swordsmanship in the Aegean Bronze Age', *art. cit.*

Chapter VII - THE HUMAN LEVEL

319 Jacques Le Goff, *Faut-il vraiment découper l'histoire en tranches ?, op. cit.*

320 Jacques Revel (eds), *Jeux d'échelles. La micro-analyse à l'expérience*, Paris, Gallimard-Seuil, 1996.

321 The site was also a form of model for archaeological excavation methodology: Michèle Ballinger, Olivier Bignon-Lau, Pierre Bodu [*et al.*], Pincevent (1964-2014): *50 années de recherches sur la vie des Magdaléniens*, Paris, Société préhistorique française, 2014, 96 p.: Nicole Pigeot (eds), *Les derniers Magdaléniens d'Étiolles: perspectives culturelles et paléohisoriques*, Paris Galllia-Préhistoire, XXXVIIe supplément, CNRS 2004, 351 p. See also the site archeologie.culture.fr/fr/a-propos/etoiles-campements-paleolithiques.

322 Jacques Revel, 'Micro-analyse et construction du social', Jacques Revel (ed.), *Jeux d'échelles. La micro-analyse à l'expérience, op. cit.*, p. 15-36.

BIBLIOGRAPHY

Andersen, Niels, « Causewayed Enclosures in Northern and Western Europe », *in* Fowler, Chris, Harding, Jan, Hofman, Daniela (ed.), *The Oxford Handbook of Neolithic Europe*, Oxford, Oxford University Press, 2015, p. 795-812.

Apel, Jan, *Daggers, Knowledge and Power. The Social Aspects of Flint- Dagger Technology in Scandinavia 2350-1500 cal BC*, Uppsala, Uppsala University Dept. of Archaeology & Ancient History, 2001.

Aurell Martin, *Excalibur Durendal Joyeuse. La force de l'épée*, Paris, Puf, 2021.

Aron, Raymond, *Penser la guerre, Clausewitz*, 2 tomes, Paris, Gallimard,1976.

–, *Introduction à la philosophie de l'histoire*, 1938, Paris, Gallimard, 1986.

–, *Paix et guerre entre les nations*, 1962, Paris, Calmann-Lévy, 2004.

Audouin-Rouzeau, Stéphane, *Une initiation. Rwanda (1994-2016)*,Paris, Seuil, 2016.

Audouze, Françoise, Schlanger, Nathan (dir.), *Autour de l'homme. Contexte et actualité d'André Leroi-Gourhan*, Antibes, Éditions APDCA, 2004.

Aujoulat, Norbert, *Lascaux: le geste, l'espace et le temps*, Paris, Seuil, 2004. Ballinger, Michèle, Bignon-Lau, Olivier, Bodu, Pierre [et al.], *Pincevent (1964-2014) : 50 années de recherches sur la vie des Magdaléniens*, Paris, Société préhistorique française, 2014, 96 p.

Bandi, Hans-Georg, « Immagini e riproduzioni di Palafitte nel XIX secolo », *in Palafitte : mito e realtà*, Museo Civico di Storia Naturale de Vérone, 1982, p. 15-24.

Barrali, Jean, Maeder, Gérard, *Précis de métallurgie,* élaboration, *structures-propriétés et normalisation*, 6ᵉ édition, Paris, Nathan, 1996. Barral, Philippe, « Des Dieux sans domicile ? », *in* Malrain, François, Poux, Matthieu, *Qui étaient les Gaulois ?*, Paris, Universcience-La Martinière, 2011, p. 131-143.

Beaune (de), Sophie, *Qu'est-ce que la Préhistoire ?*, Paris, Gallimard, 2016.

Bertholet, Denis, *Claude Lévi-Strauss*, Paris, Plon, 2003.

Blanckaert, Claude (dir.), *Les politiques de l'anthropologie. Discours et pratiques en France (1860-1940)*, Paris, 2001.

–, *Le Musée de l'Homme : histoire d'un musée-laboratoire*, Paris, Musée de l'Homme, 2015.

Blitte Hélène, Lachenal Thibault, Leandri Franck, Lehoërff Anne, Paolini Hélène, Peche-Quilichini Kewin (ed.), *Âge du bronze, Âge de guerre. Violence organisée et expression de la force au IIe millénaire avant J.-C.*, Piazzola éditeur, forthcoming 2023.

Bloch, Marc, *Apologie pour l'histoire ou métier d'historien*, Paris, Armand Colin, 1949.

Bonis, Armelle, Burnouf, Joëlle, Demoule, Jean-Paul (dir.), « Archéologie et passions identitaires », *Les Nouvelles de l'archéologie*, 67, 1997.

Bon, François, *Préhistoire. La fabrique de l'homme*, Paris, Seuil, 2009.

Bougainville (de), Louis-Antoine, *Voyages autour du monde*, 2 volumes, Paris, 1771.

Boulestin Bruno, « Ceci n'est pas une guerre (mais ça y ressemble) : entre doctrine et sémnatique, comment aborder la question de la guerre préhistorique ? », *Paleo* n° 30, t. 2, juillet 2020, p. 36-56.

Bourdieu, Pierre, *Sur l'État. Cours au Collège de France (1989-1992)*, Paris, Seuil, 2012.

Boulestin, Bruno, *Approche taphonomique des restes humains. Le cas des mésolithiques de la grotte des Perrats et le problème du canni- balisme en préhistoire récente européenne*, Oxford, Archaeopress, British Archaelogical Reports International Series 776, 1999.

Bradley, Richard, *The Passage of Arms. An Archaeological Analysis of Prehistoric Hoards and Votive Deposits*, Cambridge, Cambridge University Press, 1990.

–, « Hoards and the Deposition of Metalwork » *in* Fokkens, Harry, Harding, Antony (ed.), *The Oxford Handbook of the European Bronze Age*, Oxford, Oxford University Press, 2013, p. 121-139.

Braudel, Fernand, *La Méditerranée et le monde méditerranéen à l'époque de Philippe II*, Paris, Armand Colin, 1949.

Brück, Johanna, Fontijn David, "The Myth of the Chief: Prestige Goods, Power, and Personhood in the European Bronze Age", in H. Fokkens and A. Harding (eds.), *The Oxford Handbook of the European Bronze Age*, Oxford, Oxford University Press, 2013, p. 197-215.

Brun, Patrice, *Princes et Princesses de la Celtique. Le Premier Âge du fer (850-450 av. J.-C)*, Paris, Errance, 1987.

Briard, Jacques, *L'Âge du bronze en Europe, Économie et société, 2000-800 av. J.-C*, Paris, Errance, 1997.

Brunaux, Jean-Louis, *Nos ancêtres les Gaulois*, Paris, Seuil, 2008.

–, *Vercingétorix*, Paris, Gallimard, coll. « NRF Biographies », 2018.

–, *Les Celtes. Histoire d'un mythe*, Paris, Belin, 2014.

Buchsenschutz, Olivier (dir.), *L'Europe celtique à l'Âge du fer, VIIIe-Ier siècles*, Paris, PUF, 2015.

–, Schnapp, Alain, « Alésia », *in* Nora, Pierre (dir.), *Les lieux de mémoire*, t. 3, Paris, Gallimard, 1997, p. 4103-4140.

Bulard, Alain, « Un dépôt de neuf cuirasses découvert à Paris au xviie siècle », *Revue Archéologique d'Île-de-France*, 1, 2008, p.125-132.

Cambier, Alain, *Qu'est-ce que l'État ?*, Paris, Vrin, 2004.

Carman, John, Harding, Anthony (éd.), *Ancient Warfare. Archaeological Perspectives*, 1999, Stroud, Sutton, 2004.

Cauvin, Jacques, *Naissance des divinités, naissance de l'agriculture : la révolution des symboles au Néolithique*, Paris, Flammarion, 1998.

Certeau (de), Michel, *L'écriture de l'histoire*, Paris, Gallimard, 1975.

Chapman, John, "The Origins of Warfare in the Prehistory of Central and Eastern Europe", in J. Carman and A. Harding (eds.) op. cit., *Ancient Warfare: Archaeological perspectives*, Stroud, Sutton, 2004, p. 101-142.

Chartier, Roger, *Au bord de la falaise. L'histoire entre certitudes et inquiétude*, Paris, Albin Michel, 2009.

Chaniotis, Angelos, *War in the Hellenistic World. A Social and Cultural History*, Oxford, Blackwell, 2005.

Chapman, John, *Fragmentation in Archaeology*, London, Routledge, 2000.

Chippindale, Christopher, « The Invention of Words for the Idea of "Prehistory" », *Proceedings of the Prehistoric Society*, 54, 1988, p. 304-314.

Clark, Peter (ed.), *The Dover Bronze Age Boat*, English Heritage, 2004.

–, *The Dover Bronze Age Boat in Context 1: Society and Water Transport in Prehistoric Europe*, Oxford, Oxbow Books, 2004 & 2, 2009.

Clastres, Pierre, *La société contre l'État. Recherches d'anthropologie politique*, Paris, éditions de Minuit, 1974 (English edition, *Society against the State*, New York, Zone Books, 1989).

–, « Archéologie de la violence. La guerre dans les sociétés primitives », *Libre*, 1977, La Tour-d'Aigues, éditions de l'Aube, 1999 (English Version, *The Archaeology of Violence*, New York, 1994, Semiotext(e)).

Cline, Eric, *1177 BC.: The Year Civilization Collapsed*, Princeton, Princeton University Press, 2014 (French edition, *1177 avant J.-C. Le jour où la cvilisation s'est effondrée*, Paris, La Découverte, 2015).

Cohen, Claudine, *Femmes de la Préhistoire*, Paris, Belin, 2016.

Coles, John, « European Bronze Age Shields », *Proceedings of the Prehistoric Society*, 28, 1962, p. 156-170.

Collis, John, *The Celts : Origins, Myths and Inventions*, Stroud, The History Press, 2003.

Contamine, Philippe, *La guerre au Moyen Âge*, Paris, PUF, 1980. Corbin, Alain, *Le monde retrouvé de Louis-François Pinagot*, Paris, Flammarion, 1998.

Corvisier, Jean-Nicolas, *Guerre et société dans les mondes grecs (490-322 av. J.-C)*, Paris, Armand Colin, 1999.

Courbin, Paul, « La guerre en Grèce à haute époque d'après les documents archéologiques » *in* Vernant, Jean-Pierre (dir.), *Problèmes de la guerre en Grèce ancienne*, Paris, Seuil, 1999, chapitre 3, p. 89-120, pl. I à VIII.

Courmont, Barthelemy, *La guerre*, Paris, Armand Colin, 2007.

Coutil, Léon, « Casques antiques (Proto-Étrusques, Mycéniens, Grecs,

Gaulois et Romains », *Mémoires de la Société Préhistorique Française*, t.3, Paris, 1915, p. 163-225.

Coye, Noël, *La préhistoire en parole et en acte : méthodes et enjeux de la pratique archéologique, 1830-1950*, Paris, L'Harmattan, 1997.

Craddock, Paul, *Early Metal Mining and Production*, Washington, Smithsonian Institution Press, 1995, Londres, Archetype, 2010.

Cunliffe, Barry, *Facing the Ocean : The Atlantic and Its Peoples*, Oxford, Oxford University Press, 2001.

–, *By Steppe, Desert and Ocean : the Birth of Eurasia*, Oxford, Oxford University Press, 2015.

Darmangeat, Christophe, *Justice et guerre en Australie aborigène*, Paris, Smolny, 2021.

Delacroix, Christian, Dosse, François, Garcia, Patrick, *Les courants historiques en France*, Paris, Armand Colin, 1999.

Delpuech, André, « Il est des situations dont il faut s'accommoder», *Les Nouvelles de l'archéologie*, 147, mars 2017, p. 61-72.

Demoule, Jean-Paul, *Naissance de la figure. L'art du Paléolithique à l'Âge du fer*, Paris, Hazan, 2007, Gallimard, 2017.

–, *On a retrouvé l'histoire de France. Comment l'archéologie raconte notre passé*, Paris, Robert Laffont, 2012.

–, "L'archéologie de la France: un refoulement national ?", *in* Demoule, Jean-Paul, Stiegler, Bernard, *L'avenir du passé. Modernité de l'archéologie*, Paris, La Découverte, 2008, p. 223-245.

–, Landes, Christian (dir.), *La fabrique de l'archéologie en France*, Paris, La Découverte, 2009.

–, « Le Néolithique à l'origine du monde contemporain », *La Documentation photographique*, Dossier 8117, Paris, La Documentation française, mai-juin 2017.

–, *Les 10 000 ans oubliés qui ont fait l'histoire. Quand on inventa l'agriculture, la guerre et les chefs*, Paris, Fayard, 2017.

–, Stiegler, Bernard, *L'avenir du passé. Modernité de l'archéologie*, Paris, La Découverte, 2008.

Deonna, Waldemar, « Les cuirasses hallstattiennes de Fillinges au musée d'art et d'histoire de Genève », *in Préhistoire*, III, Paris, E. Leroux, 1934, p. 93-143.

Desfossé, Yves, Prilaux, Gilles, Jacques, Alain, *L'archéologie de la Grande Guerre*, Rennes, Ouest-France, 2008.

Deyber Alain, *Vercingétorix chef de guerre*, Chamalières, Lemme, 2017.

–, *Les Gaulois en guerre. Stratégies, tactiques et techniques. Essai d'histoire militaire*, Paris, Errance, 2009.

Diamond Jared, *De l'inégalité parmi les sociétés. Essai sur l'homme et l'environnement dans l'histoire*, traduit de l'anglais (1997), Paris, Gallimard, 2000.

Dolfini Andrea, Crellin Rachel, Horn Christian, Uckelmann Marion (dir.), *Prehistoric Warfare and Violence. Quantitative and Qualitative Approaches*, Springer ed., 2018.

Dosse, François, *L'histoire en miettes. Des « Annales» à la « nouvelle histoire »*, Paris, La Découverte, 1987.

Drews, Robert, *The End of the Bronze Age. Changes in Warfare and the Catastrophe ca. 1200 BC*, Princeton, Princeton University Press, 1993.

Duby, Georges, *Le dimanche de Bouvines*, Paris, Gallimard, 1973.

Duchet, Michèle, *Anthropologie et histoire au siècle des lumières*, Paris, Maspéro, 1971.

–, « De l'histoire morale à la description des mœurs : Lafitau », *in* Duchet, Michèle, *Le partage des savoirs. Discours historique, discours ethnologique*, Paris, La Découverte, 1985, p. 30-52.

Duday, Henri, *The Archaeology of the Death. Lectures in Archaeothanatology*, Oxford, Oxbow Books, 2009.

Dumézil, Georges, *Aspects de la fonction guerrière chez les indo- européens*, Paris, PUF/Bibliothèque de l'École des hautes études, 1956.

–, *Mythes et épopée. L'idéologie des trois fonctions dans les épopées des peuples indo-européens*, Paris, Gallimard, 1968.

Diderot, Denis, *Supplément au voyage de Bougainville*, Paris, 1772, 1796.

Eco, Umberto, *A passo di Gambero*, Milan, Bompiani, 2006.

Éluère, Christiane, *L'art des Celtes*, Paris, Citadelles & Mazenod, 2004.

Evans-Pritchard, E.E, *Les Nuer. Description des modes de vie et des institutions politiques d'un peuple nilote*, Paris, Gallimard, 1969, (English edition, 1939).

Évin, Jacques, Lambert, Georges-Noël, Lanos, Philippe, Oberlin, Christine, *La datation en laboratoire*, Paris, Errance, 1998.

Fauvelle, François-Xavier, *À la recherche du sauvage idéal*, Paris, Seuil, 2017.

– (dir), *Civilisations de l'Afrique ancienne*, Paris, Belin, 2018.

Febvre, Lucien, *Combats pour l'histoire*, Paris, Armand Colin, 1953.

Fernandez-Götz Manuel, Roymans Nico (ed.), *Conflict Archaeology. Materialities of collective Violence from Prehistory to Late Antiquity*, Themes in Contemporary Archaeology, vol 5, EAA, European Association of Archaeologists, 2017.

Fokkens, Harry, Harding, Antony (ed.), *The Oxford Handbook of the European Bronze Age*, Oxford, Oxford University Press, 2013, p. 270-290.

Fontijn, David, "Giving up Weapons", in I. Thorpe and M. Parker Pearson (eds.), *Warfare, Violence and Slavery in Prehistory*, Oxford, Archaeopress, 2005, BAR 1374, p. 145-154.

Fontijn David, *Economies of destruction. How the systematic destruction vualables created value In Bronze Age Europe*, London, Routlege, 2020.

Fowler, Chris, Harding, Jan, Hofmann, Daniela (ed.), *The Oxford Handbook of Neolithic Europe*, Oxford, Oxford University Press, 2015.

Forbes, Robert J., *Studies in Ancient Technology*, 9 volumes, Leiden, Brill, 1955-1957.

Fritz, Carole (dir.), *L'art de la Préhistoire*, Paris, Citadelles & Mazenod, 2017.

Gallay, Alain, *Pour une ethnoarchéologie théorique*, Paris, Errance, 2011.

Garcia, Dominique, « Religion et société en Gaule méridionale », dans Goudineau, Christian (dir.), *Religion et société en Gaule*, Paris, Errance, 2006, p. 135-155.

Garlan, Yvon, *La guerre dans l'Antiquité*, Paris, Nathan, 1972.

–, « L'homme et la guerre », *in* Vernant, Jean-Pierre, *L'homme grec*, Paris, Seuil, 1993, p. 65-101.

Gauchet, Marcel, *Philosophie des sciences historiques. Le moment romantique* (Texts: P. Barante, V. Cousin, F. Guizot, J. Michelet, F. Mignet, E. Quinet, A. Thierry), Paris, Seuil, 2002.

Gernez, Guillaume, *Les armes du Proche-Orient ancien. Des origines à 2000 av. J.-C*, Paris, Errance, 2017.

Gimbutas, Marija, *The Gods and Goddesses of Old Europe : 7000 to 3500 BC Myths, Legends and Cult Images*, Londres, Thames and Hudson, 1974. (French edition : *Le langage de la déesse*, Paris, éditions *des femmes* – Antoinette Fouque, 2005.

Girard, René, *Achever Clausewitz, entretiens avec Benoît Chantre*, Paris, Carnets Nord, 2008.

Godelier, Maurice, *L'idéel et le matériel. Pensée, économies, sociétés*, Paris, Fayard, 1984.

–, *L'énigme du don*, Paris, Fayard, 1996.

–, « Chefferies et États, une approche anthropologique», *in Les Princes de la Protohistoire et l'émergence de l'État*, Actes de la table ronde internationale, Naples, 1999, p. 19-30.

–, *Aux fondements des sociétés humaines. Ce que nous apprend l'anthropologie*, Paris, Albin Michel, 2007.

Goldhahn, Joakim, Ling, Johan, « Bronze Age Rock Art in Northern Europe : Contexts and Interpretations », *in* Fokkens, Harry, Harding, Antony (ed.), *op. cit.*, p. 270-290.

Goody, Jack, *The domestication of the savage mind*, Cambridge University Press, 1977, French edition, *La raison graphique. La domestication de la pensée sauvage*, Paris, Les éditions de minuit, 1977.

–, *The theft of History*, Cambridge University Press, 2006, French edition, *Le vol de l'histoire. Comment l'Europe a imposé le récit de son passé au reste du monde*, Paris, Gallimard, 2010.

Goudineau, Christian, *Le dossier Vercingétorix*, Arles, Actes-Sud, 2009.

– (dir.), *Religion et société en Gaule*, Paris, Errance, 2006.

–, *Le mythe Gaulois, in* Demoule, Jean-Paul, Stiegler, Bernard, *op. cit.*, p. 212-222.

Guilaine, Jean, « L'Âge du bronze en Languedoc occidental, Roussillon, Ariège » *Mémoires de la Société préhistorique française*, t. 9, Paris, Klincksieck, 1972.

– (dir.), *Matériaux, production, circulation du Néolithique à l'Âge du Bronze*, Séminaires du Collège de France, Paris, Errance, 2002.

–, *Caïn, Abel, Ötzi. L'héritage néolithique*, Paris, Gallimard, 2011.

–, *L'archéologie, science humaine. Entretiens avec Anne Lehoërff*, Paris, Actes Sud/Errance, 2011.

–, *La seconde naissance de l'homme. Le Néolithique*, Paris, Odile Jacob, 2015.

–, *Les chemins de la Protohistoire. Quand l'Occident s'éveillait (7000-2000 avant notre ère)*, Paris, Odile Jacob, 2017.

–, Carozza, Laurent, Garcia, Dominique, Gascó, Jean, Janin, Thierry, Mille, Benoît, *Launac et le Launacien. Dépôts de bronzes protohistoriques du sud de la Gaule*, Montpellier, Presses Universitaires de Méditerranée, 2017.

–, Semelin, Jacques, *Violences de guerre, violences de masse. Une approche archéologique*, Paris, La Découverte, 2016.

–, Zammit, Jacques, *Le sentier de la Guerre. Visages de la violence préhistorique. Une approche archéologique*, Paris, Seuil, 2001.

Guillaumet, Jean-Paul, *La paléomanufacture métallique : méthode d'étude*, Gollion, Infolio, 2003.

Haas, J., Piscitelli, M., "The Prehistory of Warfare: Misled by Ethnography", in D. Fry (ed.), War, *Peace, and Human Nature*, New York, Oxford University Press, 2013, p. 168-190.

Halleux, Robert, *Le problème des métaux dans la science antique*, Paris, Les Belles Lettres, 1974.

Hamon, Caroline, Quilliec, Bénédicte (eds), *Hoards from the Neolithic to the Metal Ages. Technical and codified practices*, Oxford, 2008, BAR international Series 1758.

Hanson, Victor, *Le modèle occidental de la guerre*, 1990, Paris, Les Belles Lettres, 2004.

Harari Yuval Noah, *Sapiens. Une brève histoire de l'humanité*, Paris, Albin Michel, 2015.

Harding, Antony, *European Societies in the Bronze Age*, Cambridge, Cambridge University Press, 1998.

–, *Warriors and Weapons in Bronze Age Europe*, Budapest, Archaeolingua, 2007.

Harrison, Richard, *Symbols and Warriors. Images of the European Bronze Age*, Western Academic, Bristol, 2004.

Hartog, François, *Le XIXe siècle et l'histoire. Le cas Fustel de Coulanges*, Paris, Seuil, 2001.

–, *Régimes d'historicités*, Paris, Seuil, 2003.

–, *Anciens, modernes, sauvages*, Paris, Galaade Éditions, 2005.

–, *Croire en l'histoire*, Paris, Flammarion, 2013.

–, *Chronos: l'Occident aux prises avec le temps*, Gallimard, NRF, 2020.

Haudricourt, André-Georges, *La technologie science humaine : recherches d'histoire et d'ethnologie des techniques*, Paris, éditions de la Maison des sciences de l'Homme, 1988.

Hayden, Brian, *Naissance de l'inégalité : l'invention de la hiérarchie durant la Préhistoire*, Paris, CNRS, 2008.

Héritier, Françoise, Copet-Rougier, Elisabeth, *Les complexités de l'alliance*, t. 1, *Les systèmes semi-complexes*, Paris, Éditions des Archives contemporaines, 1990.

Hobbes, Thomas, *Le Léviathan*, 1651, Paris, Sirey, 2007.

Horn, Christian, Kristiansen, Kristian (ed), *Warfare in Bronze Age Society*, Cambridge, Cambridge University Press, 2017.

Howard, Dan, *Bronze Age Military Equipment*, Barnsley, Pen & Sword Books, 2012.

Hurel, Arnaud, *La France préhistorienne de 1789 à 1941*, Paris, CNRS, 2007.

Ingrao, Christian, *Croire et détruire. Les intellectuels dans la machine de guerre*, Paris, Fayard, 2010.

Jacquemin, Anne, *Guerre et religion dans le monde grec (490-322 av. J.C.)*, Paris, Sedes, 2000.

–, « Guerre et offrandes dans les sanctuaires», *Pallas. Revue d'études antiques*, 51, 1999, p. 141-157.

Jablonka, Ivan, *L'Histoire des grands-parents que je n'ai pas eus*, Paris, Seuil, « La librairie du xxe siècle », 2012.

–*L'histoire est une littérature contemporaine. Manifeste pour les sciences sociales*, Paris, Seuil, 2014.

–, *Laëtitia ou la fin des hommes*, Paris, Seuil, 2016.

–, *Des hommes justes. Du Patriarcat aux nouvelles masculinités*, Paris, Seuil, Les Livres du Nouveau monde, 2019.

Jantzen, Detlef, Orschiedt, J., Piek, J., Terberger, Thomas (eds), *Tod im Tollensetal: Forschungen zu den Hinterlassenschaften eines bronzezeitlichen Gewaltkonfliktes in Mecklenburg-Vorpommern*, Teil 1: Die Forschungen bis 2011, Schwerin, Landesamt, 2014, 274 p.

Jaubert, Jacques, *Chasseurs et artisans du Moustérien*, Paris, La Maison des roches, 1999.

–, « The Chronology of Human and Animal Presence in the Decorated and Sepulchral Cave of Cussac (France) », *Quaternary International*, 2016, p. 1-20.

Kaeser, Marc-Antoine, *Les lacustres. Archéologie et mythe national*, Lausanne, Presses Polytechniques et Universitaires Romandes, 2004.

–, *Visions d'une civilisation engloutie. La représentation des villages lacustres, de 1854 à nos jours*, catalogue de l'exposition du musée archéologique Laténium, Hauterive, 2008.

Keegan, John, *Histoire de la guerre. Du Néolithique à la guerre du Golfe*, Paris, Robert Laffont, 1993. Traduction de *The Face of Battle*, Londres, Jonathan Cape, 1976. Nouvelle édition française, *Anatomie de la Bataille*, Paris, Perrin, 2013.

Keeley, Lawrence, *War before civilization*, Oxford, Oxford University Press, 1996 (French version, *Les guerres préhistoriques,* Paris, éditions du Rocher, 2002).

Kristiansen, Kristian, *Europe before history*, Cambridge, Cambridge University Press, 1998.

–, « The Emergence of Warrior Aristocracies in Later European Prehistory and their Long-Term History », *in* Carman, John, Harding, Antony (ed.), *Ancient Warfare*, Sutton, The History Press, 1999, p. 175-189.

–, « The Tale of the Sword. Swords and Swordfighters in the Bronze Age Europe », *Oxford Journal of Archaeology*, 21-4, 2002, p. 319-332.

–, Larsson, Thomas, *The Rise of Bronze Age society. Travels, Transmissions and Transformations*, Cambridge, Cambridge University Press, 2005.

Krüger Joachim, Lidke, Gundula, Lorenz, Sebastian, Terberger, Thomas (eds), Tollensetal 1300 v. Chr. Das älteste Schlachtfeld Europas, Darmstadt, Theiss, 2018.

Kruta, Venceslas, *L'Europe des origines. La Protohistoire, 6000-500 avant J.-C*, Paris, Gallimard, 1992.

L'Etoisle (de), Benoît, *Le goût des autres. De l'exposition coloniale aux Arts premiers*, Paris, Flammarion, 2007.

L'Europe au temps d'Ulysse. Dieux et héros de l'âge du bronze, catalogue de l'exposition, Paris, Réunion des Musées Nationaux, 1999.

Lafitau, Jacques F., *Mœurs des sauvages américains comparées aux mœurs des premiers temps*, 1724.

Lambot, Bernard, *Guerre et armement chez les Gaulois*, Paris, Errance, 1987.

Laming-Emperaire, Annette, *Origines de l'archéologie préhistorique en France. Des superstitions médiévales à la découverte de l'Homme fossile*, Paris, Picard, 1964.

Lanchon, Yves, Marquis, Philippe, *Le premier village de Paris, il y a 6 000 ans. Les découvertes de Bercy*, Paris, Paris-Musées, 2000.

Laurière, Christine, *Paul Rivet. Le savant et le politique*, Paris, Publications scientifiques du Muséum national d'histoire naturelle, 2008.

Le premier or de l'humanité en Bulgarie. 5e millénaire, catalogue de l'exposition au musée des antiquités nationales de Saint-Germain- en-Laye, Paris, Réunion des Musées nationaux, 1989.

Le Goff, Jacques, *Histoire et mémoire*, 1977, Paris, Gallimard, 1988.

–, *Faut-il vraiment découper l'histoire en tranches ?*, Paris, Seuil, 2014.

Lebedynsky, Laroslav, *Les Scythes. La civilisation nomade des steppes viie-iiie siècle*, Paris, Errance, 2003.

Leduc, Jean, *Les historiens et le temps. Conceptions, problématiques,* écritures, Paris, Seuil, 1999.

Lehoërff, Anne, « Les moules de l'Âge du Bronze dans la plaine orien- tale du Pô. Vestiges de mise en forme des alliages base cuivre », *Padusa*, XXVIII, 1992, p 131-243.

–, « Le travail en laboratoire au service de l'histoire de l'artisanat métallurgique du début du premier millénaire avant notre ère en Italie », *Mélanges de l'École française de Rome et d'Athènes*, 111, 1999, p. 787-846.

–, *L'artisanat du bronze en Italie centrale (1200-725 avant notre ère). Le métal des dépôts volontaires*, École française de Rome, Rome, 2007.

–, « Les cuirasses de Marmesse (Haute-Marne), un artisanat d'exception », *Antiquités nationales*, 39, 2008, p. 95-106.

–, « Les paradoxes de la Protohistoire française », *Annales HSS*, 5, septembre-octobre 2009, p. 1107-1134.

–, « Les dépôts métalliques de Cannes-Écluse (Seine-et-Marne). Étude technique des jambières du dépôt 1 », *Revue Archéologique de l'Est*, 58, décembre 2009, p. 439-451.

–, « Les armes anciennes de la collection Odescalchi (Palais de Venise, Rome) », *Jahrbuch des RGZM*, 55, 2008, 2011, p. 43-79.

–, « L'Âge du bronze est-il une période historique ? » *in* Garcia, Dominique (dir.), *L'Âge du bronze en Méditerranée. Recherches récentes*, Paris, Errance, 2011, p. 13-26.

– (dir.), *Par-delà l'horizon, Sociétés en Manche et mer du Nord il y a 3500 ans/ Beyond Horizon. Societies of the Channel and North Sea 3500 years ago/ Voorbij de Horizon. Samenlevingen in Kanaal en Noordzee 3500 jaren geleden*, Paris, Somogy, 2012.

–, « Le métal archéologique du côté du laboratoire : mythes et réalités d'un matériau » *in* Boulud-Gazo, Sylvie, Théophane, Nicolas (dir.), *Artisanats et productions à l'Âge du bronze*, Séances de la Société préhistorique française, 4, Paris, 2015, p. 97-108.

–, *Préhistoires d'Europe. De Néandertal à Vercingétorix, 40 000-52 avant notre ère*, Paris, Belin, 2016.

–, « Dire sans les mots », *in* Lehoërff, Anne (dir.), *Dossier' Préhistoire'*, *La NRF*, 622-janvier 2017, p. 125-152, part. p. 125-129.

–, « Le métal au service de la guerre dans l'Europe de la Protohistoire», in Pernot, Michel (dir.), *Quatre mille ans d'histoire du cuivre. Fragments d'une suite de rebonds*, Presses universitaires de Bordeaux, Bordeaux, 2017, p. 103-115.

–, « The Imaginary Crested Helmet of Vercingetorix : What is Creativity in Bronze Age Metal Production ?», *in* Sofaer, Joanna (ed.), *Considering Creativity : Creativity Knowledge and Practice in Bronze Age Europe*, Oxford, Archaeopress, 2018, chap. 5, p. 67-82.

–, « La métallurgie du bronze : techniques, usages et sociétés », Jean Guilaine, Dominique Garcia (ed.), *Protohistoire de la France : quarante ans de découvertes. Néolithique, Âge du bronze, Âge du fer*, *in* Guilaine, Jean, Garcia, Dominique (ed.), *Protohistoire de la France: quarante ans de découvertes. Néolithique, Âge du bronze, Âge du fer*, Paris, Herman, 2018 p. 251-263

–, « Guerres et inégalités sociales à l'Âge du bronze/Warfare and social inegalities during Bronze Age Europe », *in* Guilaine, Jean, Garcia, Dominique (ed.), *op. cit. 2018*, p. 283-295.

–, « Value, Craftsmanship and Use in Late Bronze Age Cuirasses », *in* Dolfini, Andrea, Crellin, Rachel, Horn, Christian, Uckelmann, Marion (dir.), *Prehistoric Warfare and Violence. Quantitative and Qualitative Approaches*, Springer, 2018, chap. 14, p. p. 307-326.

–, *Dictionnaire amoureux de l'archéologie*, Paris, Plon, 2021.

–, Louboutin Catherine (eds), *Archéologie en musée et identités nationales (1848-1914). Un héritage en quête de nouveaux défis au XXIe siècle*, Proceedings of the International Conference, Sain-Germain-enLaye 6-8 décembre 2017, Leiden, Sidestone, 2022.

–, Poncet, Olivier, « Un directeur historien. Auguste Geffroy (1820-1895) et l'École française de Rome », in Gras, Michel, Poncet, Olivier, *Construire l'institution. L'École française de Rome, 1873-1895*, École française de Rome, Rome, 2015, p. 103-147.

–, Talon, Marc (ed.), *Movement, Exchange and Identity in Europe in the 2nd and 1st Millennia BC. Beyond Frontiers*, Oxford, Oxbow Books, 2017.

Lemoine, Yves, *Fernand Braudel, Espaces et temps de l'historien*, Paris, Punctum, 2005.

Lemonnier, Pierre (dir.), *Technological Choices : Transformations in Material Cultures since the Neolithic*, Londres, 1993.

Leroi-Gourhan, André, *Le geste et la parole*, tome I : *Technique et langage,* tome II : *La mémoire et les rythmes*, Paris, Albin Michel, 1964, edition, coll. Espaces Libres, Paris, Albin Michel, 2022, préfaces I & II by Anne Lehoërff.

–, *Les religions de la Préhistoire*, Paris, PUF, 1964.

–, *L'homme et la matière*, 1943, Paris, Albin Michel, 1992.

–, *Milieu et technique*, 1945, Paris, Albin Michel, 1992.

– (dir.), *Dictionnaire de la préhistoire*, Paris, PUF, 1988.

Lestringant, Frank, *Une sainte horreur ou le voyage en Eucharistie xvie-xviiie siècle*, Paris, PUF, 1996.

Lévi-Strauss, Claude, *Tristes tropiques*, Paris, Plon, 1955.

–, *Le totémisme aujourd'hui*, Paris, PUF, 2002.

–, *La Pensée sauvage*, Paris, Pocket, 1990.

Lewuillon, Serge, *Vercingétorix ou le mirage d'Alésia*, Paris, Complexe, 1999.

Lidke, Gundula, Brinker, Ute, Jantzen, Detlef, Dombrowsky, Anne, Drägger, Jana, Krügger, Joachim, Terberger, Thomas, « Warfare or Sacrifice ? Archaeological Research on the Bronze Age Site in the Tollense Valley, Northeast Germany », *in* Horn, Christian, Kristiansen, Kristian (ed), *op. cit.*, p. 175-191.

Ling, Johan, *Rock Art and Seasacapes in Uppland*, Oxford, Oxbow Books, 2012.

–, Skoglund, Peter, Bertlisson, Ulf, *Picturing the Bronze Age*, Oxford, Oxbow books, 2015.

Lonis, Raoul, *Guerre et religion en Grèce à l'époque classique. Recherches sur les rites, les dieux, l'idéologie de la victoire*, Besançon, Université de Franche-Comté, 1979.

Loyer, Emmanuelle, *Lévi-Strauss*, Paris, Flammarion, 2015.

Machiavel, *L'art de la guerre*, Florence, 1519-1520.

–, *Le Prince*, Florence, 1532.

Malrain, François, Poux, Matthieu (dir.), *Qui étaient les Gaulois*, Paris, Lamartinière, 2011.

Man-Estier, Elena, Paillet, Patrick « La "scène du puits" de Lascaux ou les multiples récits issus des profondeurs du temps », in Lehoërff, Anne (dir.), *Dossier Préhistoire, op. cit.,* p. 130-135.

Mangin, Michel (dir), *Le Fer*, Paris, Errance, 2004.

Maniquet, Christophe, « Le dépôt cultuel du sanctuaire gaulois de Tintignac à Naves (Corrèze) », *Gallia*, 65, 2008, p. 273-326.

Marcigny, Cyril, Colonna, Cécile, Ghesquière, Emmanuel, Verron, Guy (dir.), *La Normandie à l'aube de l'histoire. Les découvertes archéologiques de l'Âge du bronze 2300-800 av. J.-C.*, Paris, Somogy, 2005.

Mariot, Nicolas, *Faut-il être motivé pour tuer ? Sur quelques explications aux violences de guerre*, Génèses, 53, 2003, p. 154-177.

Marzatico, Franco, Gleirscher, Paul (dir.), *Guerrieri, Principi ed Eroi fra Danubio e il Po dalla Preistoria all'Alto Medioevo*, catalogue de l'exposition, Trente, Museo Castello Buonconsiglio, 2004.

Mathieu, Franck, *Le guerrier Gaulois, du Hallstatt à la conquête romaine*, Paris, Errance, 2007.

Maureille, Bruno, *Les origines de la culture. Les premières sépultures*, Paris, Le Pommier, 2004.

Mauss, Marcel, *Manuel d'ethnographie*, Paris, Payot, 1947.

Mayor, Adrienne, *Les Amazones. Quand les femmes étaient les égales des hommes (viiie av. J.-C.-1er apr. J.-C.)*, Paris, La Découverte, 2017.

Meller, Harald (dir.), *Der geschmiedete Himmel. Die weite Welt im Herzen Europas vor 3600 Jahren*, Halle, Landesmuseum fürVorgeschichte, 2004.

–, « The Sky Disc of Nebra », *in* Fokkens, Harry, Antony Harding (ed.), *op. cit.*, p. 266-269.

Meller Harald, Schefzik Michael (ed.), *Krieg. Eine Archäologische Spurensuche*, Theiss, 2015.

Milcent, Pierre-Yves, *Le temps des élites en Gaule atlantique. Chronologie des mobiliers et rythmes de reconstitution des dépôts métalliques dans le contexte européen (xiiie-viie s. av. J.-C.)*, Rennes, Presses universitaires de Rennes, 2012.

Miller, Heather Margaret-Louise, *Archaeological Approaches to Technology*, Academic Press/Elsevier, New-York, 2007.

Mödlinger, Marianne, « European Bronze Age Cuirasses. Aspect of Chronology, Typology, Manufacture and Usage », *Jahrbuch des Römisch-Germanischen Zentralmuseums*, 59, 2012, p. 1-49.

Mohen, Jean-Pierre, « Étude comparée de deux cuirasses hallstattiennes, la cuirasse de "Grenoble" et la cuirasse "de Naples" », *Annales du Laboratoire de Recherche des musées de France*, 1970, p. 65-80.

–, *Métallurgie préhistorique. Introduction à la paléométallurgie*, Paris, Masson, 1990.

–, Bailloud, Gérard, *La vie quotidienne. Les fouilles du Fort-Harrouard*, Paris, Picard, 1987.

Molloy, Barry, « Swords and Swordsmanship in the Aegean Bronze Age », *American Journal of Archaeology*, 114-3, juillet 2010, p. 403-428.

Montelius, Oscar, *Les temps préhistoriques en Suède et dans les autres pays scandinaves*, édition française, Paris, Ernest Leroux, 1895.

Müller, Johanes, « Demographic Traces of Technological Innovation, Social Change and Mobility : From 1 to 8 million Europeans (6000-2000 BCE) » *in* Horn, Christian, Kristiansen, Kristian (ed), *op. cit.*, p. 15.

Nicolai (von), Caroline, « Historique des interprétations du xixe siècle à nos jours » *in* Testart, Alain (dir.), *Les armes dans les eaux. Question d'interprétation en archéologie*, Arles, Errance, 2012, p. 17-51.

Nimura, Courtney, *Prehistoric Rock Art in Scandinavia. Agency and Environmental Change*, Oxford, Oxbow books, 2015.

Noiriel, Gérard, *Sur la crise de l'histoire*, Paris, Belin, 1996.

Norgaard, Heide W., *Bronze Age Metalwork. Techniques and Tradition in the Nordic Beonze Age 1500-1100 BC*, Oxford, Archaeopress Archaeology, 2018

Nora, Pierre (dir.), *Les lieux de mémoires*, Paris, Gallimard, (3 vol. : « La République », « La Nation », « La France »), 1984-1997.

Pearson, Michael Parker, Thorpe, Nick (eds), *Warfare, Violence and Slavery in Prehistory*, Oxford, Archaeopress, British Archaeological Reports IS 1374, 2005.

O'Brien, William, *Prehistoric Copper Mining in Europe, 5500/500 BC*, Oxford, Oxford University Press, 2014.

Offenstadt, Nicolas, « Histoire-bataille », *in* Delacroix, Christian, Dosse, François, Garcia, Patrick, Offenstadt, Nicolas (dir.), *Historiographies, concepts et débats*, t. 1, Paris, Gallimard, 2010, p. 162-169.

Osborne, Robin, Cunliffe, Barry (ed.), *Mediterranean Urbanization 800-600 BC*, Oxford, Oxford University Press, 2005.

Osgood, Richard, *Warfare in the Late Bronze Age of North Europe*, Oxford, Archaeopress, British Archaelogical Reports IS 694, 1998.

–, Monks, Sarah, Toms, Judith, *Bronze Age Warfare*, Stroud, The History Press, 2010.

Otto, Ton, Thrane, Henry, Vandkilde, Helle (ed.), *Warfare and Society. Archaeological and Social Anthropological Perspectives*, Aarhus, Aarhus University Press, 2006.

Pare, Christopher, *Swords, Wagon-Graves and the Beginning of the Early Iron Age in Central Europe*, Oxford, Oxford University Monograph, 1998.

– (dir.), *Metals Make the World Go Round. The Supply and Circulation of Metals in Bronze Age Europe*, actes du colloque de l'université de Birmingham, juin 1997, Oxford, Oxbow Books, 2000.

Patou-Mathis, Marylène, *Préhistoire de la violence et de la guerre*, Paris, Odile Jacob, 2013.

–, « La guerre a-t-elle existé au Paléolithique ? » *in* Guilaine, Jean, Semelin, Jacques, *Violences de guerre, violences de masse. Une approche archéologique*, Paris, La Découverte, 2016, p. 23-36.

Pechoux, Ludivine (dir.), *Les Gaulois et leurs représentations dans l'art et la littérature depuis la Renaissance*, Paris, Errance, 2011.

Pernot, Michel (dir.), *Quatre mille ans d'histoire du cuivre. Fragments d'une suite de rebonds*, Bordeaux, Presses Universitaires, 2017.

–, Lehoërff, Anne, « Battre le bronze il y a trois mille ans en Europe occidentale », *Technè*, 18, 2003, p. 13-48.

Petrequin, Anne-Marie, Petrequin, Pierre, *Objets de pouvoirs en Nouvelle-Guinée. Approche ethnoarchéologique d'un système de signes sociaux*, avec la collaboration de Weller, Olivier, Paris, RMN, 2006.

Pétrequin, Pierre, Vaquer, Jean, « Masses, sphéroïdes et haches de pierre à perforation transversale », *in Signes de Richesse. Inégalités au Néolithique*, Paris, Réunion des Musées nationaux, 2015, p. 29-34.

Petrognani Stéphane, *De Chauvet à Lascaux. L'art des cavernes, reflet de sociétés préhistoriques en mutation*, Paris, Errance, 2013.

Piel-Desruisseaux, Jean-Luc, *Outils préhistoriques. Du galet taillé au bistouri d'obsidienne*, Paris, Dunod, 2007.

Pigeot, Nicole (dir.), *Les derniers Magdaléniens d'Étiolles : perspec- tives culturelles et paléohistoriques*, Paris, *Gallia-Préhistoire*, XXXVIIe supplément, CNRS, 2004, 351 p.

Philibert, Jean, Vignes, Alain, Bréchet, Yves, Combrade, Pierre,*Métallurgie, du minerai au matériau*, Paris, Masson, 1998.

Pleiner, Radomir, *Archaeometallurgy of Iron*, Prague, Archaelogical Institute, 1989.

–, *The Celtic Sword*, Oxford, Clarendon Press, 1993.

Pomian, Krzysztof, *L'ordre du temps*, Paris, Gallimard, 1984.

–, « Les archives. Du trésor des chartes au Caran », *in* Nora, Pierre (dir.), *op. cit.*, t. 3, p. 3999-4066.

Quilliec, Bénédicte, *L'épée atlantique : échanges et prestige au Bronze final*, Paris, Société Préhistorique française (Mémoire *SPF* XLII), 2007.

Randsborg, Klaus, *Hortspring : Warfare and Sacrifice in Early Europe*, Aarhus, Aarhus University Press, 1995.

– (dir.), *Absolute chronology. Archaeological Europe 2500-500 BC*, Proceedings of interna- tional conference in Verona, *Acta Archaeologica,* 67, 1995, p. 99-120.

–, « Wetland hoards », *Oxford Journal of Archaeology,* 21, 2002, p. 415-418.

Reddé, Michel, *Alésia. L'archéologie face à l'imaginaire*, Paris, Errance, 2003.

–, Schnurbein (von), Siegmar (dir.), *Alésia et la bataille du Teutoburg. Un parallèle critique des sources*, Suppléments à *Francia*, 66, 2008.

Revel, Jacques (dir.), *Jeux d'échelles. La micro-analyse à l'expérience*, Paris, Gallimard/Seuil, 1996.

Rolley, Claude (dir.), *La tombe princière de Vix*, Paris, Picard, 2004.

Richard, Nathalie, *Inventer la Préhistoire. Les débuts de l'archéologie préhistorique en France*, Paris, Vuibert, 2008.

Ricœur, Paul, « Objectivité et subjectivité en histoire », *in* Ricœur, Paul, *Histoire et vérité*, Paris, Seuil, 1955, 2001, p. 27-50.

Robion-Brunner, Caroline, « L'Afrique des métaux », *in* Fauvelle, François-Xavier (dir), *Civilisations de l'Afrique ancienne*, Paris, Belin, 2018, p. 516-544.

Rowley-Conwy, Peter, *From Genesis to Prehistory. The Archaeological Three System and its Contested Reception in Denmark, Britain and Ireland*, Oxford, Oxford University Press, 2007.

Sahlins, Marshall, *Stone Ages Economics*, Chicago, Aldine, 1972 (frenc edition, *Âge de pierre,* âge d'abondance. L'économie des sociétés primitives, Paris, Gallimard, 1976.

–, *La découverte du vrai sauvage*, Paris, Gallimard, 2007.

Sauzeau, Pierre, Van Compernolle, Thierry (dir.), *Les armes dans l'Antiquité. De la technique* à *l'imaginaire*, actes du colloque international du SEMA, Montpellier, 2003, CERCAM, Publications de l'Université Paul Valéry-Montpellier, 2007, p. 13-33, part. p. 28-31.

Schauer, Peter, *Die Schwerter in Süddeutschland, Österreich und der Schweiz*, Munich, Beck, 1971, (*PBF* IV.2), p. 193-195.

–, *Die Urnenfelderzeitlichen Bronzepanzer von Fillinges*, dans *JGZM*, 25, 1978, p. 92-130.

Schlanger, Nathan, *The « Chaîne opératoire»*, in Renfrew, Colin, Bahn, Paul G. (ed.), *The Archaeology : The Key Concepts*, Abingdon, Routledge, 2005, p. 25-29.

Scott, James C., *Against the Grain. A deep History of the Earliest States*, Yale University Press, 2017 (French edition, *Homo Domesticus. Une histoire profonde des premiers États*, Paris, La Découverte, 2017).

–, Taylor, Anne-Christine (dir.), *La Préhistoire des autres. Perspectives archéologiques et anthropologiques*, Paris, La Découverte, 2012.

Schnapp, Alain, *La conquête du passé. Aux origines de l'archéologie*, Paris, Carré, 1993 (English edition, British Museum Press, 1996).

–, *Les préadamites : une invention manquée de la préhistoire au xviie siècle*, in Lehoërff, Anne (dir.), *Construire le temps. Histoire et méthode des chronologies et calendriers des derniers millénaires en Europe occidentale*, Proceedings of international conference in Lille, 2006, Glux-en-Glenne, Bibracte, 16, 2008, p. 33-40.

–, *Une histoire universelle des ruines*, Paris, Seuil, 2020.

Scott, David A., *Metallography and Microstructure of Ancient and Historic Metals*, Los Angeles, Getty Conservation Institute, 1991.

Skogstrand, Lisbeth, *Warriors and the Other Men. Notions of Masculinity from the Late Bronze Age to the Early Iron Age in Scandinavia*, Oxford, Archeopress Archaeology, 2016.

Snodgrass, Antony, *Early Greek Armour and Weapons rom the End of Bronze Age to 600 B.C.*, Édimbourg, University Press, 1964.

Sofsky, Wolfgang, *Traité de la violence*, Paris, Gallimard, 1996. Spencer, Herber, *Principes de sociologie*, Paris, 1876-1897.

Staden, Hans, *Nus, féroces et anthropophages*, 1557, nombreuses rééditions, Paris, Métailié, 2005.

Stiegler, Bernard, *La Technique et le temps I. La faute d'Épiméthée*, Paris, Galilée, 1994.

Strahm, Christian, « L'introduction et la diffusion de la métallurgie en France », *in* Ambert, Paul, Vaquer, Jean (dir.), *La première métallurgie en France et dans les pays limitrophes*, actes du colloque international de Carcassonne, 2002, Paris, Société préhistorique française (Mémoire SPF XXXVII), 2005, p. 27-35.

Sun, Tzu, *L'art de la guerre* ou *Stratégie militaire de maître Sun*, début du ve siècle avant notre ère.

Testart, Alain, *La déesse et le grain : trois essais sur les religions néolithiques*, Paris, Errance, 2010.

– (dir.), *Les armes dans les eaux. Question d'interprétation en archéologie*, Paris, Errance, 2013.

–, *Avant l'histoire. L'évolution des sociétés de Lascaux à Carnac*, Paris, Gallimard, 2012.

Thiesse, Anne-Marie, *La création des identités nationales. Europe, xviiie-xxe siècle*, Paris, Seuil, 1999.

Thorpe, Nick, « Warfare in the European Bronze Age », *in* Fokkens, Harry, Harding, Antony (ed.), *op. cit.*, p. 234-247.

Tillier, Anne-Marie, *L'homme et la mort. L'émergence du geste funéraire durant la Préhistoire*, Paris, CNRS, 2013.

Trigger, Bruce G., *A History of Archaeological Thought*, 1989, Cambridge, Cambridge University Press, 1994.

Turney-High, Harry Holbert, *Primitive War : Its Practices and Concepts*, Columbia, University of South Caroline Press, 1949.

Tylecote, Robert, *The Early History of Metallurgy in Europe*, 1987, Londres/New-York, Longman, 1992.

Uckelmann, Marion, « Protection, apparat et culte. De la fonction du bouclier à l'Âge du bronze », *in* Baray, Luc, Honegger, Matthieu, Dias-Meirinho, Marie-Hélène (dir.), *L'armement et l'image du guerrier dans les sociétés anciennes. De l'objet à la tombe*, Dijon, Éditions universitaire de Dijon, 2011, p. 270-278.

Uckelmann, Marion, Mödlinger, Marianne, (éd.), *Bronze Age Warfare : Manufacture and Use of Weaponry*, Oxford, Archeopress, British Archaeological Reports International Serie 2255, 2011.

Vandkilde, Helle, « Bronze Age Warfare in Temperate Europe ? », *in* Hansen, Svend, Müller, Johannes (ed.), *Sozialarchäologishe Perpspectiven: Gesellschaftlicher Wandel 5000-1500 v. Chr. zwischen Atlantik und Kaukasus*, Darmstad, Von Zabern, 2011, p. 365-380.

Van Compernolle, Thierry, « L'arme : au centre ou aux marges de la cité ? », *in* Sauzeau, Pierre, Van Compernolle, Thierry (dir.), *op. cit.*, p. 585-595.

Venayre, Sylvain, *Disparu. Enquête sur Sylvain Venayre*, Paris, Les Belles Lettres, 2012.

–, *Les origines de la France. Quand les historiens racontaient la France*, Paris, Seuil, 2013.

–, Davodeau, Étienne, *La Balade nationale. t. 1 : Les origines*, Paris, La Revue dessinée, 2017.

Vernant, Jean-Pierre (dir.), *Problèmes de la guerre en Grèce ancienne*, 1968, Paris/La Haye, Mouton, 1985.

–, « La belle mort et le cadavre outragé », *in* Vernant, Jean-Pierre, *L'individu, la mort, l'amour. Soi-même et l'autre en Grèce ancienne*, Paris, Gallimard, 1989, p. 41-79.

–, *La traversée des frontières*, Paris, Seuil, 2004.

Vidal-Naquet, Pierre, *La tradition de l'hoplite athénien*, *in* Vernant, Jean-Pierre (dir.), *op. cit.*, 1968, 1985, p. 161-181.

–, *Le choix de l'histoire*, Paris, Arléa, 2004.

Volvosky, Claude, *La conservation des métaux*, Paris, CNRS, 2001.

Webber, Chris, *The Gods of Battle : The Tracians at War, 1500 BC-150 AD*, Barnsley, Pen and Sword Books, 2011.

Weber Max, *Le savant et le politique*, Munich, 1919, Paris, 10/18, 2002.

–, *Économie et société*, 1921, Paris, Pocket, 2003.

Wentink, Karsten, *Ceci n'est pas une hache. Neolithic Depositions in the Northern Netherlands*, Leiden, Sidestone Press, 2006.

Wileman, Julie Rosemary, *Warfare in the Northern Europe Before the Romans : Evidence from Archaelogy*, Barnsley, Pen and Sword Books, 2014.